Single Mothers and Sons:
A Journey into Manhood

Dr William C. Small

**FirstWorld Publishing
Dallas, TX**

Single Mothers and Sons: A Journey into Manhood
Copyright © 2017 Dr William C. Small
All rights reserved under international copyright law.

FirstWorld Publishing
5000 Eldorado Parkway, Dallas, TX 75033
www.doctorwillspeaking.com

Contents may not be reproduced in whole or in part in any form or by any means whatsoever, whether electronic or mechanical (including information storage, recording, and retrieval systems) without express written consent from the publisher.

ISBN – 13: 9780997206715
ISBN – 10: 0997206713

Cover Photo: ©Istockphoto.com
Interior & cover design: FirstWorld Publishing

Unless otherwise indicated, all scripture quotations are from the King James Version of the Bible.

Scriptures were taken from the Thompson Chain-Reference Bible, Fifth Improved Edition, copyright © 1908, 1917, 1929, 1934, 1957, 1964, 1982, by Frank Charles Thompson.

Hebrew and Greek definitions were taken from Strong's New Exhaustive Concordance Of The Bible, copyright © 1890, by James Strong, STD, LL.D. and cross referenced with Young's Analytical Concordance

To The Bible, copyright © 1982, by Thomas Nelson, Inc.

Historical references were taken from Nelson's Illustrated Encyclopedia of Bible Facts, copyright © 1980 1995, by Thomas Nelson Publishers.

The principles of leadership adapted from Field Manual 22-100, Military Leadership, copyright © 1996, by The Department of the Army.

Contents

Contents	iv
Preface	vi
Chapter 1	
Who are You?	1
Chapter 2	
Purify Yourself	38
Chapter 3	
Understanding Your Mind	70
Chapter 4	
The Essential Elements of Manhood	102
Chapter 5	
Strive for Victorious Living	129
Chapter 6	
Overcoming Obstacles	153
Chapter 7	
A Call to Leadership	182
Chapter 8	
Executive Decision Making	209

Chapter 9
Family Relationships   232

Chapter 10
Marriage and Sex   261

Chapter 11
How to Find a Virtuous Woman   282

Chapter 12
The Question of a Man's Covering   290

Chapter 13
Fight Back!   315

Can You be a Man Like Joseph?   333
Prisoner to Prime Minister   338
We Need More Uncle Toms   344

Afterword   348
About the Author   353
Recommended Reading   354

Preface

"Don't ask what the world needs. Ask what makes you come alive and go do that... what the world needs is more men who have come alive."
~ **Howard Thurman**

An African Proverb says: "If you enter a village and you can't find any good women, it is filled with no good men." As the men in every society go, so shall that society be. Single mothers are often accused of being the cause of all the ills of society because they do not have the knowledge or capacity to raise a male child up into manhood. She can keep him out of trouble until he becomes an adult male but she cannot teach him to be a man. The same people who make that kind of allegation often lament over the mass incarceration of Black men. They love to cite the statistics that says if a boy cannot read at grade level by the 4th grade he is destined for prison. Yet, you never see them volunteering to teach any boys to read. My question to them has always been: If a single mother doesn't have the knowledge necessary to teach a boy to be a man, why won't you give it to her? A mother is a child's first teacher. Whatever message she gives to him he will deliver to the world. So why not give her the information that she needs?

I have been around the world, circled the globe twice, leading young men and women and helping them make the transition from adolescence to adulthood. In teaching them about the purpose of life and the importance of fulfilling our life purpose my message was simple: if you are passionate over something that you believe is wrong, you were put here to fix it. Therefore, I have proved to myself what I have always said of others: sometimes a man is slow to learn his own lessons. I was arguing passionately that if women do not have the knowledge they need to teach their sons how to be men then men should stop complaining and give it to them. I did not recognize at the time I was making that argument that I must be the one who GOD put here to fix it. After all, I am holding the information single mothers need to lead their sons into manhood and the heart to share it compassionately.

Moms, this book is **for** you but it is written **to** your sons. It is written in a conversational style so that it will feel to your son like he is having a one on one talk with a man teaching him all that he needs to know about how to be a man, a godly man, husband and father. I recommend that you use this book to make it a joint learning experience, a family project, where you and your son take the journey into the knowledge of manhood together. Make the learning fun by reading **one** chapter a week separately (I'm not trying to sell more books but it will mean that you must buy one book for your son and one for yourself) and each of you make notes on what you learned and questions you have. This is important because some of the issues presented may be tough for him to grasp depending on his age so it is best that you read it simultaneously and prepare yourself for his questions. Then, on the same day of the week at the same time of the day share with each other what you learned. As an incentive for your son, center that discussion around a meal or a treat that he really enjoys. This will not only increase your knowledge, mom, but also create a stronger bond between mother and son.

Now, there are a few little sneaky side benefits to having this knowledge. Giving your son the knowledge he needs to think like a man will empower him to make wise decisions and help you keep him out of trouble, jail, or prison. This knowledge will empower you to do what everybody believes a single mother can't do: lead her son into manhood. It gives you the opportunity to prove to his father wrong (and maybe some of your relatives) who prophesied that not having a father would ruin his life. And it will give you the security of knowing that you did everything you possibly could to help your son complete his journey into manhood.

Young men, from this point forward everything else written in this book is about you. By the time you finish reading this book you will have more knowledge about how to be a man than more than half the men walking around on the planet. You will never have the experience that most of those guys have where their wife or girlfriend yelled at them: Be a man! She will never have to because she will know you are a man when she first meets you. That is because you will have the strength and confidence that an adult male who knows how to be a man should have.

Now, I don't believe in talking baby talk to babies and I don't believe in talking down to young men. So, even though you may only be 9 or 10 I will be talking to you and talking about issues as if you were already a grown man. A child develops their adult personality between the ages of 2 and 7. Since you already have an adult personality we might as well talk like adult men; godly men not the gross representations of what talking like a man is too often presented to be in media and in society. Alright? If something is hard for you to understand, make a note on what your questions are about it then discuss it with your mom.

Now, I had been taking notes in preparation to write this book for years but the inspiration to finally sit down and write it came from two sources. The first one was watching my daughter and her friends, seeing how they were quickly growing up to become young ladies, and realizing that they are all going to need good men to be husbands and fathers for their children. The second source was a shaving cream commercial. A rookie was in the locker room getting ready to shave with a face full of foam. A veteran player comes in and asks sternly: What are you doing? The rookie said: I'm about to shave. So the veteran says: No one uses foam anymore. Here, use this Edge Gel. The rookie looked up at him as if he was about to cry and said: Nobody told me! The way he said "Nobody told me" struck my heart and I said to myself: that's it! Nobody told me! The reason I struggled as a young man to be a good husband, father, and provider is because nobody told me what to do or how to do it. I realized then that this is the same reason every man struggles with the same issues. Nobody told them either.

The primary emotional stressors that men must contend with on a daily basis are anger, frustration, and confusion due largely to the pressure of trying to be a husband, father, and provider without the proper knowledge. Men suffer in silence as we fight to fulfill all of the demands that our families and society place upon us while we are expected to be stronger than Sampson, wiser than Solomon, and wealthier than Rockefeller. We are required to know all and be everything when no one has really shown us how to do anything. Most days we are just doing the best we can with what we have and the pressure builds because we know it's not enough.

Over 40% of men in America were born to an unwed mother. If you are a Black man that number rises to over 70%. The greatest social, cultural, and financial problem plaguing every nation across the globe is fatherlessness. The pressure on men who grew up without a father is even more intense because we had no man to guide us into the knowledge we need to meet the demands and successfully perform in the multifaceted role of a man.

Lacking the knowledge that a father should have provided is causing many men to struggle psychologically due to a lack of identity and a sense of purpose. This is why men can put sports jersey on with another man's name on their back. Only women take on another man's name. Sadly, the guy that they are trying to emulate or look to for a sense of identity doesn't even know who he is. To compound the issue society is pushing men to be more effeminate and literally forcing them to accept those who are as equals. It is already hard to define what a man is. Now we have essentially lost the definition of manhood, masculine value, vision, significance, and authority in society and in our families. We have nearly lost all the respect and reverence that children should have for men. Programs on TV condition children to believe that they are smarter than men. "This is so easy even my dad can do it!" Most of the commercials depict women alone with their children giving the impression that a daddy is not necessary.

Do you know why men like to identify with sports figures? It is because they are winners. Every man wants to be identified as a winner. But do you know why they are winners? It is because they play on a team. The word team is an acronym that means: Together Everybody Achieves More. Teams begin as a group of people coming together to achieve the same goal. They transform from a group into a team because they coalesce around a unified mindset by operating from the same playbook. Winning teams transform their individual thinking into a singular mind. They become unified in spirit, work to achieve the same goal, train their bodies to overcome opposition, and therefore they win. GOD is seeking to transform HIS men from sinners to winners; from a group to a team that will work to transform their spirit, minds, and bodies with the unified goal of transforming the world.

The book you are now reading is the playbook that will make you a winner at the game of being a provider, husband, and father. It contains the essential knowledge every man needs to successfully lead and love his wife, raise his children, produce wealth, and live a perfect and victorious life. Society says that nobody can be perfect but that is a lie and this book will show you why. We have been made mediocre by the memes and morays imposed on us by men who don't know GOD. With them perfection is impossible but with GOD **all** things are possible.

A man who can't read is no worse off that a man who won't read. Read this book young brother and you'll never be the same. The only reason you'll remain unchanged is by choice. If the average man is honest he will have to admit to himself that the knowledge he has been operating on has not led him to where he really wants to be financially. When challenged on that fact some men become bound and determined to be right and to hold on to what they know. But that mindset keeps men bound in position and stuck in their current condition.

I have seen too many men deprive themselves of a better life because the knowledge they needed to create that life came in a book. They convinced themselves that they either didn't need the book or that they couldn't afford to buy it. They do this because nobody told them that the cost of ignorance is always higher than the price of knowledge. Nobody told them that it is better to sacrifice short term need for long term gain. Men become billionaires because of what they know while other men struggle to feed their families because of what they don't know. Men who grow weary of struggling or being depressed because they can't give their wife and children everything they want, soon learn that it's better to sacrifice a couple of six packs, a pack of cigarettes, or lunch for one day to get the knowledge every wealthy man uses to help his family see better, brighter, and more prosperous days. The greatest investment that you will ever make in life will be an investment in knowledge. Investing in knowledge that is based on the word of GOD will lead you into manhood and shall cause your soul to prosper. Nobody loses the game of life that is equipped with the knowledge they need to win the game.

"Beloved, I wish above all things that you may prosper and be in health even as your soul prospers (3 John 2)."

"All scripture is given by inspiration of GOD and is profitable for doctrine, for reproof, for correction, for instruction in righteousness: that the man of GOD may be perfect, thoroughly furnished [equipped and empowered] unto **all** good works (2 Timothy 3:16-17)."

Chapter 1
Who are You?

"Our deepest fear is not that we are inadequate, our deepest fear is that we are powerful beyond measure."
~ Nelson Mandela

"When the best that you have in you is drawn out of you, the power to do whatever you want to do comes out too." **~ Dr Will**

It is impossible to succeed at anything when you don't know the truth. The primary obstacle to success in life, love, business, and every other endeavor for the average man is not having the truth about who he is and literal power station GOD created him to be. Not only has the truth been withheld from men about who they are, they haven't even been told the truth about the truth. Most men have been told that the truth shall set them free but that's not true.

"And you shall know the truth and the truth shall **make** you free (John 8:32)."

"Thy kingdom come, thy will be done **in** earth, as it is in heaven (Matthew 6:10)."

The majority of the Christian body believes that John 8:32 says "the truth shall **set** you free" when it actually says "make" you free. During the time of slavery in America if you were set free, you could be taken back into captivity. But if you were **made** or born free you were free indeed and could never be taken into slavery legally. Everyone believes Matthew 6:10 says "thy will be done **on** earth" when it clearly says "in" earth meaning in our physical body or in this earthen vessel. Jesus taught us to pray for GOD's Kingdom to come and for HIS will to be done "IN" **us** as it is in heaven. Why? The purpose is to make YOU powerful by making it possible for the Kingdom GOD to live **in YOU**; not on earth but rather **in** earth!

"The Kingdom of GOD comes not with observation: Neither shall they say lo here or lo there for, behold, the Kingdom of GOD is **within YOU** (Luke 17:20-21)."

"Know you not that **YOU** are the temple of GOD, and that the Spirit of GOD dwells **IN you** (1 Corinthians 3:16)?"

The world was given to men, the sons of GOD, as an inheritance so that we can exercise power, authority, and dominion over it. The truth or the word of GOD was given to us so that we could discover who we are, what we have, and what we are supposed to do with our lives. Knowing the truth about who you are and living in your true identity is the foundation for success in life, love, and business. When you don't know who you really are other people will give you an identity and then use your gifts, talents, and abilities to make them and their family wealthy. My people are destroyed for a lack of knowledge. Lacking knowledge about your true identity, who you really are, who GOD created you to be, and what HE created you to do positions you in slave captivity and puts you in jeopardy of losing your place in eternity. If you know the truth, the truth shall make you free and the devil can never lead you into spiritual captivity!

Who You are in Christ

Our true identity has been hidden from us traditionally by those who were commissioned to lead and guide us spiritually. It's not as if they didn't know because who you really are is described in the Bible

Single Mothers and Sons

clearly. Some never taught you who GOD says you are because what GOD said conflicts with their doctrinal traditions. They truly believe that religion requires humility. In their tradition men must see themselves as sinful, lowly, undeserving, and are not being obedient to GOD unless they are submitting to serve GOD through another man's ministry. Since many men have been conditioned to submit and be obedient, other leaders have simply taken advantage of this religious tradition and use it for their purposes. The truth is, you are not who the world and the church have conditioned you to believe you are.

You are a son of GOD and an heir to the throne of grace. As a son of GOD, that makes you equal with GOD! Now, I know that just messed with your mental muscle because you have been taught it's blasphemy to compare yourself with GOD. While it is true that this is what your preachers, parents, and relatives or loved ones have always taught, it is not true according to Father GOD.

GOD said in Psalm 82:6 "I have said, YOU are gods; and **all** of you are children of the Most High." Jesus reinforces what GOD said in John 10:34 by asking the religious leaders of His day "Is it not written in your law, I said you are gods?" This question was in reaction to the religious leader's outrage that Jesus called himself the Son of GOD. He said if the word is true (as you say it is) and the word says that GOD said **we** are gods and children of the Most High then why do you say that I blaspheme because I said I am the Son of GOD?

"What is man that you are mindful of him and the son of man that you visit him? For you have made him a little lower than the angels [Eloheim; the godhead]

Single Mothers and Sons

and has crowned him with glory and honor. You made him to have dominion over the works of your hands; you have put all things under his feet (Psalm 8:4-6)."

When the angels of Heaven saw the way GOD interacted with man they were confused and raised this question. Although they did not completely understand they did fully recognize that GOD had placed men in a position of greatness. They could see that GOD made them to be just a little lower than HIMSELF, crowned them with glory and honor, and gave them dominion over the earth.

"...I bow my knees unto the Father of our Lord Jesus Christ, of whom the whole **family** in heaven and earth is **named** (Ephesians 3:14-15)."

"If MY people which are called by MY **name**... (2 Chronicles 7:14)"

Not only does GOD say that we are gods HE also expects us to be called by HIS name! GOD's name is GOD therefore he expects **YOU** as HIS sons to be called gods. Every good father wants his children to be called by his name. Every good father named Smith wants his kids to be called Smith's. GOD is a better Father than we could ever be therefore HE wants HIS children to be called by HIS name as well. His name is GOD, the family name is GOD, ergo, "I said, you are gods!"

"The Spirit itself bears witness with our spirit that **we** are the children of GOD (Romans 8:16)."

Here we have the Holy Spirit Himself bearing witness that we are the sons of GOD. So, now we have all 3 elements of the Triune Godhead: GOD, Jesus, and the Holy Spirit declaring that we **are** indeed sons of GOD. We have evidence of the angels recognizing that GOD positioned men to represent (re/present) HIM in the earth (made in HIS image and after HIS likeness) and to rule and reign over it. My brothers, GOD, Jesus, the Holy Spirit said and the angels acknowledged that **we** are sons of GOD. What more do we need to realize that who we have been is <u>not</u> who we really are?

"Beloved, **NOW** are we the sons of GOD, and it does not yet appear what we shall be: but we know that when He shall appear, we shall be like Him; for we shall see Him as He is (1 John 3:2)."

In order to twist the word of GOD to make it fit their doctrine and tradition some religious leaders attempt to make you believe that being a son of GOD will occur in the afterlife. However, the word clearly says: Now! You do not appear to be a son of GOD like Jesus now because the eyes of your understanding have not been enlightened. But once your spiritual eyes are opened and you get to see Jesus you will have no doubt that you are a son. You will see Him as He really is and you will recognize that you are just like Him. GOD charged the religious leaders, the 5 fold ministry, to perfect you unto the measure of the fullness of His stature so that if you stood next to Jesus the world, initially, would not be able to tell the difference between you and Him. You will see that you and Jesus are one.

"Neither pray I [Jesus] for these alone, but for them also which shall believe on me through their word; that they all may be one; as YOU, Father, are in me, and I in YOU, that they also may be one in **US**: that the world may believe that YOU have sent me. And the glory which YOU gave me I have given **them**; that **they** may be one, even as **we** are one (John 17:20-22)."

Here we have Jesus praying for GOD to make you and me **one** with Him and GOD. Do you think that GOD refused to grant Jesus this request? No? You are

Single Mothers and Sons

right because I don't think so either. A good son wants to be one with his father and a good father wants to be one with his son. A good father hides his life in the life of the son so that to know the son is to know the father. GOD has made us HIS sons and has hidden HIS life in us so that as the world gets to know us they will get to know HIM. Religious leaders want to keep you in a position of being a servant of GOD in order to keep <u>you</u> serving <u>them</u> but GOD said that you are a son. You must be who **GOD** said you are not them and you must be about your Father's business not theirs.

"Know you not that **YOU** are the temple of GOD, and that the Spirit of GOD dwells **IN you** (1 Corinthians 3:16)?"

You see, who we <u>really</u> are has been taught wrong for so long that we have a problem accepting the truth of who we really are. Our minds and thought processes have been trained to operate contrary to the word of GOD. Therefore, we either never came, or have been experiencing great difficulty coming, to be who GOD created us to be. GOD said that we are gods. Jesus said we are gods. The Holy Spirit bears witness that we are gods. The Apostle Paul really upset religious tradition by teaching that we should not only think like GOD but that we should not think anything is wrong with being equal with GOD.

"Let this mind be in **you** which was also in Christ Jesus: who, being in the form [image and likeness] of GOD, thought it **not** robbery to be **equal** with GOD (Philippians 2:5-6)."

The Apostle Paul says that we need to have the same mind or to think like Jesus who thought it <u>not</u> robbery to be equal with His Father. However, that kind of thinking won't happen unless we "let" it or until we accept it as true in our minds. The problem is our religious training was designed to discipline our minds to prevent it from thinking like Jesus and believing that we could be equal with the grand deity. GOD knew this would happen so HE made it possible for us to renew our minds with the word of GOD. Since both GOD and Jesus says very plainly that we are gods, the Holy Spirit bears witness to that fact, and the Apostle Paul says we are to think it not robbery to be equal with GOD, you have to ask yourself why is it so many religious leaders would have a problem if you told them you are a god? They proclaim to be servants of GOD, experts in the word, and men whom GOD speaks to directly, so why is the word that they teach contrary to what the word of GOD actually says?

Although you would be quoting GOD religious leaders would still have an issue with you believing that you are gods. Jesus quoted GOD when He asked the Sadducees and Pharisees is it not written in your law I said you are gods. He was confronting the Bishops and Ph.D.'s of His day to make them change their traditionally held beliefs and accept the truth that GOD calls those whom HE sent HIS word to gods. The religious leaders were hostile with Jesus for saying that He is the Son of GOD. Jesus told them the truth about who we really are, GOD wrote that truth in HIS word so that we could be free of all confusion as to our identity, yet after 2,000 years of professing the word of GOD too many religious leaders still don't believe the word of GOD. They will be hostile with me for telling you that **we** are sons of GOD.

"Therefore the Jews sought the more to kill him, because he not only had broken the Sabbath, but said also that GOD was His Father, making himself equal with GOD (John 5:18)."

Jesus never actually said He was equal with GOD. So why did the Jews conclude Jesus was claiming to be equal with GOD just because He said GOD was His Father? If you say that a man is your father and you are above a certain age in Jewish custom equality with him is understood. In their custom a father, if he loves his son, makes his son equal to him. The reason he does this is because equality is a principle tenant or an essential element of love.

This is going to be hard for most Christians to understand because we have never been taught what love is, how to love, and what love is supposed to produce. I have been going to church and listening to Christian radio and TV for over 50 years. Yet, I have never heard a sermon or teaching series specifically designed to teach GOD's people how to love. So bear with me, please, as I digress to explain love from GOD's perspective.

Love is a threefold cord comprised of freedom, justice and equality. Ecclesiastes 4:12 says a threefold cord is not quickly broken. This is why real love is so strong and accounts for one of the reasons why it is so difficult to break away from someone whom you are tied to by love. When you love someone you do everything in your power to ensure they have freedom. You want them to be who they are, who they desire to be and who GOD created them to be. The three types of freedom you get when you are free in love is freedom from the fear of doing something for someone other than yourself, the freedom to love unconditionally and the freedom to forgive those who trespassed against you. Love gives you the liberty to sacrifice yourself to ensure the object of your love has justice.

There is no double standard in justice. Whatever is not good for my son is not good for me. If a place is not good for him to go, it is not good for me to go. If a word is not good for him to say, it is not good for me to say. If an activity is not good for him to do, it is not good for me to do. The laws of the household or rules of the family apply to us both when there is justice and equality. Love compels you to ensure that your love ones have equality. While I may be bigger, stronger, richer or smarter, I share my strength, riches, and intelligence with them so that my assets become theirs because in love we are one.

When the prodigal son returned home, in Luke 15:22, his father gave him things that demonstrated his love and illustrated their equality: shoes, a robe, and a ring. The father's gifts served notice to the community that the love between he and his son had not been broken. The shoes represented manhood. Boys didn't wear shoes in that day only men did. The ring was a type of credit card that allowed him to make purchases and financial decisions on the father's behalf. The robe was a sign that the son was vested with his father's authority.

When I love my son and he becomes a certain age, he is given an equal stake in the family. I treat him as an equal to give him experience and build the confidence he needs to be a man and father himself. His thoughts or input on the direction that the family business is going and on the decisions that are made are given due consideration. My son represents or re presents me to the world wherever he goes and whatever he does so he

Single Mothers and Sons

is naturally equated to me. He bears my image and likeness.

In a corporation that is owned by a father but managed by his son, the workers respond to the directions of the son as if the father gave the order. The workers know that not obeying the order of the son will incur the wrath of the father. The son does not have to tell the workers that his father gave the order. When the son speaks, it is assumed the order came from the father. The workers know the son only does what his father tells him to do and he only says what he hears the father say. Therefore, they do what the son tells them to do and they listen to what he says. That is because they know the word of the son is equal in authority to the word of the father.

GOD is semi-retired and has handed over the family business to HIS Son and sons both in heaven and in earth. As sons and heirs, joint heirs with Jesus, we are entitled to an inheritance. That inheritance comes with a duty, a charge, and a calling: to have dominion and authority over all the earth, to govern the Kingdom of Heaven and administrate the Kingdom of GOD in the earth, and complete or fulfill your individual purpose. Religious leaders believe that this duty, charge, and calling makes you a servant but these are the responsibilities of sons who are given control over the family business by the Father.

"The Spirit itself bears witness with our spirit that we are the children of GOD: And if children, then heirs; heirs of GOD, and joint-heirs with Christ... (Romans 8:16-17)"

"And because you are sons, GOD has sent forth the Spirit of HIS Son into your hearts, crying, Abba, Father. Therefore, you are no more a servant, but a son; and if a son, then an heir of GOD through Christ (Galatians 4:6-7)."

"A good man leaves an inheritance to his children's children... (Proverbs 13:22)"

"...you are all the children of GOD by faith in Christ Jesus... And if you be Christ's, then are you Abraham's seed and heirs according to the promise (Galatians 3:26-29)."

Most Christians do not to read the word of GOD because what we believe tends to conflict with what is plainly written. We put the word down because it appears too confusing. Our minds are conditioned to discard that which conflicts with what we think or believe. Ergo, it becomes difficult to accept the truth of the word when it confronts us. Traditional teaching led us to believe we are lowly worms and filthy rags in the sight of GOD when **GOD** said that WE are the **temple** of GOD and that HIS Spirit lives in us. We were taught that we are supposed to grovel and beg when we go before HIM, but **GOD** says to approach the throne of grace **boldly**! We are to approach the throne as sons of the King not as lowly subjects and servants. Jesus cannot come back to earth as the King of kings until we take **our** position as kings upon the earth. Kings always have their wishes and desires fulfilled. Therefore, we must approach GOD in faith or confident assurance that our DAD will give us the desires of our heart.

"Delight yourself also in the LORD and HE shall give you the desires of your heart (Psalm 37:4)."

"Let us therefore come boldly unto the throne of grace, that we may obtain mercy [compassion moved to action] and find grace [the power of GOD operating

Single Mothers and Sons

on behalf of a believer] to help in time of need (Hebrews 4:16)."

The unrighteous may have to approach GOD groveling and begging. However, we who are righteous or in right standing with GOD can approach HIM, not arrogantly but, boldly. Would you require your children to approach you on their knees groveling and begging when they come to talk to you or ask for something? No? It would be almost offensive if your child came to you that way. You would make him or her stand up and stop whining (Joshua 7:6-10). Yet, the devil's disciples taught our loved ones that this is how **we** must go before our Father because that is how **they** must approach HIM.

"You are a child of GOD. Your playing small does not serve the world." ~ **Nelson Mandela**

As a result of not reading and studying for themselves and by assuming their teachers knew what they were talking about, our loved ones taught you and me what the devil's disciples taught them. Now we have been conditioned (out of respect for our loved ones) to retain their teachings when confronted with the truth. This is why the preachers of Jesus' day fought to maintain their traditional beliefs more than they wanted to know the truth.

Likewise, some people today will scream at you for saying that you are a god even after you show them that it was what GOD said HIMSELF in Psalm 82:6. They will try to convince you that you are blaspheming if you were to tell them that you are equal with GOD as both GOD and Jesus said you are. Once you begin to study the word for yourself and allow it to renew your mind, you can come to realize the truth of who you really are and who GOD created you to be. The devil's

Single Mothers and Sons

disciples will keep you a servant of GOD or a spiritual child by continually feeding you only the milk of the word to keep you from reigning in dominion and authority and from receiving your inheritance as an heir. But, GOD created you to be a son. You can grow into the stature of the image in which you were created and become GOD's son by studying HIS word and being ready to receive strong meat.

"Now I say, that the heir, as long as he is a child, differs nothing from a servant, though he be lord of **all**; but is under tutors and governors until the time appointed of the father. Even so we, when we were under the elements of this world: But when the fullness of the time was come, GOD sent forth HIS Son, made of a woman, made under the law, to redeem them that were under the law, that we might receive the adoption of sons. And because **you** are sons GOD has sent forth the Spirit of HIS Son into your hearts, crying Abba Father. Therefore, you are no more a servant but a son and if a son then an heir of GOD through Christ (Galatians 4:1-7)."

Now, of course you or I could never actually be equal with GOD but GOD wants us to conduct ourselves as if we are. HE wants you and me to do what HE does and say whatever HE says so that the world can know that there is a GOD and get to know HIM through us. The word says that we were made in the image and likeness of GOD. The word "image" in Hebrew means to look alike, appear similar or to reflect. The word "likeness" means to act like, function in the same manner or to be like. A child could be the spitting image of her mother but act just like her father. GOD made us to look like HE is and to act like HE does.

Single Mothers and Sons

"But we all, with open face beholding as in a glass the glory of the Lord, are changed into the same image from glory to glory, even as by the Spirit of the Lord (2 Corinthians 3:18)."

Where R You Going?

Those who don't know who they really are and where they are going in life will have difficulty maintaining long lasting relationships. When we don't know who we are there will always be people who will try to make us into what they want us to be. If we don't know where we want to go in life there will always be people who will try to lead us to go with them; to follow their vision. It will be difficult then to continue to go along and get along with those people once we realize they were taking advantage of our uncertainty of who we are and where we should be. Ultimately, if we are uncertain of our identity or destiny we will encounter other people who will also take advantage of us financially. The cycle will continue until we come into the knowledge of who we are and where we are destined by GOD to be. Once we understand who we R we can more easily recognize our destiny and determine where we R going.

The difference between the words forward and froward is the position of the R. Froward means: not easily controlled, stubborn or willfully contrary. Having had the experiences described above could cause us to become froward and may prevent us from moving forward with people who genuinely have our best interests at heart. Those who had a bad relationship will often make the next person they encounter pay for their pain. Where are you in your current relationship with others or with yourself? Are

Single Mothers and Sons

you moving forward or being froward? Never get angry get even. The best revenge is massive success.

What is your destiny? Where are you going? A person's true destiny never conflicts with who they are in their inner being. We cannot come into the knowledge of our destiny until we know our true identity. The reason the average man has difficulty determining his destiny is due to unresolved conflict in his inner being. Internal conflict or disagreement within his own selves (body, mind and spirit) prevents him from discovering his true identity and reaching his GOD ordained destiny.

Internal conflict often arises as a result of personal trauma, pain or abuse that occurred early in our lives. Some of us cannot see who we really are because we were told by those who were close or important to us that we were bad, no good or just like our worthless daddy during our formative years. Others cannot come into the knowledge of our true identity because we were physically or sexually abused. The physical abuse creates persistent confusion internally over why we weren't protected by those who were supposed to love us. Physically abused children often become adults who struggle to find their identity because in trying to find who they are they attempt to disassociate themselves with that child who was abused.

Then there are those who were sexually abused that also try to separate themselves from the tiny personality that experienced the trauma and pain of being abused sexually. Sexually abused children often become adults who hide the internal shame they feel because of the pleasure they experienced in the course of being abused. They know old uncle Charlie wasn't supposed to touch them that way. They are angry that

Single Mothers and Sons

he did that to them but at the same time they feel shame because it felt good. Conflict and confusion as to why it felt good cause young boys who were abused by a man feel like they are gay. Conflict and confusion over the pleasure makes some young women feel perverse. They conclude that something must be wrong with them or that their only personal value is associated with their bodies which causes some of them to become prostitutes.

Pain is what we experience when an event is occurring. Suffering is what experience long after the painful event has passed as we continue to relive the event over and over in our minds. Suffering causes internal conflict. The suffering must cease and that internal conflict must be resolved in order for a person to discover who they really are and where they are destined to go.

We have to reconcile with suffering to cause it to end. There has to be forgiveness for the perpetrator for what they did and we have to forgive ourselves of the blame and shame that we place on ourselves because of it. There has to be an atonement (at-one-ment) with GOD to erase the sin consciousness, guilt, and shame that we continue to carry. It has to be cast aside and we must get free of that mental space where we kept ourselves captive so that we can BE free. No one, not even GOD, can do this for us. We have to do it ourselves. Then we can stop doing the things we do, saying the things we say (particularly about ourselves) and thinking the things we think. If we want to know who GOD intended us to be or our true identity, our mind, actions and words must become one. The key to resolving internal conflict lies in making what we do, say and think agree. Our mind, body and spirit must agree that whatever happened is just something that happened to us, it is NOT who we are!

The things we do, say, and think emerge from the core of our being and reveal the essence of who we made ourselves to be internally. Those three are analogous to the body, spirit and mind respectively. The conflicts of life arise when what we do, say and think do not agree or when our body, spirit and mind are in conflict constantly. Our body, spirit, and mind are 3 entities in one being that vie for control or supremacy that must be brought into agreement. Jesus said "How can two walk together except they agree?" We cannot have peace or harmony or reach our GOD ordained destiny when our selves: mind, body and spirit are in conflict constantly. If our 3 selves don't agree our lives will be stormy and we will have lack and poverty even in the midst of great prosperity.

Internal conflict causes us to act contrary to the will of GOD for our lives (aka sin) and thereby leads us away from purpose and destiny. Reconciling this conflict is in actuality what Hebrews 10:25 "forsake not the assembly of ourSELVES together" was attempting to teach us before someone misinterpreted it as a command to "go" to church. That verse, when kept in context, is teaching us to refrain from sin. Refraining from sin will prepare us to discover our identity and fulfill our destiny. The key to refraining from sin is resolving the conflict between mind, body and spirit. Our mind, body and spirit are actually separate "selves" in one being that each have their own wants and desires and attempt to make their own decisions. Thus the exhortation from GOD was to "assemble our SELVES"; to bring the mind, body and spirit into harmony or in agreement with HIS word. This is affirmed by Romans 12:1-2.

"I beseech you therefore, brethren, by the mercies of GOD, that you present your bodies a living sacrifice, holy, acceptable to GOD, which is your reasonable service. And be not conformed to this world, but be you transformed by the renewing of your mind, that you may prove what is that good, and acceptable, and perfect will of GOD."

Now, the word harmony in Greek is "sumphoneo" which means to be in accord or to agree. It is also where we derive the English word "symphony". The purpose of a symphony is to arrange musical notes in a manner that produces harmonic accord. A chord in music is three notes in perfect harmony.

Symphonic harmony is the state that we must reach in our being in order to discover who we are and eventually reach our GOD ordained destiny. It is imperative that we complete or fulfill the purpose that GOD sent us here to accomplish. That is the only way that we will hear "Well done thy good and faithful servant; enter ye into the joy of the Lord." Therefore, it is critical that we forsake not the assembly of our 3 selves together. Our mind, body and spirit must agree or come into harmonic accord in order to find our true identity and discover our GOD ordained destiny. Assembling our mind, body and spirit in unity will put our hearts in symphonic tune with the earth and the universe. Being in tune with the earth and universe gives us the ability to hear the melodic voice of GOD clearly, helps us to discover our true identity and gives Holy Spirit the authority to lead us into our destiny.

Single Mothers and Sons

What we have in Christ

Romans 8:17 says that those who are in Christ are joint heirs with Jesus. Heirs are entitled to an inheritance. As joint heirs with Jesus what inheritance are we entitled to receive? We are entitled to receive an inheritance from the Kingdom of GOD which is the financial system of the Kingdom of Heaven that GOD uses to provide for his sons on earth. Read my books Money DOES Grow on Trees and Secrets of the Fortune 500 http://amzn.to/1yUYIIR http://amzn.to/1DxyegF which you can find on amazon.com to get in depth knowledge on how to access your inheritance. Take advantage of the entrance that GOD gave you into the treasury room of heaven. You are an heir to the riches of the Kingdom of GOD therefore you should **not** be struggling financially!

Unto **you** it is given to know the mystery of the Kingdom of GOD (Mark 4:11)."

You have the right to expect to be treated like royalty because you are a royal heir. Prince William of England is entitled to an inheritance, he lives like a prince, gets treated like royalty, and is rich, simply because he is an heir of the queen. You are an heir of the King of Kings. You are supposed to be wealthy and treated like royalty because you are a child of the Most High GOD! Just as Prince William is treated as the queen is treated, you are entitled to be treated as GOD is treated. Religious people would cry that is blaspheme; that is sacrilege but this is exactly why most religious people are poor! They love to wallow around in false humility. They believe that GOD is a cruel master who will strike them down if they don't act humbly; less than what or who

Single Mothers and Sons

they really are. But again, this false humility is the very reason they remain in poverty.

There was a young man named Mephibosheth that was the grandson of King Saul and the son of Jonathan King David's best friend. David promised Jonathan before he died that he would take care of his children. So he asked a former servant of King Saul to find out if any of them were still alive. He told David about Mephibosheth who had been hidding in a place called Lodebar. His nurse thought that as the new king, David would kill off all the heirs of Saul or his relatives. In her haste to flee she fell with the boy and made him permanently lame in his feet.

"Then King David sent and fetched him out of the house of Machir, the son of Ammiel, from Lo-debar. Now when Mephibosheth, the son of Jonathan, the son of Saul, was come unto David he fell on his face and did reverence. And David said, Mephibosheth. And he answered, behold your servant! And David said unto him, fear not: for I will surely show you kindness for Jonathan your father's sake, and will restore you **all** the land of Saul your father; and you shall eat bread at my table continually. And he bowed himself, and said, what is your servant, that you should look upon **such a dead dog as I am**? Then the king called to Ziba, Saul's servant, and said unto him, I have given unto your master's son all that pertained to Saul and to all his house... as for Mephibosheth, said the king, he shall eat at my table, as one of the king's sons (2 Samuel 9:5-13)."

David was trying to restore Mephibosheth into his rightful place of royalty and position him to receive his inheritance. However, he had been taught all of his life that David would kill him. So, fear led him to genuflect in a false humility and act as if he was unworthy to stand before the king and receive his inheritance. Fear, false beliefs, and bad teaching made Mephibosheth not only lame of feet but also lame of heart. False humility is offensive to GOD because it makes the sons that HE created to be powerful appear to be pitiful. Bad teaching, false doctrine, and religious tradition have made the men of GOD lame of feet: unworthy to stand before GOD and unable to walk with HIM. It has also made them lame of heart because they don't feel powerful enough to stand up to false teaching.

"And when you **stand** praying... Mark 11:25)"

Kings kids don't fall on their face before their father. Mephibosheth fell on his face for the same reason men fall on their face to pray before GOD. They have been taught to be humble or act like they are unworthy to be in HIS presence because HE might kill them if they don't. We can continue to wallow in false humility, or we can receive the inheritance that we are entitled to, that GOD wants to give us, and eat continually at the kings table. You can live in the abundance that GOD wants to give you or you can live on the Aid for Dependent Children, Section 8 kind of subsistence that religious people would lead you to. I don't know about you, but as for me and my house, we will be SERVED WITH the Lord!

Another thing we have in Christ is GOD's Word. We have the logos or written word and we are entitled to receive the rhema or inspired word once we learn how to diligently study. We have the power contained in the word of GOD as well as the authority to utilize that power. The word will work, if you work it!

We have GOD's Will: the perfect will and the permissive will of GOD; the boulema and thelema.

Single Mothers and Sons

GOD's perfect, boulema, will is what HE intended everything to be when HE created heaven, earth and mankind. GOD's permissive, thelema, will is what HE allows mankind to do because of the authority and sovereignty that HE has given us in the earth. GOD's perfect will for us is to live like royalty, but he will allow us, by HIS permissive will, to be lowly and live in abject poverty if we want to.

We have the Holy Spirit who, according to Acts 1:8, gives us the power to be a witness to the world of not only the preeminent existence of the True and Living GOD but that both HE and HIS power reside in us.

Finally, we have Jesus, Son of the only Living GOD, who is the only deity among the more than 140,000 religions world-wide **BOLD** enough to declare "**I** am the way the truth, and the life. No man comes unto the Father but by **Me**! In Him we have **all** things that pertain unto life and godliness.

What we can do in Christ
"I can do all things through Christ which strengthens me (Philippians 4:13)."

"To whom GOD would make known what is the riches of the glory of this mystery among the Gentiles; which is Christ in you, the hope of glory (Colossians 1:27)."

The word "Christ" has three different Greek meanings: 1) chrio; the anointing, to equip, 2) Christos; the anointed one, and 3) kurios; supreme authority or the anointed one and His anointing. The anointing is the power that GOD lends natural men to enable them to do supernatural things. The anointing is the grace (the power of GOD acting on behalf of a believer) that

Single Mothers and Sons

GOD equips you with whenever HE gives you a job to do. It is the power that makes all things that appear to be impossible possible.

I can do all things through the anointing or the power of GOD which strengthens (endunamoo; empowers) me.

To whom GOD would make known what is the riches of the glory of this mystery among the Gentiles; which is the anointing or the power of GOD **in** you, the hope of glory.

The word "glory" is being used here in a manner that indicates a job, mission, or purpose has been completed or fulfilled. We give a loved one, for example, a day of glory after they have graduated high school or college. The Greek word for this is "kauchaomai" which means to exalt, celebrate, or rejoice in the context of the completion or fulfillment of an assignment or mission. Thus, the word glory should be translated to either completion or fulfillment in this verse.

To whom GOD would make known what is the riches of the fulfillment of this mystery among the Gentiles; which is the anointing or the power of GOD in you, the hope of completion. That is, the hope of completing the mission or assignment that GOD has given you the anointing or HIS power to fulfill.

There is a reason GOD placed you here. None of us were born just to suck up air, eat, drop excrement, and die. There is a purpose that GOD wants you to complete or fulfill that will benefit mankind before you exit this planet. That job or assignment is unique to the knowledge, gifts, talents, and abilities that HE placed in you. It is a job that nobody can do but you.

Single Mothers and Sons

Therefore, whenever GOD speaks to you it will be pertaining to something that HE wants you to do. With GOD everything is always about going and doing. If you analyze the name of GOD you will notice that two thirds of HIS name spelled forward is GO and two thirds of HIS name spelled backward is DO. GO & DO is a GOD Ordained Divine Opportunity to achieve glory. All of the heroes in the Hebrews 11 hall of fame of faith obtained glory because GOD said go and do, and by faith they went and did.

Now, we have five voices that we have to contend with on a daily basis that are trying to control what we go and do. Those voices are: the voice of our spirit, the voice of our mind, the voice of our body (when you want a cookie that is your body speaking), the voice of GOD, and the voice of the devil who always tries to pretend that he is GOD. Therefore, we must know how to tell the difference between all the others and the voice of GOD.

The voice of GOD when heard outside of us is thunderous, sounds like rushing rivers, and is powerful. See John 12:28-29, Ezekiel 43:2, and Psalms 29:4. GOD's voice will always be in concert and never in conflict with HIS word. The devil's voice is deceiving, tempting, and tormenting. See Matthew 4, Genesis 3, and Mark Chapters 5 and 9. The devil will try to use the word in an effort to make us believe that he is GOD speaking but his word will always be a twisted version of GOD's word.

When GOD speaks to us from the inside it comes up in a still or quiet manner that harmonious or melodic in tone. Until our body is made a living sacrifice unto GOD whenever we hear the voice of GOD our inclination is to go in the opposite direction; to run and

Single Mothers and Sons

hide. (Note: whenever a preacher says that he ran from "the calling" to preach he is telling you that GOD called him while his body was still in rebellion which means his mind was too. It also means he is a dangerous dude.) This is the reason after something happened you said: something told me to or something told me not to. That something was the voice of GOD trying to guide, direct, and protect you but you chose to do the opposite of what HE said to do.

Our instinct to go in the opposite direction is the reason I believe GOD chooses to speak to us quietly and melodically. This reminds me of a teacher I had in high school. Whenever he tried to give us personal advice and we didn't agree he would respond in a quiet musical tone: allllriiiight sucka! At the end of the day we would find out that he was right and would have to do what he said anyway. I believe, therefore, that GOD speaks using harmony or the musical scale to lead us into harmony with HIS will as well as to teach us a lesson.

The musical scale is: do, re, me, fa, so, la, ti, do. Now, the first note is pronounced doe but it is actually do because with GOD everything is related to go and do. Since we tend to run in an opposite direction from what GOD said we usually find our self in difficulty and eventually have to go back to the point where we disobeyed GOD when HE told us to "do". Consequently, we end up going back up the musical scale but only after changing the notes ti, la, so, fa, me, and re into: tired, lazy, sorry, fat, meals, and recover. We spend so much time running from GOD getting in trouble and becoming depressed in the process that we become tired, lazy, sorry and fat from eating so many meals that we need to recover. Notice at the beginning and the end of the scale you will find the word "do". This is teaching you that you can run and hide but at the end of the day you will always have to "do" what GOD said. There is power, riches, and glory or fulfillment waiting for us if we would just do whatever GOD gave us an assignment to do.

"And He [Jesus] is the head of the body, the church: who is the beginning, the firstborn from the dead; that in **all** things He might have the preeminence (proteuo; first or first example). For it pleased the Father that in Him should all fullness dwell (Colossians 1:18-19)."

GOD made Jesus after HIS likeness to provide us with an example of what HE wanted us to be like. GOD sent Jesus here to do various exploits to be an example of what HE expects us to do. That means, whatever we have seen Jesus do in the word it was put there as an example to show us that we can do it also.

What we can do in Christ is utilize His power to cast out demons, heal the sick, mend the broken hearted, etc. We can control our environment, just as Jesus controlled the wind and the waves of the sea, just as Jesus walked on the water and Peter followed after, we can do this and more if we only have the faith to believe that we can.

"I will lift up my eyes unto the hills from whence comes my help. My help comes from the LORD... (Psalm 121:1-2)"

GOD Prospers HIS Sons

"A man's gift makes room for him and brings him before great men." ~ Proverbs 18:16

GOD's word promises that HE will make our names great and place us before great men and I am living proof that GOD keeps HIS promises. I was a US Army

Single Mothers and Sons

Intelligence Analyst where I was responsible for briefing White House Senior Staff Executives, U.S. Senators, Congressmen, Generals, and foreign dignitaries on matters concerning intelligence. I had some of the world's most powerful people literally sitting at my feet because I had information they needed. A blue collar boy from Buffalo should not have been in that position. Room was constantly being made for me and I was placed in positions that I shouldn't have been in because I was gifted. That happened because GOD's word promised to bring me before great men and HE delivered!

I must stress, however, that I am nothing special. And I am not trying to brag about me. I am sharing my experiences to brag about GOD! When we faithfully follow GOD's word, HE is faithful to equip, empower and strengthen us. Having GOD as a business partner or your CEO is an unbeatable asset. Operating on the principles of GOD's word will lead to massive success both in business as well as in life, love and family.

After retiring from the Army I went back into the entertainment business promoting concerts and parties. There was a very hot comedy show on tour that was selling out box offices all over the country. I noticed there was a gap in their tour dates and locations that I could easily fill so I put in an offer to book the show. The problem I encountered was there were veteran concert promoters who were well known, well established, and highly financed that wanted to book the same show at the same venue where I had planned to produce it. I beat the veteran promoters who had big reputations, large organizations, and more cash because GOD gave me a game plan. HE showed me what to do, what to agree to, and I got that

Single Mothers and Sons

contract! I'm not bragging about me, I'm telling you about GOD.

I was in California during the late 80's where the car driven by young urban professionals in that area was the Volvo. Rather than buying new cars I always went to an auction to find a late model used one at a bargain price. I hate paying interest so if I couldn't find what I wanted at the auction I would go to a dealer and pay cash. In the process of negotiating with the salesman I ended up buying a clean and loaded 85 Volvo for $3,200 cash. Volvos were in high demand so I should not have gotten it for that price. However, I did what the Spirit of GOD told me to do and said what HE told me to say and I got the car for that price anyway. About a week or two later the salesman called me up and asked to meet me for lunch. The reason he wanted to meet with me was to teach him how I got him to sell me that car for that price. He said "I didn't make a dime on that sale." I had no choice but to confess to him that it wasn't me, it was GOD.

Another incident related to this car is the favor I received with car insurance. I had been with Allstate for years so I insured it with them but they charged me $1,600 per year. Paying that high premium made me feel like I was paying a car note. Paying interest on a depreciating liability disturbs me. So I asked GOD what to do and the Spirit of the Lord said switch to GEICO. I went into the office to get a quote and the woman said your premium will be $843. I was dejected because it appeared GEICO would cost $86 more than Allstate. So I asked, is that quote for every 6 months? The lady said, "No, for the year!" I wrote her a check for $420 so fast it made my head spin. GOD has always

Single Mothers and Sons

blessed me in this way when I listen and do what HE says.

During this time I was living in Monterey, California which is located 95 miles south of the Oakland/San Francisco Bay area and about 450 miles north of Los Angeles. Being a young single man on the weekends I jump in my car drive to the bay or take a flight to LA (because it was a 6 hour drive) and party in those cities. In the process of playing the jet setting, smooth dressing, parting playboy I ran up the debt limit on a couple of credit cards. I didn't realize what I had done until I noticed that I was paying the equivalent of the average home mortgage on those credit cards every month and the balance wasn't moving. I felt like a slave working for nothing because paying this debt was taking almost all of my money. So I cried out to GOD and asked HIM what to do to get out of debt captivity.

I cut back my partying lifestyle to direct that money towards those bills. Then I started getting assignments that sent me on temporary duty. On those assignments you get extra money for travel, lodging, and food. I lived like a man from Zimbabwe in seedy motels and spending only $20 on food each day. Every penny I saved I paid it on those cards. Just before coming home I received a check for a little over a thousand dollars. I only needed nine hundred and change to finish paying off the debt. I made that payment and was so happy to finally be debt free.

When I got back home I received a letter from the payroll office stating that I had been over paid $3,000 and they wanted that money back yesterday. When you owe the government money and they say they want their money NOW they mean it! So I decided to go to the office to see if I could work out a payment plan. I

Single Mothers and Sons

was so dejected I didn't want to drive. I walked so that I could have time to think about how this happened and ask GOD to help get me out of this debt.

A guy met me at the service counter and I explained about the letter I had received. He went to pull my file and when he returned he said "We don't have a record that you owe anything." I said "Can I have that in writing!" He said, sure, and pumped out a letter on the spot. I walked out of there letter in hand and once again a free man; instant debt cancellation. If you do, GOD will!

GOD Protects HIS Sons

The Spirit of GOD saved my life many times throughout my life. The first time it happened I was about 2 years old. I wandered out into the street and suddenly I heard car tires screeching. I turned and saw the car coming right at me but my reaction was to just sit down. When the car stopped the bumper was less than an inch from my head. The next time occurred when I was around 5 or 6 shortly after I had begged my mother to get baptized. I wanted to be a preacher and in my little mind I thought you had to get baptized to be a preacher. I used to just about memorize each sermon and would perform in front of my mom who got a real kick out of it.

One night I was awakened by what felt like a hundred pairs of hands holding me down on the bed. They were forcefully pushing on every part of my body and holding my head down so that I couldn't move. I heard a voice that sounded like it might be the voice of the devil saying "We're going to kill you!" So I yelled "Jeeessssussss!" and, bang, they were gone. Then I heard a voice that sounded like the voice of GOD that said "Don't worry, you're not going to die."

Another night while sleeping I was awakened by a strange light in the room. You know how the light looks in a room at night when the lamp shade is removed. I knew that I had turned off the lamp before going to sleep. Now I'm awake and wondering who turned the lamp on. But the lamp wasn't on. I looked to my left and I saw a pair of feet standing on the pillow. I looked up and there was this giant sized individual standing there. From his feet up to the area just below his shoulders was bronze colored. He appeared to be wearing a pair of brown overalls. The area of his body from his shoulders to his head was a very bright white that was more like just light than color. I asked him "Who are you?" I saw his lips moving but I couldn't hear any sound.

I didn't want him to know that I was scared so I hooked my left arm around his ankles, hooked my legs around his waist, and pulled him down to the bed. I jumped on top of him and yelled in his face, "Who are you?" Again, his lips moved but made no sound. That is when I noticed that he didn't have eyes. In his eye sockets were flickering red and yellow flames. Suddenly, the light was sucked out of the room all at once and he was gone. The Spirit of the Lord revealed later that he was an angel that protects me while I sleep. I wasn't supposed to see him but the spirit world opens up to us while we sleep. What we believe are dreams are sometimes activities that we observed in the spirit world that lets us see into the future. The portal closes right before we wake up but I became conscious before it closed and was able to see the angel.

Single Mothers and Sons

On my way out of a supermarket one night I was surrounded by six guys. One guy stepped in front of me and yelled to another guy who was standing a little further away and asked him "Is this the one?" The kid said "Yeah, that's the one who tried to jump me!" Now, I have to admit that I used to fight for any reason or no reason. I had fought a lot of kids in the neighborhood but I never fought this particular kid because whenever he saw me he would just run away. The guy in front of me started questioning me in an effort to distract me from what the other guys were doing behind me. At that moment, GOD gave me 360 degree vision so I could keep my eyes on the guy in front of me and see the others taking out their knives. One guy had gotten down on all fours behind me to set me up for what was called a "road block". The guy in front was going to push me over the guy on the ground and they would commence to stabbing and kicking.

GOD told me what to do. When the guy in front moved to push me I had to step to the side, make him fall over, push through the two standing to my left and run. I was about 3.5 blocks from the street where I lived. Once I started running it took about 3.5 seconds for me to turn the corner onto my block. The two guys who I had pushed through tried to chase me but they couldn't keep up with the speed GOD had given me. I still had 360 degree vision as they chased me so I didn't have to look back. I saw them slow down to a trot, stop and look at each other as if to say, did you see that! Some people get saved by the bell however I have continually been saved by grace.

The last story I will share regarding GOD saving my life is I was driving one winter on a highway covered with snow and ice. I was making the transition from

Single Mothers and Sons

one highway to the next on a curve when my car went into a 360 degree spin. That joker was spinning like a top. I managed to get the car out of the spin but now it was sliding sideways. There was no guardrail there only grass and about a 3-4 foot high embankment. When the car slid up to the grass area I could feel it starting to tip over. I didn't know what to do so I yelled "Jeeeeeesusss!" and, bang, the wheels hit the ground and the car came to a dead stop. It was like somebody grabbed the car and just stopped it. You know who did it right? GOD promised when I was a little boy the day the devil tried to kill me that I wasn't going to die. GOD has kept HIS promise faithfully in spite of me.

GOD Creates Provision for HIS Sons

I have to remind you once again here that I'm not bragging about me. I'm telling you about GOD. I cannot explain why I have received so much favor in my life. But I have always loved GOD, always loved reading the word, and always enjoyed fellowshipping with other men who know the word well enough to run me to the book. They would share something that I read but never received the revelation they saw. So I would run to my book so I could see it too. Other than that there is nothing special about me. I believe that what GOD has done for me HE will do for everyone.

As a boy I used to play on garage roofs by myself like I was fighting bad guys, monsters, dragons and such. One day I was playing where a group of garages from one street lined up back to back with the garages from the next street. I sat at the edge of one roof tired, thirsty and hungry. I said something like "GOD I'm hungry." I looked down in between the two garages and there was a fence and growing on the fence was a

Single Mothers and Sons

grapevine. On that grapevine as the biggest, bluest, sweetest, juiciest grapes I had ever seen or tasted in my life. To this day I have NEVER been able to find a grape in a store that tastes like the ones GOD provided. Nobody knew that grapevine was there except me and the spiders that protected it from the insects.

I had a job as a section supervisor where there were 3 others who supervised sections along with me. I had the top performing section because I believed in leading my people to operate in excellence. The only thing I would do besides counseling them on their performance; complementing where they were strong and giving guidance where they were weak, I would grab a random 10% of their work each day and review it. If I found 10% of that 10% had errors that meant to me that they had an overall 10% error rate or they were working at 90% efficiency.

I never bought into that nobody can be perfect nonsense. Anybody who wants to be 100% can be. Most people just need someone to push them to it. So, I pushed my people, they performed, and I rewarded and promoted them accordingly. Rather than asking me how I got my people to perform brilliantly the other supervisors went to our boss and complained that I was trying to make them look bad. They wanted to see if he could transfer me. He looked for a job for me and one was available.

Now, I was a non-commissioned officer however this job was for a commissioned officer. Nobody wanted it because it was a kiss of death possibly career ending job for an officer. The job was an Operations Liaison Officer whose duty was to bridge the communications between the Brigade and Battalion elements that were responsible for the same mission. However, the

Battalion Commander, Lieutenant Colonel, had to report to the Brigade Commander, Lieutenant Colonel, and these boys "hated" each other. Of course, I didn't find this out until I took the job.

To make a really long story short I was able to work the liaison mission well enough to get these two men to actually become friends. Being in that position led me to another job where I became responsible for briefing White House Senior Executive Staff, Senators, etc. That position also led me to be promoted to the senior ranks in only 8.5 years where it took the average person 12-15 years to make it. My peers wanted me transferred and my boss had set me up for evil but GOD turned it into good.

GOD Gave HIS Sons Authority and Dominion

This will be the final example in my testimony. There are people reading this who still think that I'm bragging about me so this one is going to be just too much for them. I could not tell you with certainty that GOD wants every man and woman to operate in dominion and authority over the earth and without giving you an example of how HE led me to exercise that power.

"But strong meat belongs to them that are of full age, even those who by reason of **use** have their senses exercised to discern both good and evil (Hebrews 5:14)."

Those who are not mature enough in Christ to receive strong meat are going to have trouble believing this one. In Buffalo, NY it snows in January. We have had some legendary record braking snow fall there during that month. I was given an assignment by a preacher to teach a Saturday morning class on the topic of faith.

Single Mothers and Sons

This was an important assignment because for most people faith is a major area of struggle. While I was studying one day I heard a weather report that said the city and surrounding area would be blanketed with snow on the very day I was to teach. I asked GOD what to do and HE said command it to not snow. I spoke to the clouds and commanded them not to snow in Buffalo and it did not snow. The surrounding suburbs were crushed but Buffalo only received a light dusting that simply blew in on the wind.

When GOD said that HE wanted men to reign as Kings and have dominion and authority over ALL of the earth HE meant it. One of the reasons GOD sent Jesus is to show us how to do it. Whatever we've seen Him do we can do. Colossians 1:18 says GOD made Jesus to be the Head of the church "that in all things He might have the preeminence" or that He would be the first example to us in ALL things. We saw Jesus curse a fig tree, we can do it too. We saw Jesus heal the sick, we can do it too. We saw Jesus rebuke the wind and the waves, we can do it too.

Everything Jesus showed us that He could do was but an example of what GOD intends for YOU to have the power to do. The only catch is you must first overcome yourself, overcome the world, and become perfected as Jesus is. You can go to the Father to receive HIS grace and power but you cannot get to the Father unless you first become "like" HIS Son.

"...With men this is impossible; but with God all things are possible." ~ Matthew 19:26

"...If you can believe, all things are possible to him that believes." ~ Mark 9:23

Single Mothers and Sons

"...Ask, and it shall be given you; seek, and you shall find; knock, and it shall be opened unto you." ~ Luke 11:9

"If you live in me, and my words live in you, you shall ask what you will, and it shall be done unto you." ~ John 15:7

What We are Supposed to do in Christ
- Recognize that you are a son of GOD
- Make the conversion into perfection and Christ likeness
- Have dominion and authority over the earth
- Govern the Kingdom of Heaven on earth
- Administrate the Kingdom of GOD on earth
- Complete or fulfill your created purpose
- Become wealthy and live abundantly
- Leave an inheritance of wealth and a lifestyle of faith for the next generation

Chapter 2
Purify Yourself

"And every man that has this hope in him purifies himself, even as HE [GOD] is pure (1 John 3:3)."

Purification of a man begins with purification of his heart because purification must occur in a man at the core or center of his being. The Bible uses the word "heart" as metaphoric references in 3 ways. It refers to a man's spirit, his mind, and the central cause for the situations he finds himself in. That is, the heart of the man, the heart of the mind, and the heart of the matter. When we are born again the heart of the man, his spirit, is cleansed or made new. The heart of the mind remains infected and affected by sin and therefore must be cleansed too. GOD purified our spirit but HE charged us, made it **our** job, to purify our own mind and body.

"Do not you yet understand that whatsoever enters in at the mouth goes into the belly and is cast out into the draught? But those things which proceed out of the mouth come forth from the heart; and they defile the man; for out of the heart proceed evil thoughts, murders, adulteries, fornications, thefts, false witness, blasphemies (Matthew 15:17-19)."

It is easy to tell when the heart of a man needs to be purified by the words that come out of his mouth; "...out of the abundance of the heart the mouth speaks (Matthew 12:34)." A journey of a thousand miles does **not** begin with the first step it begins with the first thought. You must have a thought of taking the step in your mind for your body to respond to before it will move. The situations and circumstances that we find

Single Mothers and Sons

ourselves in life are the direct result of the thoughts we have been thinking. Once we complete the process of purifying our mind it will end or eliminate some of the calamity in our lives.

Purification of the mind is a process that you must initiate and complete on your own. Contrary to popular belief, GOD is not going to do this for you. You must do this for GOD, Jesus, your family, and for yourself <u>by</u> yourself. GOD will help you after you reach a certain point. But you must diligently do what you can do then GOD will do what HE can do.

I used to drink like a fish. I loved to drink and I loved everything about drinking. I loved the way it tasted. I loved the way it smelled. I loved the way it made me feel. I loved the fact that it changed my personality, made me funny, and made me the life of the party. Drinking is what I and my friends did and we had fun doing it. One day we were having a bar-b-q and I was cooking so I started drinking and grilling about 10 in the morning. I drank all day and by 3 AM the next morning I was sitting in a club still drinking. In the club I always drank top shelf, man style, so I was drinking Chivas Regal neat. I took a sip and suddenly that scotch started tasting like dog dookie smells. Then the Spirit of the Lord said to me: "Why are you drinking that?" In my drunken madness I answered: "Yeah, why AM I drinking this? I put that glass down and decided to never pick up another one again. Over a period of time of being determined not to drink and fighting with and losing my friends over it, GOD took away my love and desire for it. It has been 35 years now since I had a drink because I have no desire for it.

I also had what some might call a sex addiction. I loved women and women loved me. Getting them to make love with me was easy. Throughout my days of womanizing I was a GOD loving Bible reading young man. One day I was reading my Bible when the Spirit of the Lord interrupted me and asked: "How many women have you had sex with?" I tried to count them while listing them by name. By the time I got up to 82 I became embarrassed and had to stop and repent because while I could remember their faces I couldn't remember a lot of their names. GOD warned me then that my next child was going to be a girl and if I didn't repent all of my sin will be visited on my daughter.

I felt bad and had fully intended to repent but I met this big booty cutie and forgot all about GOD's warning. When she told me that she was pregnant the memory of GOD's warning struck me like lighting. I fell down and repented at that moment, which was in 1993, and I have been celibate ever since. I still love women and I still love sex but the lust that I had for sex is gone.

Purification is a process of making yourself quit engaging in sin and being lured into lust so that GOD can then remove the desire in our heart for sin and lust. Since the seduction of Eve ("...when the woman saw the tree was... desired to make one wise..." ~ Genesis 3:6) and the fall of Adam in the Garden satan has used the same three things against men to cause them to fall to their desires: the lust of the flesh, the lust of the eye, and the pride of life. He always uses them because they always work. He even tried to use them in the temptation of Jesus.

"Being forty days tempted of the devil in those days He did eat nothing: and when they were ended, He afterward hungered. And the devil said unto Him: If you be the Son of GOD, command this stone that it be

Single Mothers and Sons

made bread [lust of the flesh]... And the devil, taking Him up into a high mountain, showed unto Him all the kingdoms of the world in a moment of time [lust of the eye]. If you therefore will worship me, all shall be yours [pride of life] (Luke 4:2-8)."

"And when the devil had ended all the temptation, he departed from Him for a season. And Jesus returned in the power of the Spirit into Galilee... (Luke 4:13-14)."

If satan will try to use Jesus' desires against Him, you know that he will do it to you. Therefore, we must determine to make ourselves become disaffected from the world and disinfected from sin by purifying ourselves. Then the Holy Spirit, just as it did with Jesus, will come to aid and comfort us.

In order purify yourself or become pure you have to purge (pur**G**e) yourself. Eliminate the "g" in the word purge and you will get the word pure. To purge and become pure you must begin by removing the G or get the garbage out of your mind, body, and physical presence. The first step in the purification process requires stopping your lustful activities completely and getting rid of everything and everyone that you were doing it with. Once you have purged the garbage out of your life and you have been diligent in keeping it out, the inner "G" or the power of GOD will come in to help you finish the job permanently. If you get the garbage out but don't let GOD in, satan will return with new garbage seven times more powerful than that which you purged (Luke 11:26).

There is a process of purification and there is also a process of sin that, if we don't complete the process of purification, will lead us into total depravity. There are 7 (seven) steps in the process of sin. Purification gives us the power or godly will to stop at the first step

Single Mothers and Sons

because without lustful desire sin has no power. The seven steps in the process of sin are:
- Observation – we see something that we desire
- Stimulation – our flesh or body is activated by it
- Admiration – we start gain a mental acceptance of it
- Experimentation – we decide to try it; just once
- Participation – we begin to do it more often
- Consummation – we plan activities around it and select friends or associations based on it
- Reprobation – we lack the godly will to quit, become depraved, live in iniquity, and die in sin

"...the wages of sin is death; but the gift of GOD is eternal life through Jesus Christ our Lord (Romans 6:23)."

"If any man defile the temple of GOD, him shall GOD destroy; for the temple of GOD is holy, which temple you are (1 Corinthians 3:17)."

"...if the Spirit of HIM that raised up Jesus from the dead dwell **in** you, He that raised up Christ from the dead shall also quicken your mortal bodies by HIS Spirit that dwells in you (Romans 8:11)."

It is said that you cannot help a drug addict, for example, until they hit rock bottom and have no place to look but up. Reprobation is rock bottom. It is a type of spiritual death due to iniquity that puts a man one step away from physical death. If he does not find a way to repent once he becomes reprobate he is already knocking on death's door. He has to revive his spiritual life in order to save his natural life. The only way to come back to spiritual life is by the aid of the Holy Spirit. The Holy Spirit will not only save a man's spiritual life but He will quicken or revive his mortal body as well. A body that had been ravaged by sin can be made new again. However, spiritual intervention to save him from reprobation only comes through personal repentance.

The longer you deviate from the path of righteousness the more you become deviant. The primary attraction to deviation from the path of righteousness is through association with other people. Association leads to assimilation into other people's sins. Sinful assimilation ultimately leads to iniquity. Sin is something you fall into. Iniquity is something you plan to do. Iniquity is a consequence of forming a connection to people and becoming joined for a common sinful purpose and making yourself a companion in the fulfillment of your lustful desires together.

We need purification to eliminate the lust within us that draws us into sin and iniquity through our associations with other people. This is why the Bible warns us to not be unequally yoked to unbelievers. But, you know as well as I do that some church going believers can lead you astray too. The other problem is we cannot get through life without associations with other people and we have a tendency to allow people to pull us off our path too easily. Therefore, we have a duty to chose our path righteously and establish our relationships accordingly.

When we are searching for an identity while trying to show the world a picture of who we are we use people to help the world receive a sense of our identity. We choose people to surround ourselves with that give the world a reflection of our real self and our true direction. The problem with using people to help identify yourself is they will frame you.

Single Mothers and Sons

When you try to present the world with a picture of who you really are, you have the picture but then there is the frame. The frame surrounding our picture has 4 parts that are comprised of people, places, activities, and things. That is, the people you associate with, the places you go, the activities that you get involved in, and the things you do modifies your picture and often gives the world a different view of you. If the picture you want to show the world is righteous but the people, places, activities and things that you surround yourself with are illicit, the frame is going to change how the world sees your picture. Therefore, purifying yourself also involves analyzing and eliminating the people, places, activities, and things in your life that can hinder the purification process, modify the world's image of you, and cause you to backslide.

"I beseech you therefore brethren by the mercies of GOD, that YOU present your bodies a LIVING sacrifice holy, acceptable unto GOD, which is YOUR reasonable service (Romans 12:1)."

The Apostle Paul declares that it is **our** responsibility to purify ourselves; to make ourselves holy and acceptable to GOD and describes it as our reasonable service to GOD or as the least that we could do for HIM considering how much HE has already done for us. This reinforces the fact that not only is purifying ourselves our responsibility but also that GOD is NOT going to do this for us as many preachers lead us to believe.

Leading people to believe that GOD is going to do this for us leaves people languishing in sin and leaning on foolish axioms such as: "GOD ain't finished with me yet". I try to shake people awake when I hear them say that by saying: "You are 40! GOD is not finished with

Single Mothers and Sons

you because HE is through! Once I get them to come down off the roof I ask them: When do you think GOD is going to be finished with you and why do you think it is taking so long? Do you think that it has something to do with what you are either doing or have not done? People rarely give an answer to those questions because they don't want to reveal their private sins. So I gently touch them and tell them: GOD saved you and HE has done what HE is going to do so now you have to finish you. You have to purify yourself. Otherwise, you are going to fool around to the point where GOD will not only be finished with you, HE will be through.

"And be not conformed to this world: but be you transformed by the renewing of your mind, that **YOU** may prove what is that good, and acceptable, and perfect, will of GOD (Romans 12:2)."

It is our job to refuse to conform ourselves to the ways, thoughts, and ideals of the world. It is our responsibility to transform ourselves from sinner to saint by cleansing, purifying, or renewing our mind; changing the way that we think from the ways of the world to the way of GOD. It is our duty to prove (dokimazo – pass the test) to show what is that good, acceptable, and perfect will of GOD to the world. Accepting our responsibility faithfully will lead us into the perfect will of GOD for our lives. Purifying ourselves will help lead those who see our example and choose to believe into the will of GOD for their lives as well.

Many wise men of history who spent their entire lives in search of the key to the mystery of alchemy (the process of turning lead into gold) never discovered that alchemy was simply a reference to GOD's purification process or plan for a man.

Single Mothers and Sons

Every man is born with the appearance of being as worthless lead or coal when in reality he is as valuable as diamonds and gold. Alchemy, is the process of transforming our lower self (which causes us to behave bad and therefore makes us look bad) into our higher self. It is a process of transforming from the mental and spiritual state that makes us a lead weight on our family, friends, and community into being worth our weight in gold.

Wealth and poverty are not states of money they are states of mind. The mystery of alchemy is simply the purification process that transforms a man's mind and spirit in a way that makes him a source of value to himself and others and allows him to evolve from poverty to wealthy through the proper use of his personal currency. His personal currency is the knowledge, gifts, talents, and abilities that he was born with inherently.

Jesus revealed the secret to alchemy when HE said, "where your heart is there will be your treasure also." Those who have been purified in the heart of the man and the heart of the mind can uncover the treasure that was hidden in their heart at birth. Every time GOD gives you a tough job to do, such as being an ambassador of Heaven and administrating the Kingdom of GOD on earth, there are reasons but there are always rewards. One of the reasons we must purify ourselves or change alchemically is so that we can represent (re/present) Jesus righteously. The reward is access to the treasury room of Heaven.

The Truth about Perfection

"Be you therefore **perfect** even as your Father which is in Heaven is perfect (Matthew 5:48)."

Single Mothers and Sons

"All scripture is given by inspiration of GOD and is profitable for doctrine, for reproof, for correction, for instruction in righteousness: that the man of GOD [YOU] may be **perfect**, thoroughly furnished, unto all good works (2 Timothy 3:16-17)."

"But let patience have her perfect work, that YOU may be **perfect** and entire, wanting nothing (James 1:4)."

"But the GOD of all grace who has called us unto HIS eternal glory by Christ Jesus, after that you have suffered a while, make YOU **perfect**, establish, strengthen, settle you (1 Peter 5:10)."

The scriptures above are just a small sample from a multitude of Bible verses that admonish or encourage us to be perfect. If GOD directs **you** to be perfect even as **HE** is perfect, WHY then do we have so many people who believe to their dying breath that NOBODY can be perfect? WHY do so many religious leaders declare that you are committing blasphemy if you said that you are perfect? If it is impossible for a human being to be perfect in this human flesh then WHY was Jesus determined to be the preeminent example of how a man in flesh can be perfect?

"...let GOD be true, but every man a liar... (Romans 3:4)." GOD would not command you to be as perfect as **HE** is if it were not possible for **you** to be perfect. GOD would not call for you to do a job without equipping or empowering you with whatever you need to get the job done! If HE commands you to do something, GOD is already certain that you can make it happen.

Part of the purification process involves cleansing our mind from unproven doctrines, falsely held beliefs, and traditional religious thinking. False doctrines and teachings have hindered the body of Christ collectively and prevented us individually from coming into the truth of the of the word of GOD. Consequently, the truth of who **we** really are in Christ Jesus and what He has given us the power to do has been hidden from us. This is why the church appears to be powerless to heal sickness and disease and impotent to transform people's lives.

"Beware lest any man spoil [Greek: Sulagogeo – seduce; make merchandise] you through philosophy and vain deceit, after the tradition of men, after the rudiments of the world, and not after Christ." ~ **Colossians 2:8**

The primary culprit that has kept GOD's people impotent and powerless is the false doctrine that we cannot be perfect. The traditional philosophy that nobody can be perfect is a rudiment of the world and is vain as it does not lead men to be productive. It is deceitful in that it makes men believe they are being pious. That philosophy is CLEARLY meant to contradict the word of GOD in an effort to seduce men to be used or made merchandise by other men. If a man won't teach you right, he won't treat you right. The word instructs, admonishes, and warns us that we **must** become perfect. Again, GOD would not tell is to be perfect if we couldn't do it. And GOD will not give us a job or an assignment without providing the provision to get it done. Ergo, HE gave us the 5 fold ministry and charged them with the duty to lead HIS children into perfection.

"And HE gave some, apostles; and some, prophets; and some, evangelists; and some, pastors and teachers; for the **perfecting** of the saints, for the work of the ministry, for the edifying of the body of Christ (Ephesians 4:11-12)."

Single Mothers and Sons

The 5 fold ministry's assignment is to lead GOD's people into perfection and He gave them the power or anointing needed to get the job done. However, their collective acceptance of the false religious doctrine that no man can be perfect has made them fail to carry out their charge. Just about every preacher you know teaches that the word perfect in this scripture translates in Greek to mean "mature". However, there is NO, I mean absolutely NO, Greek dictionary or lexicon that defines the word "perfect" as mature. The Greek word for perfect that may be misinterpreted to mean mature is "teleios" or "full age". The word "age" here is not a reference to a person's chronological age but rather a time period; the fullness of time, or the end of an era. The phrase "full age" is not a reference to maturity but rather a state of perfection.

"...strong meat belongs to them that are of **full age**, even those who by reason of use have their senses exercised to discern both good and evil (Hebrews 5:14)."

It is easy to misinterpret the phrase "full age" in this verse to mean mature because it is being expressed in the context of comparing spiritual adults to spiritual babes. However, you can know that it is not saying "strong meat belongs to them that are mature" simply by reading the very next verse after 5:14.

"Therefore leaving the principles of the doctrine of Christ, let us go on unto **perfection**... (Hebrews 6:1)"

Full age in Hebrews 5:14 is one of the English translations of the Greek word "teleios" or perfect: "strong meat belongs to them that are perfect" or to them who have been perfected in the measure of the stature of the "fullness" of Christ. It also means to be complete because those who have been perfected in Christ Jesus are complete in Him.

"Beware lest any man spoil you through philosophy and vain deceit, after the tradition of men, after the rudiments of the world, and not after Christ. For in Him dwells all the fullness [perfection] of the GODHEAD bodily. And you are complete [perfected] in Him, which is the head of all principality and power (Colossians 2:8-10)."

Misinterpretation of the word perfect to mean mature has caused the majority in the body of Christ to remain spiritual babes and thus have failed to become perfected in Christ. The majority of church going adults in the body of Christ are still living with the "I love Jesus and Jesus loves me" mentality of a spiritual baby. Therefore, they must be fed baby food from the word of GOD because they can't handle strong meat. Consequently, the Sunday School lessons for Christian adults has to be taught out of those quarterlies that keep you going around and around over and over the same basic information.

This is just like the adult children of Israel who kept going around in circles covering the same territory over and over. It took them 40 years to make a trip that should have taken 11 days. 11, by the way, is the Bible number of perfection and is a symbolic representation of 1 who has been perfected standing next to the 1 and only begotten Son. Anyway, ALL of those adults died in the wilderness except for 2 of them. It should have taken them only 11 days to reach the state of perfection and thereby qualify for the promise. But they died in the wilderness because they refused to let go of their slave mentality and grow up into spiritual adulthood. Therefore, GOD could not allow them to enter the

Single Mothers and Sons

Promised Land. Sadly, this is exactly what we are seeing today. People who went to church for 40 years are dying as spiritual babes, never reaching spiritual adulthood, seeking the Promised Land, but being laid to rest in the wilderness.

So now, let's be clear about the definition of the word perfect in Ephesians 4 since we know now that it does not mean mature. You need to know then that there are ten (10) definitions in the Greek language for the word perfect. The word "perfect" is used in all 10 of those ways in the New Testament. Therefore, wherever we see the word "perfect" in a verse we have to examine the context where it appears to make sure that we are applying the right meaning to the word so that we can obtain the proper understanding of that verse. So, let's examine Ephesians 4 and apply the definitions that fit within that scripture's context.

One Greek meaning of the word perfect is "replete" (pleroo). That is, to be **supplied** with everything we need to fulfill the purpose for which GOD gave us life. Another Greek definition for the English word perfect is katartizo which means "complete, repair, fit, prepare, and restore. This definition of perfection is a reference to the perfection process whereby we may become complete in Christ and cleansed from all unrighteousness. This is the definition that fits in the context of Ephesians 4.

"And HE gave some, apostles; and some, prophets; and some, evangelists; and some, pastors and teachers; for the **perfecting** [completion, reparation, fitness, preparation, or restoration] of the saints, for the work of the ministry, for the edifying of the body of Christ (Ephesians 4:11-12)."

Single Mothers and Sons

GOD wants us to do the work of the ministry of Jesus Christ and thereby edify the body of Christ but we must be perfect in order to get the job done. Therefore, HE called for the 5 fold ministry to lead us into perfection or to be complete, repaired, fit, prepared, or restored to fulfill the mission. Again, GOD is not going to give you an assignment to do without equipping you to get it done. So, HE gave us Apostles, Prophets, Evangelists, Pastors, and Teachers to lead us through the perfecting process completely so that HE can then trust us with HIS power or the anointing necessary to do the work of Jesus' ministry without controversy due to human failings.

"Having therefore these promises, dearly beloved, let us cleanse **ourselves** from all filthiness of the flesh and spirit, perfecting holiness in the fear of God (2 Corinthians 7:1)."

The 5 fold ministry must keep GOD's charge and lead HIS people through the perfecting process so that: 1) we might be at peace, not in opposition or enmity with GOD, 2) we might be made whole with nothing missing, nothing broken; perfect, entire, and wanting nothing, and 3) so that we can be endued with the power of GOD to do the work of the ministry. Perfecting is supposed to occur sometime at an early stage of our spiritual development. GOD sent HIS servants to lead us through this stage of development because the average man would likely not have yet learned to discern the voice of the Spirit of the Living GOD. Ergo, he may not yet be disciplined enough to heed His teachings well enough to perfect himself in true holiness.

"Till we all come in the unity of the faith and of the knowledge of the Son of GOD, unto a **perfect** man, unto the <u>measure</u> of the <u>stature</u> of the <u>fullness</u> of Christ (Ephesians 4:13)."

  The English word "perfect in this verse is translated from the Greek word "teleioos" which means complete as well but it also means to be consummated or become accomplished at the task of becoming one with or like as another as husbands and wives become one when they are in perfect union with one another. You might have heard somebody say before "they've been married so long they are starting to look like each other." This is what happens when we become consummated or one, in perfect union, with Christ Jesus. We begin to appear to be as He is to the point that without wisdom the world wouldn't be able to tell us apart from Him. This is why the number 11 in the Bible represents Christ likeness. When the world sees a person who has become 1 in Christ standing next to the number 1 son of GOD, 11, it is hard to tell the difference between the two without the wisdom to know the difference.

  Now, there is a phrase that is used over 430 times in the Bible and that phrase is: it came to pass. Everything comes into our life for a reason and it only stays for a season. Everyone's life and everyone's ministry came to pass because it is only programmed to last a season. You do not have your entire life to get the work of the ministry for which GOD placed YOU in the earth for fulfilled. You are assigned a season of perfecting which includes the purification process. And you have a season of execution which concludes at the point of completion and fulfillment of your heavenly purpose. This is why GOD set a time limit for the 5 fold ministry, a standard for how long they would do the work of their ministry which is indicated by the word

Single Mothers and Sons

"till" or until, and what the finished product should look like so that they would know when it is complete.

"**Till** we all come in the unity of the faith and of the knowledge of the Son of GOD, unto a **perfect** man, unto the measure of the stature of the fullness of Christ (Ephesians 4:13)."

Every organization has an administration along with a mission, objectives, and goals. Examining Ephesians 4:11-13 you can see clearly the administration of the 5 fold ministry. There are 3 or a trinity of missions: 1) perfecting of the saints, 2) the work of the ministry of Jesus, and 3) edification of the body of Christ. There is also 3 or a trinity of objectives: 1) unity of the faith and knowledge of Christ, 2) become perfected, and 3) to lead us to stand in Jesus' measure and stature. Now, verse 14 reveals the 5 fold ministry's 3 goals.

"That we henceforth be no more children, tossed to and fro, and carried about with every wind of doctrine, by the sleight of men, and cunning craftiness, whereby they lie in wait to deceive (Ephesians 4:14)."

It is crucial that the TRUE ministers of the 5 fold ministry accomplish their goals in order to help men obtain victory over their selves and overcome the world because the devil knows scripture. He will use other men who are FALSE ministers of the 5 fold ministry to toss us about on every wind of false religious doctrine. And as I illustrated earlier, He will use the word to try to make you bow down and submit to his will just like he did with Jesus. If he tried to do it with Jesus, he will have NO problem trying to do it with you. Therefore, it is crucial also for you to remember that you only have a season to get your job done. The longer you go without being perfected, purified, and empowered the longer you will have to endure satanic trouble.

Single Mothers and Sons

Graduation in Perfection

Brothers, once you come into the unity of the faith with Jesus and the knowledge of Him to the point where you are complete, repaired, fit, prepared, and restored up to the measure of His stature in His fullness it is time for your instruction by the 5 fold ministry to end. When you are in the measure of the statue of Jesus' fullness if the world saw you standing next to Him, they should not be able to tell (initially) the difference between you and Him. Once you reach that level of maturity in Christ, grasshopper, it is time for you to leave the 5 fold ministry and begin the work of completing and fulfilling your created purpose.

The reason they make the desks so small in the 3rd grade is to force you to leave when you get too big for the chairs. They make the chairs little so that it won't be comfortable for you to sit around in 3rd grade when you should be in high school. One of the rules of high school is once you graduate you can't come back. If you came back after graduation the Principal will ask you: What are you doing here? You may say well, I have been going here for 4 years, my mother went here, and my grandmother went here, so this is where my family always goes. However, the Principal will make you leave and tell you that if you want to take more classes you have to go to a school of higher learning, sweetheart. You cannot come back here!

Once you have been perfected you have to leave the 5 fold ministry of begin to operate in the ministry or purpose that GOD has for your life. You go to pre-K for a season. Then, you go to elementary school for a season. Then, you go to middle school for a season. Then, you go to high school for a season. Then, you go to college for a season. Then, you have to get a job; you've got to get to work! At some point you have to leave going to school and begin to do and be what the school trained you to do and be. If you were going to law school at some point you must go and be a lawyer. The same is true for teaching under the 5 fold ministry. After you have been taught all you need about Jesus Christ at some point you must go out into the world and BE like Christ; you have to stop going to church and start BEING church. You have to stop learning under the 5 fold ministry of Christ and start doing the work of the ministry of Christ that GOD has ordained for you to do in **your** life.

"And as they went on their way they came unto a certain water: and the eunuch said, See, here is water; what does hinder me to be baptized? And Philip said if you believe with all your heart, you may. And he answered and said I believe that Jesus Christ is the Son of GOD. And he commanded the chariot to stand still: and they went down both into the water, both Philip and the eunuch; and he baptized him. And when they were come up out of the water, the Spirit of the Lord caught away Philip, that the eunuch saw him no more: and he went on his way rejoicing. But Philip was found at Azotus: and passing through he preached in all the cities till he came to Caesarea (Acts 8:36-40)."

Once the student has learned the lesson he either has to leave the teacher or GOD will make the teacher leave him. In this case GOD sent the teacher to another place to preach. GOD's men have been conditioned to believe that they **must** remain with the same preacher in the same church all of their life. It almost takes a bomb to get a person to leave a church. People have gotten into the habit of worshipping their preacher and making them a type of idol god. Since GOD cannot get the people to leave and their preacher chides them for wanting to leave GOD has been taking away the preacher. Some have been going to other churches to preach. However, many have been dying suddenly who are yet young men in their 40's, 50's, and 60's. Don't make your preacher an idol god and cause him to be taken out. Once you know it's time to go you have a duty to leave and allow yourself to be led where GOD would have you to be.

I heard the pastor of a 26,000 member church tell a story about how his pastor kicked him out of his church. He said that his pastor recognized that it was time for him to start his own church. So the pastor called him in front of the church, gave him his blessing to start a church, asked 100 tithe paying members to volunteer to go with him, and he sent him off. When he came back that Wednesday for Bible Study his pastor asked him: What are you doing here? He said I came for Bible study. He said his pastor told him: Get out of here and go to your own church for Bible study! He said "I was so hurt I didn't know what to do but after a while I realized that it was the right thing to do." Once you have learned everything you can from a teacher it is time to move on. Remaining there will not only stop you from growing it will also cause you to regress. Rather than becoming a man in Christ you will remain a boy.

Reposition Yourself to Receive Heaven's Reward

"In my Father's house are many mansions: if it were not so I would have told you. I go to prepare a place for you (John 14:2)."

Single Mothers and Sons

When you approach the gates of heaven at the end of your days the only way you will get to hear "well done thy good and faithful servant, enter ye into the joy of the Lord" is if you have completed the mission or purpose that GOD sent you here to fulfill. GOD is not interested in how "good" you were while you lived. HE will only want to know if you completed your heavenly assignment while you were alive.

The English word "mansion" here comes from the Greek word "mone" (pronounced: mon-ay') which of course means residence or place of abode. But now, look at the scripture carefully. Does it say in my father's house there are **only** mansions? No, it says there are many mansions. We know that a mansion is the highest level of residence or place of abode on earth and we know by the universal principle of: as above so below, everything in the earth is merely a reflection of things in heaven. Ergo it stands to reason that a mansion is the highest place of abode in heaven as well. It also stands to reason that there are lower places of residence in heaven. Since there are ghettos on earth do you think that there might also be a ghetto in heaven? Who do you think would get to live in the mansions of heaven? More than likely it would be those who fulfilled their purpose on earth, right? So, who do you think might have to live in heaven's ghetto? I don't know if there is a heaven's ghetto. Just in case on the off chance that it might be I would rather get my heavenly assignment done, get up there and hear well done, and get to live in an eternal mansion. Amen?

I believe GOD where HE says that HE wants to bless us abundantly while we yet live on earth as it is in heaven. The reason most people don't receive a reward

Single Mothers and Sons

from GOD's "living will" is simply because they have not been taught how to receive it. With a little more knowledge about how and why GOD blesses people, you could be experiencing exceeding, abundantly, above all you could ask or think kind of blessings. Read my books **Money DOES Grow on Trees** (http://amzn.to/1yUYIIR) and **Secrets of the Fortune 500** (http://amzn.to/1DxyegF) for more information on how to achieve abundant living. As it is now we are taught to just be thankful for the subsistence, Aid For Dependent Children, Section 8 kind of blessings from GOD wherein HE provides money, food, shelter, and clothing as a form of charity because HE knows that we have a "need" of these things.

Religious people who are satisfied residing in the spiritual projects, living on spiritual child support, spiritual welfare, and heaven's food stamps in life maaaaay be the ones who will have to live in the ghetto of heaven. However, if you believe GOD will bless you far beyond anything you could imagine, complete your heavenly assignment and you can get to live in a heavenly mansion! You could probably get the job done under your own power but it will be much easier if you first become perfected and purified because GOD then will lend you his power.

"This I say therefore and testify in the Lord, that you henceforth walk **not** as other Gentiles walk, in the vanity of their mind (Ephesians 4:17)."

You see, religious people lack the level of power and provision that GOD wants to give them because they believe that walking in false humility will cause them to be elevated in the sight of GOD. They think that making themselves downtrodden; appearing to be nothing more than a lowly worm and a filthy rag will put them at the head of the line at the gates of Heaven. They look mealy-mouthed and say I'm grateful for every little blessing the Lord gives me because they think to GOD that is ingratiating. They don't know that to GOD this is false humility and is irritating particularly when they come crawling before the throne in prayer. GOD said to "...come boldly unto the throne of grace..." in Hebrews 4:16, not crawling, crying, and begging.

I hate to use a criminal as a metaphoric representation of how GOD operates in an illustration but we don't see any examples of "good" men in the movies commanding their sons to stand up and be men. There is a scene where Johnny Fontaine is whining and crying to the Godfather because a studio executive refused to give him a part in a movie. He says "Godfather, I don't know what to do; I don't know what to do." The Godfather jumps out of his chair, grabs him, and says "You can act like a man! What's the matter with you! Is this how you turned out, a Hollywood boy that cries like a woman? Heh heh, what can I do; what can I do?"

This reminds me of how GOD confronted Job as he was whining, crying, and complaining with his friends. GOD came to him and said "Who is this that darkens counsel by words without knowledge? Gird up now your loins like a man; for I will demand of you, and you will answer me (Job 38:2-3)!"

GOD, like most fathers, hates it when HE hears HIS children whining and complaining. HE hates it when we act like we are helpless and can't do something because we are trying to be humble. True humility is when you CAN do something but you don't because

Single Mothers and Sons

GOD hasn't said so yet. True humility is doing what GOD said to do instead of doing what you want to do. False humility is a product of having never been perfected. The 5 fold ministry has not taken its charge therefore GOD's people are tossed to and fro with every wind of religious doctrine. Thus, the world perceives GOD's people to be unstable and is becoming increasingly unwilling to follow Jesus. Why would people want to move from a lowly state in the world to a lower state in Christ?

Take Back Your Power and Authority

"Beloved, **now** are we the sons of GOD, and it does not yet appear what we shall be: but we know that, when He shall appear, we shall be like Him; for we shall see Him as He is (1 John 3:2)."

The disciples of satan lie in wait to deceive the children of GOD to prevent us from becoming perfected in an effort to reduce the number of soldiers in the army of GOD. Can you imagine how confused the enemy is going to be in the day of Armageddon when he comes out to fight with Jesus, he sees millions and millions of people who look just like Jesus, and he can't tell who the real Jesus is? He will flee in terror knowing that it is impossible for him to win. Ergo, it is critical that we cast off false doctrine, come into the knowledge of the truth, and be perfected in Christ. The truth is, we not only <u>can</u> but we **must** be perfected in Christ Jesus.

"But speaking the truth in love, may grow up into Him in <u>ALL</u> [not some, all] things, which is the Head, even Christ (Ephesians 4:15)."

"And He [Jesus] is the head of the body, the church: who is the beginning, the firstborn from the dead; that in ALL things He might have the preeminence. For it pleased the Father that in Him should ALL fullness dwell (Colossians 1:18-19)."

"I can do all things through Christ which strengthens me (Philippians 4:13)."

If the true teachers of GOD carry out their 5 fold ministry charge GOD's children will grow up into Christ in **all** things. That is, whatever we have seen Him do, **we** will be able to do. Jesus is the preeminent or the first example for us in **all** things. Therefore, we **can** do all things that we have seen Jesus do through Christ [the anointing] which strengthens us or gives us the power to do it. Not just in some things, but all things.

"For unto us a child is born, unto us a Son is given: and the government shall be upon His shoulder: and His name shall be called Wonderful, Counselor, The mighty GOD, The everlasting Father, the Prince of Peace. Of the INCREASE of His government and peace there shall be no end (Isaiah 9:6-7)."

"From that time Jesus began to preach and to say: Repent for the Kingdom of Heaven is at hand (Matthew 4:17)."

Jesus taught many things but He preached only ONE thing: "Repent for the Kingdom of Heaven is at hand." The most overlooked and rarely preached reason why Jesus came to earth was to deliver or give man access to the Kingdom of Heaven. You will find a scene in the book of Job Chapter 1 where satan entered heaven after he had been cast out yet there was no commotion or alarm related to his presence. GOD simply started having a conversation with him. GOD never asked satan what are you doing here, HE asked him where have you been? The reason satan could enter heaven without alarm and didn't get treated like a burglar is because he obtained the right to be there from Adam.

"...The first man Adam was made a living soul; the last Adam was made a quickening spirit (1 Corinthians 15:45)."

You see, Adam was a son of GOD, the first Jesus, which is the reason Jesus is called the last Adam. Adam not only had dominion and authority over all the earth, like Jesus, he also had authority in Heaven up to but not including the throne of GOD. When Adam yielded his authority to satan authority to enter Heaven was included. Jesus came not only to undo what Adam had done but also to restore to you and me what Adam had given away. Thus, when Jesus preached "repent for the Kingdom of Heaven is at hand" He was alerting us to prepare ourselves to receive authority and access in Heaven as sons of GOD.

I know the point I stated above is controversial because I have taught it before in churches and men's conferences specifically. Invariably, there is always that <u>one</u> guy who gets upset at the revelation that Adam had authority in heaven. He gets hell bent on trying to make me prove to him from the Bible that this is true. So, I have to calm the boy down by saying, listen, I am a teacher. My job is to teach you things that you don't know. When it comes to revelation that is controversial instead of coming from the Bible I must prepare your mind to receive revelation by leading you from what you know to what you don't know.

So I ask, have you ever scheduled office hours with a professor? The reason you did that most of the time is because you didn't understand some things. More often than not to help you understand he shared information that wasn't presented in class and wasn't written in the book. Well, the Holy Spirit does the same thing. While studying with the Holy Spirit you will receive rhema and logos information. That is, revelation on things that are not written and clarification on that which is written. There are numerous scriptures that prove that statement is true. If a man can't receive revelation that means it is being hidden by GOD from him or it was **not** meant to be revealed to him. That means there is nothing wrong with the teaching or the teacher. Something is awry in the student's relationship with GOD.

"And He [Jesus] said unto them, Unto **you** it is given to know the mystery of the Kingdom of GOD: but unto them that are without, all these things are done in parables: That seeing they may see, and **not** perceive; and hearing they may hear, and **not** understand; lest at any time they should be converted and their sins should be forgiven them (Mark 4:11-12)."

Contrary to common Christian belief GOD does not want everyone to understand HIS word, does not want everyone's sins to be forgiven, and does not want everyone to be saved. The reason is because of the hardness of their hearts. HE knows that they may say that that they want to be saved and they will come to have their sins forgiven but they are only looking for absolution and will go right back out and sin anyway. This is precisely what we see happening in church today. People go to church figuring that it will give them some sort of credit in heaven but they leave church and go right back into their sinful ways. They can have their hands thrown up for Jesus in church then go right home and throw their legs up for Jimmy. If you cannot receive revelation that is not a reflection on me because the Holy Spirit reveals hidden

Single Mothers and Sons

knowledge to those He wants to give it to. The following verses will prove for you that at least that is true.

"…there is nothing covered that shall not be revealed; and hid, that shall not be known (Matthew 10:26)."

I thank you, O Father, Lord of heaven and earth, because you have **hid** these things from the wise and prudent and have **revealed** them unto babes (Matthew 11:25)."

"…you have heard of the dispensation of the grace of GOD which is given me to you ward: which in other ages was **not** made known unto the sons of men, as it is **now** revealed unto his holy apostles and prophets by the Spirit (Ephesians 3:2&5)."

"…who has known the mind of the Lord, that he may instruct him? But **we** have the mind of Christ (1 Corinthians 2:16)."

Receiving revelation from the Holy Spirit works on the ask, seek and, knock principle. He will share the knowledge of heaven and earth that Jesus has in His mind with those who diligently seek it. Jesus wants to share that knowledge with those who love Him like David ("a man after mine own heart") loved GOD so that we can be as He is. Heart equals mind; David sought after what was on GOD's mind. We have to love GOD and Jesus enough to seek after their mind and have a desire to know how they think. Amen?

Getting back to the subject at hand… We reside on earth but we are actually citizens and ambassadors of the Kingdom of Heaven. In every country where the United States has an embassy that embassy is sovereign US territory. A representative territory of the US is set up in a foreign country that is governed by the

Single Mothers and Sons

US Ambassador and operates on the same laws, rules, and regulations of the US government. The government of the US comes to that foreign nation and the people in the embassy are charged with administrating that government.

When the Holy Spirit came to the foreign territory of earth He established the embassy of the Kingdom of Heaven on earth. As members of the "body" of Christ and ambassadors of the Kingdom of Heaven we are charged with administering the government of Heaven on earth. Jesus is the "Head" of the church and we are the body. Isaiah Chapter 9 says "the government shall be upon His **shoulder**" not His head. The shoulder is a part of the **body** therefore the government of the Kingdom of Heaven on earth rests upon you and me as citizens and ambassadors of Heaven and members of the body of Christ.

"Now then we are ambassadors for Christ as though GOD did beseech you by us: we pray you in Christ's stead, be you reconciled to GOD; for HE has made Him to be sin for us, who knew no sin; that **we** might be made the righteousness of GOD in Him (2 Corinthians 5:20-21)."

This scripture teaches us that GOD wants us to occupy the role as ambassadors for Christ. However we must first be reconciled to GOD, go through the purification process to become sin free, so that we can represent the government of Heaven righteously.

"...the wealth of the sinner is laid up for the just (Proverbs 13:22b)."

As we administrate the government of the Kingdom of Heaven on earth we are also charged with administrating the financial system that Heaven operates on. That system is called the Kingdom of

Single Mothers and Sons

GOD. As administrators of the Kingdom, like Joseph, we are also in charge of the Kingdom's treasury so there is no reason why you and I should not be living abundantly. GOD did this to restore to HIS children not only the power and authority but also the treasure that satan stole from Adam. Thus, just as Pharaoh did with Joseph, GOD has positioned us to rule over HIS house, the Kingdom of Heaven, up to but not including the throne of GOD. My brothers, we have to get over the false religious and elementary or childish ideology that we are not worthy. GOD is expecting HIS sons, HIS men, to be rulers over HIS Kingdom.

"You shall be over my house and according unto your word shall all my people be ruled: only in the throne will I be greater than you (Genesis 41:40)."

"Therefore leaving the principles of the doctrine of Christ let us go on unto **perfection**; not laying again the foundation of repentance from dead works, of faith toward GOD, Of the doctrine of baptisms, and of laying on of hands, and of resurrection of the dead and of eternal judgment (Hebrews 6:1-3)."

"But speaking the truth in love, may grow up into Him in **all** things, which is the Head, even Christ (Ephesians 4:15)."

We are no longer children or babes in Christ my brothers. It is time therefore that we stop walking around on the elementary knowledge on which the church was founded like the Children of Israel did; wondering in the wilderness 40 years when it should have only taken 11 days. Some of us have been going to church for 40 years and are still feeding on the same old Sunday school information that you received when you were a kid. We have to move on to the advanced knowledge that GOD is trying to reveal to us today so that we can grow up into and have the mind of Christ. Thus, we will be equipped with what we need to rule His kingdom effectively.

"Jesus didn't come that we might have church He came that we might have life. However, we do church better than we do life so much of what we do in church has no effect on our life." ~ **Bishop T.D. Jakes**

The purpose of the Bible is to show us the plan of GOD for our lives which is to return to us what the devil stole from Adam. The Garden of Eden was the first embassy of Heaven on earth; the Kingdom of Heaven on earth in which Adam was the Ambassador. The Bible, from Genesis to Revelation, is GOD's plan to move man back to the Garden, reclaim the embassy, and free the hostages. However, this time the embassy will reside **in** men internally to prevent us from giving it away to satan again physically. GOD has given you an opportunity to have a peace within you that passes all understanding; to live in the secret place of the Most High. That is Eden, the Garden, the Kingdom of Heaven. GOD made you to lie down in green pastures beside still waters, in the shadow of the Almighty, and to restore your soul. The new Eden, the Kingdom of GOD and Heaven, that secret place is now **in** you.

"He that dwells in the secret place of the most High shall abide under the shadow of the Almighty (Psalm 91:1)."

"...behold, the Kingdom of GOD is within you (Luke 17:21)."

GOD has a job for us to do and it is time that we get to being about our Father's business of leading and managing the Kingdom of Heaven on earth until He returns. That job begins with the perfecting of the saints and the purification of the hearts and minds of GOD's men. Are you ready to go to work? Let's GO!

And he called his ten servants delivered them ten pounds and said unto them, occupy [Greek: pragma – do business] till I come (Luke 19:13)."

Chapter 3
Understanding Your Mind

"You've got to win in your mind before you can win in life." ~ **John Addison**

A man cannot change his life until he first changes his mind. Periodically, you have to do a quality check on what you have been thinking and verify the knowledge that you have been using as a guide for your life to see if it is valid. If you have goals and aspirations that you have failed to fully achieve, you must review the knowledge that you have been operating on to see whether it is properly serving you. If what you know has not been working for you, you have to eliminate the old information and obtain new knowledge to use as the foundation upon which to build your game plan or chart a new direction.

This is hard for most men to do for many reasons but there are three primary reasons we don't discard unproductive information: 1) philosophy, we love what we know, 2) paternity, we love the person who gave us the information, and 3) identity, we associate what we know with who we are.

Pride often prevents us from accepting the fact that we are wrong. We know what we know and we are not going to let anyone tell us any different. Loyalty prevents us from recognizing that the parent, grandparent, or other loved one who shared their wisdom could have been wrong. When people who love us share wisdom they are doing it out of love. They were sincere when they shared their wisdom but they were sincerely wrong. They inadvertently shared wisdom that put us on the wrong path and are now long gone but out of a sense of loyalty we are still trying to hang on to the last advice grandmamma gave us. The world's worse vice is advice from a respected loved one. You must periodically evaluate your information, regardless of where it came from, to see if what you know has been working for you. If the knowledge you have been operating on has not led you to where you want to be, it is time to discard it and replace it with new information.

My mom loved me dearly so I can tell you unequivocally that she would never give me bad information intentionally. However, she gave me counsel concerning my sons that changed their lives and that I have regretted following the rest of my life. As a kid I used to sit with her in the kitchen while she cooked and we would talk about different issues. One of the things I admired about her is that she was very smart. We were talking about cancer one day and she said she believed lung cancer didn't come from smoking the tobacco but rather inhaling the sulfur from the matches. A teacher held a discussion in class about the cause of cancer and when I shared my mom's belief about the origin the teacher and the entire class laughed me to scorn. My mom was sincere when she said those things but she was sincerely wrong.

The third major reason why it is difficult for most men to discard old information is it creates a crisis of identity. The word "information" is comprised of the syllables: in, form, ation. The word "in" in this context means: inner, within, or on the inside. The word "form" means: to shape or develop and the suffix "ation" means: the act or process. When you combine the meaning of those syllables you get the "true" meaning of the word information: the act or process of

Single Mothers and Sons

forming, shaping, or developing a person on the inside. Old information then becomes difficult to discard because it shaped and developed who we are. If I have been living on knowledge that shaped and developed my identity that is incorrect then who am I really?

The person that you were when you were 13 should not be the same person that you are at 33. You have to allow the information you receive throughout the course of your life shape and develop your life so that you are always growing and evolving as a person. Allowing new information to help you grow and evolve personally will lead to a transformation mentally, spiritually, and financially as well as lead you to live abundantly.

I was going to church every week, reading my Bible, and watching a lot of TV ministries in an effort to increase my knowledge and build my faith. I had gotten caught up in that whole faith based charismatic movement and I sent them "tons" of money. I did that because I truly believed that giving money was a demonstration of great faith and that a high level of faith is what moved the hand of GOD. I'm telling you, I sincerely believed that until I went from simply reading my Bible to studying it.

All of the TV ministers frequently quoted the same scripture from Romans 10:17 "So then faith comes by hearing and hearing by the word of GOD." I operated in faith, guided my life, and began to form my identity as a Christian based on what I was told this scripture meant. I was determined to stand in faith based on what I thought this verse meant even though I knew that it was not working for me. It wasn't until I started studying on my own that I realized what this scripture was actually saying.

Single Mothers and Sons

"So then faith comes by hearing and hearing the word of GOD." This scripture is plainly telling me that growing or increasing your faith has nothing to do with giving money, planting seeds, and all of that. Faith comes by hearing and hearing the word of GOD!

Now, the word hearing being used twice may seem redundant or it can give the impression that hearing is something that must be done repeatedly. While that impression is correct in terms of learning (teaching requires repeating until learning takes place) that is not what this scripture is actually saying. The English word "hearing" is used twice because it came from two different Greek words that translate to the same word in English although they mean two different things in Greek. The first word "hearing" comes from the Greek word: "akoe" meaning a process of listening or having heard. The second word "hearing" comes from the Greek word: "akouo" which means understanding. Since I had been studying voraciously, scriptures were beginning to line up in my mind quickly so these verses came to my memory:

"...the LORD gives wisdom: out of HIS mouth comes knowledge and understanding (Proverbs 2:6)."

"Wisdom is the principal thing; therefore get wisdom: and with all your getting get understanding (Proverbs 4:7)."

"He that gets wisdom loves his own soul: he that keeps understanding shall find good (Proverbs 19:8)."

So then, faith comes not by giving and giving your money into charismatic ministries. Faith actually comes by having heard and understanding the word of GOD! This verse is telling me that you cannot increase your level of faith without having heard the word of GOD along with having an accurate understanding of

Single Mothers and Sons

what you heard. This is why studying your Bible is so crucial. Receiving understanding works on the ask, seek, and knock principle. Ask and you shall receive, seek and you will find, knock and it SHALL be opened up unto you. After you have been studying and seeking to understand the Bible diligently, the Holy Spirit comes to open it up for you. You need the Holy Spirit to be your teacher because 1) no man can ever be a better teacher; the Holy Spirit can lead and guide you into ALL truth whereas a man can only lead you into the truth that he knows, and 2) no man has the knowledge of who you really are and what GOD sent you here to do; you need the Holy Spirit to lead you into that truth.

"But the anointing which you have received of HIM lives **in** you, and you need not that **ANY** man teach you: but as the same anointing teaches you of **ALL** things, and is truth, and is no lie, and even as it hath taught you, you shall live in HIM (1 John 2:27)."

Sadly, people and even preachers will try to lead you away from obtaining understanding through studying by implying that if you don't have a preacher telling you what the word means the understanding that you are receiving is your OWN understanding and not the truth. Ergo, they use scriptures like the following to discourage you from studying and to shake your confidence in the Holy Spirit's ability to lead and guide you into all truth:

"Trust in the LORD with all your heart; and lean not unto your own understanding. In all your ways acknowledge HIM and HE shall direct your paths (Proverbs 3:5-6)."

The flaw in their attempt to prevent you from studying is that the word "heart" in this verse means

Single Mothers and Sons

"the mind" ("You shall love the Lord your GOD with all your heart and with all your soul and with all your mind ~ Matthew 22:37"). Trust in the Lord comes from the love that we have for HIM based on the experience we've had with HIM and HIS faithfulness to HIS word. Acknowledging GOD is demonstrated through prayer and study of HIS word. Confidence that GOD is directing your path and not satan comes by being able to distinguish HIS voice from others through much prayer and spending time studying the word of GOD. Filling your mind with the knowledge of the word of GOD and diligently applying it to your life until you reach the point of understanding is how you build love, trust, and faith in GOD. You cannot get there from here unless you spend time studying on your own receiving guidance and understanding from the Holy Spirit.

There are 3 different levels of comprehension of the word of GOD: knowledge, wisdom, and understanding. Knowledge is the word of GOD. There is no knowledge in the world apart from the word of GOD. So, knowledge is simply knowing what GOD said. Wisdom comes when we apply the word of GOD or do what it says. In this context, wisdom is the diligent application of the knowledge of the word of GOD in your life. Therefore, wisdom is diligently doing what you know that GOD said to do. Understanding is having a complete or full grasp of the reason GOD said to do what HE said to do. When you can see GOD's reason, motivation, and strategy for what HE said in HIS word clearly and it matches up with HIS word perfectly that is when you have understanding. So, understanding is simply knowing **why** GOD said what HE said.

Why Understand the Mind?

Since we now have a good definition for the word understanding how do we apply that knowledge to understanding our mind? Why is it important as men that we understand how our mind functions? The answer in short is understanding our mind helps to lead us out of sin and into righteousness and prosperity. The spiritual battleground where you must fight the devil and win is located in our head or the battleground of the mind.

Wealth and poverty are not states of money they are states of mind. If you can recognize the attributes of your mind that led you into poverty and change them, it could lead you to become wealthy. Again, the only way to change your money is to change your mind. If you can change your mind sufficiently, you will be able to complete or fulfill your GOD ordained purpose and reach your GOD ordained destiny. Reaching your GOD ordained destiny will equip you to lead your children into their GOD ordained destiny because daddy determines destiny. The key to reaching your destiny and receiving your reward will be learning to understand your mind, how it works, why it is hard to accept new information, and how to defeat the devil.

"...they that are after the flesh do mind the things of the flesh; but they that are after the Spirit the things of the Spirit. For to be carnally minded is death; but to be spiritually minded is life and peace. Because the carnal mind is enmity against GOD: for it is not subject to the law of GOD, neither indeed can it be. So then they that are in the flesh cannot please GOD (Romans 8:5-8)."

This scripture is alerting us to the fact that we only have two ways of thinking: carnally and spiritually. It is also teaching us that one way of thinking is beneficial to us and the other is not. To be carnally minded is death, but to be spiritually minded is life and peace. Why? The carnal mind is enmity (hostile, in opposition, an enemy) against GOD.

When you see chili con carne on a restaurant menu the words "con carne" tells you that the chili has meat in it. The English word "carnal" comes from the Latin word "carnalis", which means meat. The word "mind" in this scripture is a reference to the way we think or how we use the knowledge in our head. Since carnal means meat and mind is a reference to the head, GOD is simply saying: *"Don't be a meat head!"* Thinking like a meat head is thinking that is in opposition to GOD. That type of thinking makes us hostile toward GOD, an enemy against HIM (even when we don't intend to be), and leads to death. But to be spiritually minded on the other hand or to think like GOD thinks makes us a friend of GOD. Being spiritually minded makes us subject to GOD's word, HIS will, and gives us access to long life, prosperity and peace.

When you are a saved, church going, Bible believing man who has not been purified or perfected you will continue to be carnal. No matter how hard you try to be a good man of GOD, you will still be a meat head. If your mind has not been transformed from conforming to the ways of the world you will continue to suffer in the issues of the world around you. 2 Timothy 3:12 says all that will live godly in Christ Jesus shall suffer persecution. However, your suffering will not be due to living godly it will be due to continuing to live in the carnality of your mind. The devil will have ready access to torment and persecute you because you still have one foot in the camp of the enemy. You see, when you lived in sin you were in satan's gang. Once you become

Single Mothers and Sons

saved you can't just walk out of his gang, you have to be jumped out. You suffer because being only half-way out of the gang of the enemy is causing you to take beatings periodically.

"The steps of a good man are ordered by the LORD... (Psalm 37:23)"

If you can't see your steps yet it's because they are still on order. Once you are enlightened (in-lightened) enough to light your ascent and prevent a fall, GOD will deliver your steps and install them. The process that you must go through before GOD will enlightened you is found in Romans 12:1-2. GOD is not going to complete that process for you. It is a work that you must do on yourself by yourself that is YOUR "reasonable service". We often hear the TV and mega ministry preacher prophesying on what GOD is "about to" do in your life. The only reason GOD would be "about to", "getting ready to", or "fixin' to" do anything for you is because HE is waiting for **YOU** to do what you can do before HE can do what HE can do. If you have been going to church, languishing in the pew, hoping and praying for a financial breakthrough, but nothing is happening for you it's because GOD is waiting for you do to what HE expects you to do. Then, HE will do what HE has been fixin' to do for you. The steps of a good man are arranged in this order: you do, GOD will; you do, GOD will; you do, GOD will; and so on... and so on.

Men are a lot like fish. If fish stop swimming they will die. Men are subject to thermal dynamics and the Law of Entropy which is where we derive axioms like "use it or lose it". When we stop using our brain or using our muscles they will atrophy or begin to deteriorate. For many men life is like walking on a treadmill because they are not really going forward but if they stop trying to move forward they will roll backward. Recede is to go backward and proceed is to go forward. In every endeavor toward success in order to pro/ceed you have to go through a pro/cess. Whatever the endeavor GOD orders the steps that lead to success. You must spend some time in or on each step because there is knowledge and experience that will empower you to proceed to the next step. The steps prepare you to stand on the stage and stand in the spotlight. Some men jumped on stage because they wanted to be in the spotlight but they didn't realize that with the spotlight comes heat. Life is like a university. You don't have to take the classes but you do have to take the tests. If you don't take the steps, you won't be able to take the heat. Thinking carnally makes men believe that they can skip the steps or don't have to go through the process.

Since you have not yet renewed your mind from carnality you will continue to make decisions to resolve issues based on the ways of the world instead of the word of GOD. Proverbs 4:23 says keep your heart with all diligence; for out of it are the issues of life. The issues that we have in life my brothers arise as a result of what is residing in the heart of our mind. Completing the Romans 12:1-2 process (purify our bodies and transform our minds) provides the grace that we need to live in abundant peace. If we fail to complete that process, although saved, we will continue to live in carnality. The Apostle Paul showed us how he continued to suffer with issues due to carnality after he had gotten saved.

"...we know that the law is spiritual: but I am carnal, sold under sin. For that which I do I allow not: for what I would, that do I not; but what I hate, that do I. If then

Single Mothers and Sons

I do that which I would not, I consent unto the law that it is good.

Now then it is no more I that do it, but sin that dwells in me. For I know that in me (that is, in my flesh) dwells no good thing: for to will is present with me; but how to perform that which is good I find not. For the good that I would I do not but the evil which I would not, that I do. Now if I do that I would not, it is no more I that do it, but sin that dwells in me.

I find then a law, that, when I would do good, evil is present with me. For I delight in the law of GOD after the inward man: But I see another law in my members, warring against the law of my mind, and bringing me into captivity to the law of sin which is in my members. O wretched man that I am! Who shall deliver me from the body of this death (Romans 7:14-24)?"

"And lest I should be exalted above measure through the abundance of the revelations there was given to me a thorn in the flesh, the messenger of Satan to **buffet** me... For this thing I besought the Lord thrice that it might depart from me. And HE said unto me, my grace is sufficient for you: for my strength is made perfect in weakness (2 Corinthians 12:7-9)."

You see, Paul is explaining how he continued to vacillate in and out of sin and the buffeting or beatings he endured periodically as a result. He wanted to do good but something inside of him kept leading him to do that which he **knew** he should not do. This is how we as saved, church going, Bible believing men can still cheat on our wives, lie, steal, and even murder.

GOD has given us power or grace to overcome sin and thereby end the suffering that is a consequence of carnality. Forget that nonsense about grace being the unmerited favor of GOD. That definition is like cotton candy because it has neither substance nor nutritional value. Grace is actually the power of GOD acting on behalf of the believer. GOD gives us grace or power to overcome the issues of life and eliminate the thorn in our flesh through the purification and perfection process. Once we have done all that we can do to perfect and purify our self GOD will then do what HE can do.

"HE that is our GOD is the GOD of salvation; and unto GOD the Lord belong the issues from death. But GOD shall wound the head of HIS enemies, and the hairy scalp of such a one as goes on still in his trespasses (Psalm 68:20-21)."

Now, GOD is a good Father; a far better DAD than we could ever be. You might pluck your boy upside the head when he can't seem to follow your instructions. Well, GOD will do the same to us to get our attention when we can't seem to follow HIS word. Just like you would teach your son how to keep from killing himself in the world, GOD is trying to teach us how to keep our self safe from satanic attack as well. Sometimes the little digs and nicks we have been enduring are a consequence of GOD alerting us that we have unresolved issues which are keeping us carnally minded and therefore in enmity with HIM. The suffering comes to alert you that you still have to go through perfection and purification to purge yourself of sin. Otherwise, the issues that persist in your life due to carnality could lead to death.

You have a Helper
"Be still and know that I AM." ~ **GOD**

Single Mothers and Sons

"I have found David the son of Jesse, a man after mine own heart, which shall fulfill all my will (Acts 13:22)."

The word "heart" in this context means the mind as well. David wanted to know what GOD thought. GOD made David the King of Israel because he always sought the mind or thoughts of GOD on what he should do whenever he was about to take a major step. He understood that GOD knows the end from the beginning so he would ask GOD what would be the end of his actions before he began. He would be still and wait to know what GOD knows before he would go. And he would only do what GOD said to do. If GOD said no, he wouldn't go.

GOD gave every man life for a purpose; to fulfill HIS will that HE ordained for our lives. There is something that GOD sent you here to do that is unique to you which will transform the world in some unique way. Nobody can get that job done but you. If you do not discover what your purpose is and get the job done, GOD's will won't be fulfilled and the world will be deprived.

Therefore, GOD gave you a helper, the Holy Spirit, to lead and guide you into the truth of who you really are and what HE sent you here to do. GOD would not establish a vision for your life and send you to fulfill the vision without giving you provision. GOD will provide food, clothing, shelter along with provisions of knowledge, information, direction, guidance, people, power, and divine association to help you fulfill HIS will. The Holy Spirit is given as provision for divine association to act as a mentor, if you will, to your spirit to help it guide you to do what GOD sent you here to do. You must learn to have peace within yourself or **be**

still so that you can hear the Spirit of GOD speaking to your spirit. Then you will **know** where GOD is guiding you and what HE sent you here to do. Discovery of your purpose does not come by thinking it comes by hearing the voice of the spirit of GOD.

Programming Your Mind

Contrary to popular belief the process of thinking and believing does not occur in our brain. Our brain is simply the central processing unit for our body and contains the software it needs to perform its functions. The process of thinking and believing occurs in your soul. The words spirit and soul are used interchangeably in traditional religious doctrine. The truth is your soul is the mind of your spirit. Your spirit has a body similar to your physical body therefore it has eyes, ears, and can speak. Your soul ultimately sends instructions to your brain and attempts to lead your body to function according to its will. Therefore, it is critically important to understand the while GOD gives us a renewed spirit when we are saved it is up to you and me to program our soul or spirit mind with the word of GOD. We must use the word of GOD to program our spirit mind to respond to the leading of the Holy Spirit. Then, it will have the knowledge to inform our brain to direct our body to respond to GOD's will for our lives.

Like purification and perfection, programming our soul with the word of GOD is not something that GOD does for us it is something **WE** have to do for our self. The Holy Spirit then takes the word we fed our soul and uses it, like yeast, to cause what it already knows to grow. Be advised however that the Holy Spirit only works with the word of GOD. You can feed your soul a diet of books, newspaper articles, academic studies, and so on but the Holy Spirit doesn't use any of that. You can use that information to help those you are teaching to understand the word more clearly. But, if you want to empower your soul dramatically, feed it the word of GOD constantly because the Holy Spirit uses the word only to enlighten your spirit.

As I said earlier, your spirit has eyes and ears. Those eyes and ears must be opened by the Holy Spirit to allow your soul to become your personal prophet or spiritual guide. Your eyes and ears need to be able to see into the future as directed by the Holy Spirit so that it can lead you to go and be what GOD wants you to go and do. Without spiritual eyes opened to see and ears opened to hear your access to the knowledge of GOD for your life by the Holy Spirit will be limited. And your capacity to complete and fulfill your created purpose will be diminished.

Just like thinking and believing does not occur in your brain understanding does not occur in your brain either. The process of understanding happens in the mind of your spirit. You must have your spirit enlightened by the word of GOD and the Spirit of GOD in order to understand the word of GOD. Otherwise, it becomes just a big confusing mass of unusable nonsense. That, however, is exactly the way that GOD wants it to appear to satan and his minions so that they will lack the ability to utilize the power that comes with understanding the word effectively. The only one that is authorized to give understanding to your spirit besides Jesus is the Holy Spirit. Understanding is restricted to those who study the word and diligently seek it and those whose mind is not operating carnally. Hence, the reason Jesus gave the Holy Spirit the standing directive: "He that has ears to hear, let him hear (Matthew 11:15)." We have a multitude of scriptures that show how Jesus carefully limits access to understanding the word of GOD. Oh, you can read it like satan obviously does but you won't understand it unless the eyes of your understanding in your spirit are enlightened.

"Unto you it is given to know the mystery of the kingdom of GOD: but unto them that are without, all these things are done in parables: that seeing they may see and not perceive; and hearing they may hear and not understand; lest at any time they should be converted and their sins should be forgiven them (Mark 4:11-12)."

"But blessed are your eyes for they see: and your ears for they hear. For verily I say unto you that many prophets and righteous men have desired to see those things which you see and have **not** seen them; and to hear those things which you hear and have **not** heard them (Matthew 13:16-17)."

"And I say unto you, ask and it **shall** be given you; seek and you shall find; knock, and it shall be opened unto you. For every one that asks receives; and he that seeks finds; and to him that knock it shall be opened (Luke 11:9-10)."

"...behold, two of them went that same day to a village called Emmaus which was from Jerusalem about threescore furlongs. And they talked together of all these things which had happened. And it came to pass that while they communed together and reasoned, Jesus himself drew near, and went with them. But their eyes were <u>held</u> that they should **not** know Him (Luke 24:13-16)."

Single Mothers and Sons

"And it came to pass as He sat at meat with them He took bread, and blessed it, and brake, and gave to them. And their eyes were opened, and they knew Him; and He vanished out of their sight (Luke 24:30-31)."

What is the Mind?

Again, the mind is often confused with the brain but they are two different things. The brain is to the body what a Central Processing Unit (CPU) is to a computer. It houses various programs and information and then utilizes them to lead the body to perform various functions. The mind is the CPU of your spirit that works for the spirit in the same manner as an advisory board does for a CEO. The mind feeds your brain information in an attempt to make it lead your body to perform various functions. The mind's primary purpose is to process and store information.

The main weakness in the functionality of the mind is information received first is more likely to be perceived as true when presented with new or conflicting information. This is the reason it is very hard to change a person's mind from what they believe is true. The old information or "tapes", if you will, must be located, erased and the new information stored whenever it is accepted as true. The mind itself has two areas wherein it processes and stores information: the conscious and subconscious which are analogous to the RAM and ROM respectively of a CPU. That is, Read Access Memory; can be changed easily, and Read Only Memory; must be reprogrammed.

Every person has three parts of themselves that comprise their being: a spirit, brain and body. Most people refer to these 3 parts as spirit, soul, and body but that is not true and here's why. Your body is the carrying case for your spirit. Your brain is the CPU that gives your body functionality or tells it what to do. Your body houses your spirit and soul and allows it to operate legally on this side of eternity. Your spirit is who you are; it is the real you. Your soul is the "mind" of your spirit. Your soul, **not** your physical brain, is what gives you the capacity to think and believe. The body also gives your spirit access and authority to operate in this 3 dimensional physical world. Your spirit is actually a heavenly body that can live and function in eternity but needs a physical body to function in the earth. The spirit and soul cannot remain in the earth without a physical body. So when the brain is damaged to the point where it can no longer command the body to function the spirit has to leave the body. This is why people whose body is relatively healthy die when they have a brain disease. When the body no longer responds to the brain to allow the spirit to function purposefully the spirit and soul leave.

I know that I am repeating myself but it is important to remember that the soul is the "mind" or CPU of the spirit. The soul or mind of the spirit communicates with the brain of the body in an effort to influence the body to go and do what GOD is directing it to lead our body to do.

It is crucial that we understand that the soul has a distinct function within the spirit. The English word "soul" comes from the Greek word "psuche". It is where we derive the word "psyche", which means the mind. The English word "spirit" comes from the Greek word "pneuma", which means a current of air. The spirit of man is the life of man. The air or spirit of GOD was inspired or breathed into man by GOD and he became a living soul like GOD (Genesis 2:7). GOD is spirit; every man is spirit (the real you inside of your body) that is made in the image and likeness of GOD and has the capability and capacity to think like GOD.

There is 3 million years of space for information to be stored in our brain which gives us the capacity to be all knowing like GOD is. With the power of the Holy Spirit we have the capability to absorb GOD's thoughts and simultaneously put our own thoughts into captivity. This is why the Bible says: "We have the mind (the same mind) of Christ." The Holy Spirit gives our spirit the authority to access the capability and capacity of the mind of Christ so that we can overcome spiritual blindness, understand the word of GOD, and be renewed in the mind of our spirit.

"...be renewed in the spirit of your mind and... put on the new man which after GOD (or like GOD) is created in righteousness and true holiness (Ephesians 4:23-24)."

"...you have put off the old man with his deeds and have put on the new man, which is renewed in knowledge after the image of HIM that created him (Colossians 3:9-10)."

The soul and spirit are eternal entities so they will survive physical death but the body will not (Luke 16:19-31). The reason the soul must survive with the spirit is to make judgment day a fair and just event. If I had no memory of my life and the things I had done, it would not be just or fair to judge me for what I had no knowledge of doing. I would be legally incompetent to stand trial.

The soul is the spirit's data processing center; the CPU of the spirit. The soul houses our institutional and historical memory. It stores the knowledge, information, experience and values that establish our core beliefs. The soul and the brain processes these before they are allowed to be housed in its dual core storage area known as the conscious and subconscious. This virus protection process is designed like a firewall. It examines all that we come in contact with to see if it agrees with what we already have on file in order to protect our core beliefs from corruption.

Like a board of directors, the mind is comprised of active members that direct this process. Each member has positive and negative attributes. It has 5 internal members and 2 external. The internal members are: will, intellect, emotion, imagination and desire. Flesh and spirit are external members, but they both have voices that can influence decisions the mind makes. Feeling is the voice of flesh, conscience is the voice of spirit and reason is the voice of the mind.

Components of the Mind

Will - The will is an internal force that transforms the thoughts of our mind into action or being. Will can either conform to the word of GOD or manifest the evil desire of a mind that is yet carnal. Will serves as Chairman of the mind's advisory board and runs the meeting. No decisions are acted upon unless they are authorized by the will. Therefore, the main struggle among other members of the mind is for control of the will. Each member has its own agenda that it wants to bring to the table and it needs control or approval of the will to get that agenda implemented.

Intellect - The intellect provides you and I with the ability to perform rational thought. The mind is the area within our tri-partite being where life decisions are made. However, it's through the rationalizing process of our intellect that decisions are made to accept or reject the things of GOD. Therefore, people must be intellectually trained to be wise and diligently apply the word of GOD to their lives without compromise and taught how to think and make decisions in line with the word of GOD. Then they will come to the proper conclusions and choose the freedom of light over the prison of darkness. You see, it is not changing man's laws that emancipates a man's intellect, it is the liberation of his mind through the word of GOD that makes men free (John 8:32).

The intellect is seated to the right of the will at the advisory board table and is the will's chief advisor. Intellect occupies the seat of human reasoning and logic and tells the will what to consider and what not to consider. Your intellect, which is developed by information, education and life experience in the world, will keep your mind from receiving the word of GOD. The problem is the intellect is limited by the knowledge and information that it has on hand. If our intellect is under informed our will is going to be under served, ergo, our decisions will lead us to underperform in life. So, it is critical for your soul to be programmed with the word of GOD.

Emotion - Emotion is an aspect of the conscious part of the mind that is heavily influenced by the body and/or the flesh. Flesh in this context is not the natural body but rather a man's sin or carnal nature that was born into his spirit at birth. Emotion is a state of feeling; an internal (physical and mental) response to external stimuli placed on the mind and body. There is an inherent dichotomy to emotion in that it can cause a person to either draw near to GOD or run away from HIM. Yielding to emotion is yielding to flesh. Flesh

(Greek: sarx) is the inherent lust we are born with that drives us to sin. Yielding to flesh leads to corruption (Galatians 6:7-8). Every time we yield to flesh it becomes stronger and stronger until it not only influences but dominates the system. When flesh is strong, our spirit will be weak.

Emotion can also be described as a strong surge of feelings triggered by an outside stimulus. Emotion and intellect are close associates and it exerts great influence on intellect. Emotion sits to the left of will and attempts to lead will to consider the circumstances instead of the facts in an effort to get what it wants. An indication that fleshly emotion is trying to influence intellect is when people make "not all" or "not always" arguments when confronted with the truth. Intellect has the confidence of will. Hence, emotion provides intellect with a sense of urgency to influence will to make a quick decision; to act or react to the circumstances without proper consideration.

Emotion often likes to buy things to soothe itself when it is feeling unfulfilled. Madison Avenue advertisers know how emotion works to override intellect because they hired psychologists to teach them how our mind works. This is another reason why we must understand how our minds work. Advertisers know emotion will induce intellect to respond to sales because it is driven by one of the Seven Deadly Sins: Greed. They know that psychological obsolescence creates the perception of scarcity and shortage so even though there is no need for what is on sale greed will drive emotion to get intellect to react quickly. Emotion is targeted constantly with advertising (adversary's enticing) stimuli that warns "You'd better buy that now! The sale ends today! It may not be here when you come back! This one is new and improved. Buy this now and you can get the girl, the guy or it will make you sexy!" If couples learned how to fulfill one another mentally and emotionally it might keep us from buying our way into debt captivity.

Imagination - Imagination is the creative mechanism of the mind that provides the will with images. Those mental images can enable one to visualize the plan of GOD or they can exalt themselves above the things of GOD. Imagination is our will's link to the mind's creative center and the external world outside. Imagination is the vehicle the mind uses to transport itself into the spirit world or the underworld. The Greek word for imagination is "pornos" from which we derive the English word pornography. Through the imagination we can devise million dollar dreams or craft ungodly schemes. Imagination can be used, therefore, for either good or evil. Imagination is companion to and seated to the left of emotion on the mind's advisory board. It is only an acquaintance to the intellect and it conspires with emotion to form a picture of the circumstances for the will to see the urgency of what it is being confronted with.

Desire - Desire provides the mind with access to that which we were genetically coded to be or do. We are born with both a sin nature and a divine purpose. We are all genetically coded with a predisposition to commit the sins of our fathers at birth, which is the reason we must become born again. A man could give birth to a child, for example and never have any contact with that child. Yet, that child may take on the same characteristics as his father and begin to commit the same sins his father before him committed. I have seen guys serving time in prison for burglary who have sons they've never had contact with. Yet, their boys can't seem to keep their grubby little hands off of other people's things. This occurs because the boys' desire hooks into the part of them that is genetically coded to sin. On the other hand, everyone was sent here by GOD for a particular purpose or to complete a particular task that no one can do but us. Once our desire attaches to the vision of what GOD created us to be or do, as influenced by the word of GOD, we will begin to desire to do things that will bring that vision to pass.

Desire and imagination are good friends. Desire is seated next to imagination and directly across from will. Desire is also driven by one of the Seven Deadly Sins: Lust. Desire is a place of lust, craving, covetousness or longing and can be either positive or negative depending upon how a person is living. If I am living in the flesh, my desires will be controlled by my flesh. If I am living in the spirit, my desires will be controlled by my spirit. When desire wants something it cannot have, it gets imagination to show emotion a picture in an effort to excite it. Once emotion becomes excited it tries to influence intellect. Intellect listens to both of them present the positive aspects of their proposal as imagination provides a pleasant picture. The intellect then directs the will to the image and influences it to act without considering the negative consequences.

Flesh - Flesh is Chairman Emeritus of the mind's advisory board when the spirit is in control. Flesh is always invited and is always present at the meetings because it used to be in charge before we were born again. But, flesh is no longer an active member because it is retired. Still, it has great influence on the other members as one would who used to be in control.

Single Mothers and Sons

Constant movement is an attribute of flesh once it is activated. It is always moving and never sits down because it wants direct access to each member. Flesh always seeks a way to devour or dominate the will and cause it to become reprobate through the mind's other components.

The flesh contains our inner nature or genetic makeup. The flesh is genetically coded to sin and disobedience. It became upset when we gave our lives to Jesus. Flesh used to be Chairman of the Advisory board of the mind when we were involved in sin. At that time, all of the lust and desires of the flesh could be fulfilled. The flesh controlled our emotions, intellect and imaginations and gave itself everything it wanted. Once we became saved, our spirit empowered our will by the word of GOD and reduced flesh to emeritus or pre-retirement status. Still, flesh gets to attend the meetings. The will, empowered by the spirit, basically forced flesh into retirement. Therefore, a war is still waging in our mind for control of our will. Flesh is always seeking to regain dominance. This is why we must refresh our minds daily with the word of GOD.

You see, flesh knows that our spirit is responsible for the will being in control. So it does not want the spirit to provide input or the word of GOD into the decision making process. The advantage flesh has is it controls the tongue unless it is taken over by the will. Flesh uses the tongue to interfere with our deliberative thought process because deliberating thoughts must stop and pay attention when our mouths begin to speak. GOD created the world by speaking and being made in HIS image and likeness we have the power to shape our world by the words that we speak. A lust for control is also the reason why flesh fights against the baptism of

Single Mothers and Sons

the Holy Spirit. The baptism of the Spirit gives control of the tongue to our spirit. Both flesh and spirit need the tongue to speak what they want into existence. Therefore, the tongue is an important instrument because words are creative. The world was framed by GOD's words. Words said by your father to your mother are the means by which you were born. Confessing the word is the means by which you were born again.

Spirit - Your spirit is the real you. However, your flesh presents itself to the world as the real you. Therefore, it acts as a hindrance to your spirit. When you accept Jesus into your life, your spirit is the only thing that gets born again. Your mind and flesh do not become born again. Therefore, the mind must be renewed and the flesh must be controlled or brought under subjection to the word of GOD by the Holy Spirit.

"I beseech you therefore brethren, by the mercies of GOD, that ye present your bodies a living sacrifice, holy, acceptable unto GOD, which is your reasonable service. And be not conformed to this world: but be ye transformed by the renewing of your mind, that ye may prove what is that good and acceptable and perfect will of GOD (Romans 12:1-2)."

The Holy Spirit can stand inside the waiting room outside the meeting of the advisory board of the mind. It cannot come in and speak, however, unless will gives it permission. Since the Holy Spirit is governed by spiritual authority, it has no authority in the material realm unless it's given authority by something natural. Flesh needs no permission to speak and neither does emotions, intellect, imaginations or desires because they are natural. But, the Holy Spirit cannot say a word or deliver the word of GOD until the will gives it permission. Ergo, there is a battle waging in the mind between flesh and Holy Spirit for control or influence over the will.

When the board of the mind meets to resolve the issues of life, each component struggles to have its resolution enacted. While the members deliberate, the Holy Spirit sits outside waiting with the answer. He has been in contact with GOD who knows all things. The Holy Spirit's presence goes unnoticed because he is out of sight. He becomes out of mind, in effect, as the members of the mind and flesh engage in conflict. After a while, the Holy Spirit knocks in an effort to get them to realize that he is standing at the door with the answer to their situation to try to keep them from devising an answer through the confluence of the mind. Human logic may bring temporary relief but rarely provides a long term solution. Therefore, you must learn to purify yourself, renew your mind, and allow the Holy Spirit to be the primary advisor to your will rather than your intellect.

Renew your Mind

"A double minded man is unstable in all his ways (James 1:8)."

In order to renew our minds, we have to first become born again. Renewing the mind requires that we overcome the old man or our old nature. Becoming born again gives us the capacity to do that. It will be futile to try to create a new mind in you when you still have an old nature. That will make you double minded or schizophrenic. This is why many church people appear to be crazy or unstable with some even looking like they might have a devil. Jesus likened mixing a new mind with an old nature to putting new wine into old wine skins. The pressure created by the fermentation process will cause the old skins to burst. Similarly, the pressure created by the process of renewing the mind without a renewed spirit will cause a person's old mind to warp and become vulnerable to satanic attack.

Renewing our minds requires that we also have to learn how the mind functions because renewing the mind involves clearing out old information. Renewing the mind is difficult because the things we learn first are preeminent in our subconscious and we tend to fight to hold on to that which is first. This is what is referred to by some as the law of first mention. Things that are learned first remain preeminent in our minds until they are challenged or corrected. Information that we come in contact with is received by the conscious mind. It is then validated and stored on tape in the subconscious mind. Any information that the conscious mind is presented with that contradicts the information stored in the subconscious mind is rejected. Unless the subconscious mind is confronted with irrefutable facts that proves the information it has is invalid, it will not accept it. However, once the conscious mind becomes aware that information in the subconscious mind is invalid, it will accept it, but it will not erase the previous information. The mind will retain it for future reference.

What happens, in effect, is a piling on of new information on top of old instead of building pure truth. The structure of the information contained in your subconscious mind then becomes unstable. It will topple over and crash if it becomes overloaded or unbalanced with contradictory information.

Single Mothers and Sons

Consequently, a person will find himself agreeing with information that is presented to his conscious mind even though he knows it is not true. Once he hears that information, a tape will be played in his subconscious that has the correct information on it. He will know the information is wrong. Yet, depending upon **who** presents the information, how he feels or what he wants, it produces cognitive dissonance in his mind and he may accept the information anyway. The presence of cognitive dissonance is how some of us become unstable, tossed to and fro with every wind of doctrine, and easily led astray.

Creating cognitive dissonance in our mind is the same process those in media, politics, and advertising use to take control of our minds in an effort to move us to think, behave and believe in a way that is contrary to our own best interests. Our intellect is arrested through a process of repetitive words, images and sounds. During this process we are told that we are being smart, intelligent, free thinkers, and sometimes cool when we allow ourselves to be captured by their mind control process. Our natural intellect, overtime, is replaced by an artificial intellect and the programmers begin to do our thinking for us. This is how we can be led to do things we that know we are not supposed to do. We do them because we refuse to believe the programmer is doing anything but telling us the truth.

Once other people begin to do our thinking, we lose autonomy and our world becomes their world or the one they create for us. You or I cannot come along and try to free others from the grips of the programmer because they become so inert and hopelessly dependant on the programmer that they will fight to protect him. It is dangerous to try to save those who are not ready to be saved from their programmers because they will, invariably, kill the savior.

Once we break free of the programmers and begin to receive correct information, we have to erase the old tapes by refusing to accept or respond to the old information when we hear it. The process of capturing our minds was loaded with repetitive stimuli so the process of freeing our minds calls for repetitive action as well. Repeatedly refusing to accept old information and rehearsing the new information out loud each time we hear the old will in effect record the correct information over the incorrect information in time. Eliminating old, wrong or contradictory information from our subconscious mind will bring stability to our minds by creating balance. Removal of the old information also eliminates confusion because contradictory information will not be available for us to access in the decision making process. When we have not adequately done this, our conscience or spirit will make us aware of it.

Your conscience is actually the voice of your spirit, whereas, reason is the voice of the mind and feeling is the voice of the flesh. We have all had that experience where we said "Something told me to... or something told me not to..." We might have been driving home, for example and something inside of us said "Turn here". But we did not turn there because that was not our usual way home. Two blocks further down the street we had a car accident. When we realize what happened, we will say "Something told me to turn off that street." You might have been planning to go to a party one night and something on the inside of you said "Don't go". Desiring greatly to go to that party you

Single Mothers and Sons

ignored the instruction. Not long after you arrived a big fire erupted and you were injured. Once you realized what happened you will say "Something told me not to go to that party".

That something is a product of you spirit being directed by the Holy Spirit of GOD or the spirit of truth. It knows all things and is in constant communication with our spirit every day. Since our conscience is the voice of our spirit, it will let us know when the information that we are acting on is not valid or in conflict with the truth. It will also let us know when we are about to approach danger. The conscience is designed to assist us in making the correct or moral decisions in life. However, most of us have not disciplined ourselves to listen to the voice of our spirit and act on the instructions we receive from it. We have to know why the spirit is telling us to do what it is instructing us to do before we do it. Or we will try to go through the validation process over again when we want to act on information and do that which we know is wrong. In situations like that, your spirit will not argue with you. It will simply give you the truth and then allow you to do whatever you want.

The decisions that we make puts us on a course, for example, to have that car accident. There are other routes we could have taken to get home but we decided to take the collision course. The desire of our heart, then, was to have an accident. Now, we did not know an accident was waiting down the road. However, our conscience or our spirit that receives information from the Holy Spirit did know. It tried to influence our mind to make a decision that would avoid the accident. Yet, we chose to follow our desires instead of the instructions of our conscience. In effect, we chose to have the car accident.

This works both ways. The key is following your conscience. You may desire to be wealthy and it may be in GOD's plan for you to be wealthy. So your conscience will lead you into the way to achieve the desire of your heart. Yet, if you do not follow the instructions your conscience is giving you, you will miss the opportunity to become wealthy. Your spirit will always instruct you in the direction that GOD wants you to go. On the other hand, it is also programmed to allow you to have the desires of your heart. We have to learn that our conscience gives us wise counsel to do the things that GOD would have us do. Then, we must learn to make sure whatever our conscience is leading us to do becomes the desire of our heart. The word of GOD says:

"Through wisdom is a house built and by understanding it is established; and by knowledge shall the chambers be filled with all precious and pleasant riches. A wise man is strong, yes, a man of knowledge increases strength. Because by wise counsel you shall make your war and in the multitude of counselors there is safety (Proverbs 24:3-6)."

You see, GOD fully intends to lead and guide us into all truth. However, we have to learn what we need to know so that GOD can take us where HE wants us to go. We also have to know some things so that we can remain in the place where GOD wants us to be. It is one thing to know how to get there. Knowing how to stay there is a whole other ball game.

Chapter 4
The Essential Elements of Manhood

"The combination of active and completive virtues is one of the most enduring themes in three thousand years of experience of what it means to be a man."
~ **Waller Newell**

If you ask the question: "what is a man" in a public forum of men and women it will spark a fierce debate. The ideal of what a man is changes depending on which person you ask. It appears to be painful for people to come to a consensus on what a man is. The average woman under 50 has difficulty defining what a man due to the phenomenon of nearly 3 generations of males that have been languishing in psychological adolescence well into adulthood as a result of fatherlessness. Men appear to have difficulty defining what a man is for the same reason. Arguments and fights ensue when a woman believes that she is not getting what she needs from her husband or boyfriend who has the image of a man but falls short on the knowledge of what a man should be. Communication becomes frustrating to infuriating when she utters the phrase "be a man" or "be a real man" when neither one of them knows what she really means.

It is important therefore for every man to have a very clear idea of what a man is and become determined to demonstrate the ideal of what a man is to his wife and children. The essence of what a man must be is demonstrated by how he takes care of his family and whether or not he can retain his integrity with GOD and be true to his wife in times of tough temptation. A real man is one who has a combination of brains,

Single Mothers and Sons

brawn and heart. A real man loves his wife as Christ loves the church; he will sacrifice for her and always put her first. A real man understands that his duty is to guide his children into their destiny. A real man knows that his job as a father is to guide, guard, and govern; direct, correct, and protect. No matter how intelligent, capable and tough his wife is a real man does this for her as well.

It is equally important for every man to have knowledge on the essential elements that go into making a male a man. When men begin to apply this knowledge to their lives diligently it will help women identify a "real" man when they see him. It will keep women from discarding and dismissing the faithful man when they meet him, and save them from packing on even more emotional baggage from having relationships with guys who appear to be men but are in reality just big boys. Understanding the essential elements of manhood provides men with knowledge to reinforce in themselves and to teach their sons about what a man should be.

The phrase "essential element" means a thing cannot be what it is supposed to be if it is missing this thing or things. The essential elements of a cake, for example, are flour and sugar. Without sugar a cake is just bread. Baking the other cake elements together without flour would just make a mess. There are 15 elements that are essential to an adult male's character and nature if he is to be a real man and have the maturity and responsibility to properly lead a family. A guy who does not have the essential elements of manhood may be an adult male in stature but he is still a boy in essence. When a woman sees any of these essential elements missing in a man that she was dating, she must watch him in her rear view mirror as she is leaving.

Essential element of manhood #1: Integrity. Integrity is a state of complete mental, emotional, intellectual, moral and ethical development where a man becomes mature or single. That is, whole within himself and connected and one with GOD. Integrity is proven when these attributes are tested and a man is found to remain strong in his commitment to GOD, his wife, and his family. A man retains his integrity at all costs because he understands that integrity is more easily kept than recovered.

You will know if a man has integrity once his character or the distinctive qualities of his personality or nature are tested. A person with integrity is actually who he appears to be. Like Popeye ("I am what I am") a man with integrity is not pretentious. You will find him to have a consistency of personality and character. When he is under pressure, you will find him steadfast and unmovable.

Imagine someone with their fingers interlaced. Then imagine two people standing on each side of that person trying to pull their fingers apart. A man with integrity is strong and mentally tough enough to keep his fingers interlaced. This is an illustration of what will happen if a woman comes along and tries to pull him away from his wife on one side and satan tries to pull him away from GOD on the other side. The strength of his character makes him tough enough to keep his fingers interlaced or to remain connected with GOD and one with his wife under an extreme amount of pressure. By the strength of his character a man can

Single Mothers and Sons

get a woman to marry him, but without integrity he can't keep her from divorcing him.

Essential element of manhood #2: Excellence. A man with excellence transcends other men in quality, merit or skill. He is highly sought after and nearly without peer in business and society because no one can do what he does quite the way he does it or as well as he does it. He breeds this quality into his family. His children become eminently good, powerful and productive as a result of his example and influence.

Each person was created to be unique like a snowflake. There is no one who has your DNA, finger print, retinal pattern, palm print, foot print, etc. There is no one with your unique set of knowledge, gifts, talents, and abilities that was given by GOD to fulfill your unique purpose. We were ALL born, built and bred for excellence. Men who are excellent simply step up or grow into what they were originally created by GOD to be.

Sadly, however, men and boys have difficulty reaching this level of quality these days because we are trained and conditioned through the education system and society to be mediocre. 70% is enough to pass to the next grade level and we advance without being pushed to excellence; or pushed to achieve greatness. Most of us succumb to the pressure of our peers to not appear very smart because nobody likes anybody who knows everything.

Men of excellence are internally driven to exceed well beyond mediocrity and have learned to advance to a high level where they don't have many peers. They take the hard jobs that no one else wants and do the job better than anybody who has ever done it before. Men of excellence do what is right because it is right and they do it right the first time.

Essential elements of manhood #3: Bravery. Every a man must have intestinal fortitude or the courage to stand in the face of adversity and drive on. Being brave is not being without fear. Bravery is having the capacity to defend one's self or family in the face of fear. There is a difference between bravery and bravado or swagger. Many young people today think that having swagger or "swag" is cool. However, according to the dictionary swagger is: a **superficial** show of confidence. A real man does not have swagger, he has real bravery. A man must possess the bravery to tenaciously defend his wife and family. He must have the quality of bravery internally in order to teach his sons to be brave because a chump can't raise a champ.

Now, bravery is a very important element of manhood because physical security is a primary need for a woman. She has to know that her man can defend her and keep her safe physically or she will begin looking for a man who has the quality of bravery. "Fontes fortuna juvat" – fortune favors the brave.

Essential element of manhood #4: Knowledgeable. Knowledge is science. In order for a man to effectively serve a family he must have a grasp of knowledge in six sciences: religion, law, finances, medicine, politics, and history. If his family has a problem the solution is will more than likely reside in one of those areas. A man does not need to be an expert in any of them but he does need to have working knowledge of all of them.

Single Mothers and Sons

In math, whenever you don't have the answer... it's a problem. In order to solve the problem you need knowledge on the process, steps or formulas that will lead to the answer. In a family whenever the family has a problem and a man doesn't have the answer or the knowledge needed to produce the answer it compounds the problem.

Some guys treat marriage like its game of checkers and pride leads some guys to act like it's a game of check-HER. If marriage can be compared to a game at all it would be the game of chess. Before a man gets married he must get his life in check. Once he has himself in check he then needs a check-MATE.

Adult males become prideful when they lack knowledge. Pride is a defense mechanism that can arise once a man sees in a woman's eyes that she knows that he lacks knowledge on how to be a man, husband, father, and leader. When women begin to pressure prideful men to be what they are supposed to be and operate in what they are supposed to know ("Be a man!"), it is like throwing a match on gas. A prideful man is puffed up, full of hot air, and is combustible. A man who is full of pride can't take the heat so he explodes. A lack of knowledge mixed with too much pride is what often ignites domestic violence.

Prideful men can't allow themselves to be reduced in the eyes of the woman in lives so they will try to use their physical strength against her to relieve the pressure and "prove" they are a man. Once you recognize that a man lacks knowledge and is full of pride it means that he is potentially a striker. It is wise, therefore, not to argue or fight with him. He is best just left alone.

Essential element of manhood #5: Prudent. A prudent man is intelligent, successful, and understanding. He is a wise guide in the management of a family's affairs and sees no value in having an extramarital affair. He has learned to circumscribe his desires and keep his passions within due bounds. His passion and desire is reserved and released for activities with his wife. He is a proper example for his children.

Essential element of manhood #6: Patient. A patient man is able to bear the trials and tribulations of life calmly without complaint. He has the discipline to not retaliate immediately when provoked and understands that reacting emotionally is a luxury only women and children can afford. He has the intestinal fortitude to remain steadfast despite opposition, difficulties or adversities.

The majority of men who are locked up in the penitentiary for violent crimes committed an act as an emotional response to something someone else had done or they are there as a result of making a hasty decision. Rashness is the parent of misfortune. I have never seen a man fall into misfortune that was not preceded by a hasty act or where he made a decision without due caution. Men who react emotionally or hastily are dangerous because we have too much power in our hands and we can destroy things very quickly. Therefore, men must be logical rather than emotional in their response to any situation. Patience is a virtue or a type of strength. This is why the virtuous woman and the patient or faithful man is a perfect match.

Essential element of manhood #7: Faithful. Faithful in this context is not a reference to sexual fidelity; it is merely a byproduct of it. A faithful man is reliable, trustworthy, established, stable, consistent, and dependable. He is a guardian of his wife's virtue and has the ability to nurture and care for his children. Men who don't have a faithful quality are not ready to lead and care for a wife and family because while they are in the house they are often emotionally unavailable.

The foundation of a faithful man's faithfulness centers on his faith in GOD. He models this character quality in himself after the experiences he has had with GOD being faithful to HIS word. Having personal knowledge of the faithfulness of GOD has led to an increased level of faithfulness within himself. The faithful man has prepared himself to receive the power that comes with a higher level of faith by following the instruction from 2 Peter 1:5-7 and adding to **his** faith a few of the characteristics and qualities found in GOD HIMSELF:

- Virtue - strength, power and moral energy
- Knowledge - the word of GOD or truth
- Temperance - self control or discipline
- Brotherly kindness - employing virtue on behalf of others
- Godliness - the outer expression of an inner virtue
- Love - compassion and empathy for another
- Patience - cheerfully waiting regardless of circumstances

"Most men will proclaim everyone his own goodness but a faithful man who can find (Proverbs 20:6)." "Who can find a virtuous woman? For her price is far above rubies (Proverbs 31:10)."

Single Mothers and Sons

The perfect man for a virtuous woman is a faithful man. The effort to keep a virtuous woman, one with strength power and moral excellence, from a faithful man is the reason why the adversary wages a persistent attack against women using men. The union of a faithful man and virtuous woman is too powerful for the devil or his demons to deal with and are a threat to his very existence. Therefore, he works to harden women's hearts against men using deceived men so that when the faithful man comes along they will reject him. "He's too nice!"

Faithful men see their families as the beginning and the end of their existence. Faithful in family is the reason, in their hearts, why GOD placed them here. Faithful men also recognize that the only hands GOD has in the earth are the ones attached to the end of our arms. The only power Jesus has in the earth to fulfill His mission is through His bride; she has to put Him on (Galatians 3:27) so that He can have the power to do what He needs to do.

Similarly, a faithful man needs a virtuous woman to put him on like a jacket. The mission or purpose of a jacket is to cover and protect but it cannot do what it was designed or created to do unless someone puts it on. Once someone puts it on, it receives the power it needs to do what it was designed to do. Once a virtuous woman "puts on" a faithful man, he obtains the power and strength to complete his mission or purpose as well as to cover and protect her while she protects and covers him.

Essential element of manhood #8: Loyal. A loyal man is unswerving in allegiance to his wife and family but his first obligation is to GOD. Loyalty is a

Single Mothers and Sons

quality that makes a man want to sacrifice his life to save the lives of his loved ones. His sons learn loyalty through him making it their responsibility to protect their mother and sisters in his absence. Loyal men are law abiding and work hard to get ahead rather than devise schemes to get over.

Loyalty is the character quality the scripture is urging us to grow into that said "Submitting yourselves one to another in the fear of GOD." Submission simply means: to get under, support, or help our spouses to complete or fulfill the mission they were assigned by GOD to do. Husbands must submit and be loyal to our wives but we owe our first loyalty to GOD. As we follow HIS guidance to submit ourselves one to another, we must NOT do anything that GOD would not want us to do. If we are struggling to pay bills or we don't have the money needed to fulfill our mission, for example, we can't allow our spouse to convince us to rob a bank.

Some men accuse their wife of not having their back or lacking loyalty when they refuse to support them in a mission that is wrong, unethical or criminal. He tries to make her feel guilty when he is the one who actually lacks loyalty. A man that is loyal to his wife would not ask her to do something he knows she does not want to do. It is a statement that he doesn't care if she goes to jail or will feel badly once she helps him. He simply wants to do what he wants to do. And he appears to have a need to drag someone else into disloyalty before GOD with him. A man who is loyal will always do what is right for his wife regardless of what she might want him to do.

Essential element of manhood #9: Honest. An honest man is believable and truthful when tested over time. He has an unwavering quality of being a decent, fitting and proper husband. An honest man strenuously protects the reputation of his name. He knows that he only owns two things in this world: his word and his name. Everything else that he owns can be taken away but he can only lose his good name by not keeping his word. Honesty is the quality that determines a man's credibility or whether or not he is credit worthy.

If a man has good credit it is a good indication that he is fairly honest because a credit report is actually a credibility report; an assessment of whether a man's word and name is good. When you receive a loan you have to give your word that you will pay on time and then you have to sign your name. If you don't pay or fail to pay on time they put a mark next to your name that says your word is no good. The way that a man spends his money and pays his bills is an indication of the condition of his heart; for where your treasure is there will be your heart also.

Essential element of manhood #10: Selfless. A selfless man is one who believes it's important to place the needs of others before his own. This quality drives some women crazy because they can't argue with him. In every case where it doesn't make a difference he is going to let her have her way. It may make him seem weak to her when he won't fight for what he wants but what he wants is for her to have what she wants.

Selflessness can appear to be weakness to some women until they understand that selflessness is a type of strength. Selflessness is what the Bible calls "meekness" which means to have one's "power under control". Jesus is called meek because he could have

Single Mothers and Sons

called down 10,000 angels to help him down from the cross. However, He kept His power under control in order to complete His mission and please His Father. A meek or selfless man's main desire is to please those he loves in his quest to maintain peace and harmony within his family. One of the things a man needs most in his home is peace. Therefore, he will give his wife whatever she wants so that he can have peace.

"...the meek shall inherit the earth; and shall delight themselves in the abundance of peace (Psalm 37:11)."

Selfless is also synonymous with egoless. Our ultimate mission in life as men is to become egoless and to awaken to the reality to who GOD created us to be. That is, to be reborn out of our current selfish, self centered, or prideful ego state into an egoless state where we become conscious to who we really are. In order for a man to actually be "born again" he must first become selfless. Then he can truly experience life and love in peace.

Essential element of manhood #11: Responsible. Responsible men are accountable and answerable to their wives. They are able to hold the duty, trust and position of husband and father. Responsible men understand they must be able to respond to the needs of their wife and family. Thus when it is time for them to respond they have the ability to respond appropriately. A man who has the ability to respond, then, can be given responsibility.

Growing up in a home under the nurture and guidance of a mother and having a job when a boy is young is simply the training he needs to be able to handle the responsibilities he will have as a man. A boy learns to be accountable to his mother so that he will have no problem being answerable to his wife. He learns to perform his duty and retain trust in his position on a job so that he will know how to execute his duty and retain trust in his position as husband and father. A man can never be given the responsibility of a wife and family unless he has demonstrated that he has response ability or the ability to respond properly.

Learning to submit to the authority of his father gives a boy the discipline he needs to be, not just an adult male but, a responsible man. The best place for a boy to learn discipline is in the home from his father. However, there are only two places where a boy can learn discipline (besides the military): either the play pen or the state pen. If a boy does not learn discipline at home, he will be forced to learn it from men in jail. Learning discipline teaches a boy to be responsible. Giving a boy duty and responsibility will teach him to be a man and will keep him out of the penitentiary.

Essential element of manhood #12: Good. A good man has a positive moral quality that is beneficial to his family. The quality of his good character makes him a strong powerful leader. Others follow him because they want to not because they have to. He is the epitome of a winner. He is a courageous intelligent decision maker, is often well spoken of, highly regarded, and a man who can make his family wealthy.

A good man understands that a candle does not lose anything when it lights another candle; it only spreads more light. Thus he is eager to help his wife and children become the best they can be. A good man also the type of man who:
• Conforms to the moral order of the universe
• Has a praiseworthy character

- Advances prosperity or well being
- Is useful or beneficial to others
- Has economic utility or satisfies an economic desire
- Has the qualities to get results
- Is an example by which bad men are revealed to women

Essential element of manhood #13: Kind. A kind man is benevolent, eager to serve and gracious to his wife and family. He is observed by others to be giving, easy to get along with, and has a loving manner. Kind men have a natural state of being where it's easy to see that being kind is not what they do, it's who they are. The one thing kind men hate, however, is when people mistake their kindness for weakness.

A man who is kind has the ability to easily influence others as they see no danger in opening themselves up to him. Influence means to breathe into or inspire. It is similar to influenza which is caused by someone breathing on you and causing the infection they have in them begin to grow in you. When a person influences, inspires or breathes into you, a part of them or some of what is contained in their spirit and character goes into and becomes a part of your spirit. Their influence begins to affect how you think, effect what you do, and infect your life. A man who is kind has the capacity to inspire and therefore affect, effect and, infect his wife and children with his characteristics and qualities which helps him to more effectively lead them.

People don't care how much you know until they know how much you care (Dr Cornell West "borrowed" this maxim from me). Thus kind men are excellent teachers who have the ability to lead their family to do extraordinary things.

Essential element of manhood #14: Love. A man with the quality of love lives his life and loves his wife with passion, devotion and tenderness. His love is expressed through freedom, justice and equality. A flower must willingly give up its life to allow us to express our love. A man who not only has love but IS love will be willing to die to his own life in order to express his love to his wife and children.

Women appear to be born with a natural capacity to love whereas men appear to have to learn to love and then learn to BE love. This is why, at the end of his dissertation on love, the Apostle Paul said in 1 Corinthians 13:11 "When I was a child, I spoke as a child, I understood as a child, I thought as a child: but when I became a man, I put away childish things." That is, things like pride, envy, anger, selfishness, lying, evil thoughts, and so on. Adult males who have not learned to put away childish things are yet childish. Adult men must first learn to love before they can be led within themselves to put away childish things. Until they learn to BE love, and be as Jesus is (who IS love), understanding of the word of GOD and the secret knowledge of the universe will be cut off or darkened to them.

"But when that which is perfect [love] is come, then that which is in part shall be done away. For now we see through a glass, darkly; but then face to face: now I know in part; but then shall I know even as also I am known (1 Corinthians 13:10 &12)."

1 John 4:18 says: "There is no fear in love; but perfect love casts out fear..." Wherever fear is not present trust can exist. Once men learn to perfect themselves in love their wives can then freely trust them. Then, GOD can

trust them to have access to the understanding of his word, the knowledge of the universe, and the power to transform the world that comes with it.

The secret to success in life is to stay in love! Love gives us the fire needed to ignite other people, the insight to recognize the good qualities in them, and a passionate desire to do things for them. A person who is not in love doesn't have the kind of excitement that helps propel them ahead. The quickest way to get ahead is to help others achieve. You can have everything you want in life as long as you help as many people as you can get what they need. It takes love to make that kind of sacrifice. There is nothing more powerful, motivating and exhilarating in life for a woman than to be IN love with a man who IS love.

Essential element of manhood #15: Blessed. Every man who is blessed was empowered by GOD to prosper. He has inherent knowledge, gifts, talents, and abilities that when marketed properly someone will pay him for handsomely. Blessed men understand that when GOD said HE gave them the power to get wealth HE was actually talking about his wife. A single man can become rich but a man with the right wife can become wealthy.

In order to be blessed or endowed with the power to prosper, a man has to complete the perfection and purification process known scientifically as alchemy. Alchemy in mythology was a secret process of turning lead into gold. However, the mystery has been revealed as the process of transforming our lower self into our higher self. Alchemy is process wherein a man changes himself from being virtually useless to becoming highly valuable. He sheds that selfish, cheating, stealing, lying, etc., character quality and puts on a new prudent, patient, faithful, loyal, honest, selfless, etc. identity. A man who was once a lead weight now becomes a valuable commodity to the world, his wife, and family.

In His famous "Sermon on the Mount" Jesus recites a number of character traits traditionally known as the **"beatitudes"** that are held by those who are blessed or have completed the alchemical process. This list is actually a series of attitudes that a man must "be" in mind, body and spirit in order to be blessed, empowered to prosper, or to BE as Jesus IS. Jesus said blessed are those who "BE":

• Poor in spirit – this is the opposite of greedy or selfish. A person who is poor in spirit gives freely and does not worry about hoarding or putting things away for rainy days because he has faith that GOD will always provide.

• Mournful – to have empathy or compassion for others; is apt to teach to give others knowledge needed to overcome their state or condition. Mournful people are effective teachers because they teach out of love.

• Thirsty for righteousness – to be in right standing with GOD; wants to do what is right because it is right.

• Merciful – is not quick to punish or condemn others for their faults, mistakes, or misjudgments.

• Pure in heart – are those who have a natural abundance of love and affection for all people

• Peacemaker – reconcile disputes between others; helps lead people back into the grace of GOD.

An African proverb says: "If you enter a village and you can't find any good women, it is filled with no good men." When you cannot find men as they ought to be you won't find women as they should be. Women are always affected by men. It seems reasonable to conclude then that if you find a wise man, you should be able to find at least one wise woman. However, in a corrupt environment a wise man is too well ordered, too good to be true, and is rejected by the very women who are seeking a blessed man.

The reason the Bible is written in patriarchal position is not because men are superior to women. It's because GOD knew that if men were in order the women and children would be alright. A well ordered man comes fully equipped with all of the essential elements of manhood. The problem in modern times is a woman cannot see anything in a well ordered man's life that he would "need" her for. Besides being made suspicious by the world, society and church that nobody can be perfect, this is one of the reasons good women reject the well ordered man. She chooses instead the unordered, undisciplined or unrighteous man because she can see where she can help "fix" him to become what she needs him to be. But ultimately, because women are affected and infected by men, she only becomes as **he** is.

In order for a woman to become the best woman she can be, her husband has to be the best man that he can be before they get married. The male who is only an adult boy will have difficulty being the man a woman needs but the male MAN always delivers. Therefore, the best man for a woman is a perfected man who has all 15 of the essential elements of manhood.

Why are there 15 Essential Elements of Manhood?

I don't really want to add this section because it is a little heady and it exposes my inner nerd. However, I

Single Mothers and Sons

feel compelled to include it because I always get the question: Why are their 15 essential elements of manhood? So I will try to explain it as briefly as I can. It contains some powerful information, but if you are not really interested in the answer to the question you may want to go on to the next chapter.

Man was made by GOD to operate in the same way as the earth and universe. He was organized by GOD to be in harmony with his environment in order to be an effective ruler over and keeper of it. Everything in the earth and universe is currently moving from duality to unity; from being separate to becoming one. The reason we can see further and further out into space is not just because of the Hubble Telescope but because the universe is getting smaller. Consequently, everything that pertains to humanity must also move from duality to unity.

When we see a number that has dual elements, like 15, we must move that number into its unifying factor or force which in this case is 6 (1+5=6). All of the numbers that appear in the Bible have a meaning. The number 6 represents the number of man in that man was created on the 6th day. The 6th verse in **every** chapter of Genesis contains a reference to mankind, a man, or men. If a man's mother was standing up when he was born, he would come into the world upside down or with his head pointing toward the ground, emblematic of the number 6.

An adult male must have 15 qualities that form the totality of his character in order to be organized into a whole or complete man. That is, a man who is in union or harmony with himself, the earth and the universe. The union of 1 and 5 make 6, which is the bible number

Single Mothers and Sons

of man. The combination of all 15 essential elements in unity makes a man whole, complete, or perfect.

The essential elements of manhood are actually the 15 character qualities of Jesus Christ. An adult male must have all of these qualities to create a harmonious home environment and to be an effective leader for his family. Having all of these qualities prepares him to be the "perfect" man, husband, and father. He understands that a man establishes the environment of the home and the woman sets the temperature. If the heat gets turned off in the house the temperature will go up.

Now, this is the point where we depart from the wisdom of the world, society, and even traditional church teaching because we are instructed by all three that "nobody's perfect", "no one CAN be perfect", "the only one who was perfect was Jesus", etc. However, GOD said the reason HE gave man the five-fold ministry in Ephesians 4:11 (4+11=15) to make him perfect. In order to become "perfect" a man must become as Jesus is; to measure up to Him in mental, physical and spiritual stature. Every man must become as Jesus is in order to be well pleasing to GOD. The growth process that a man must go through in this regard is represented by the position of the numbers and the movement of the hands on the face of an analog clock.

The number 12 is authority; the seat of GOD. It represents "eternal perfection" in the union of the trinity 1+2=3. We were created in heaven or the spirit realm and resided with GOD before we were born into the earth. We move metaphorically across the face of the clock once we depart the spiritual realm of heaven with each number representing a stage of growth until

Single Mothers and Sons

we ultimately get back to the 12 or return to GOD. Hopefully, we will return to HIM triumphantly or in glory having completed or fulfilled the purpose for which we were sent into the earth.

The Bible number 1 means "union", 2 means "unity, and 3 means "divinity". We are still in divine union with GOD while in the first trimester of development in our mother's womb. The number 4 means "the world" which is the beginning of the second trimester, or the 4th month. That is when most mothers began to "show" that our presence in the world is imminent. The number 5 means "grace" or power. As we are in our final stages of development babies are endued with power while we are yet unborn. This is how John the Baptist was able to recognize Jesus in Mary's womb while John was only a 6 month old fetus (Luke 1:36-41). We are born at the number 6, upside down, and our primary goal at this point is to turn our lives right side up, get our head to the sky, change our mind, orient our way of thinking toward GOD, and become upright in stature.

We need the 5 fold ministry to provide the knowledge that is designed to empower us to turn toward GOD and become complete. That is, whole within ourselves and connected and one with GOD. The number 7 means "completion". Once we become complete within ourselves we are born again and ready to begin a new life. The number 8 means "new beginning". This is the point where we are positioned to move up to the next level physical and financial existence and obtain victory over our self by turning 180° (1+8=9) within ourselves. We turn from being up-side down in our mind, body and spirit morally and spiritually to being right-side up (from 6 to 9) or in line with heaven.

Single Mothers and Sons

This is the position where most people who go to church every week get stuck in their spiritual growth and development. If we don't get beyond the number 8 level of development, we will be condemned to renewing ourselves daily because we will vacillate in and out of sin continually. This was the Old Testament condition of men which is where we remain until we grow beyond being born again. Every time we sin we will have to start over and over and over again. This is why the symbol for infinity is the number 8 turned on its side. Rather than being 180° out of phase with GOD at the position 6 level of growth, we remain stuck at the 240° mark in our growth and transition back to GOD (2+4=6); operating in the mind of man rather than the mind of Christ, after the rudiments of the world rather than after Christ; going round and round, over and over, like the children of Israel in the wilderness.

While we may have progressed into adulthood physically and morally, spiritually we remain stuck at a child-like level of development. Sadly, the overwhelming majority of people who attend church every week are stuck in this position. Yet, neither they nor their pastors can figure out why they go to church every week, some several times per week, but they never grow. They become born again and get stuck; physical adults but still spiritual babies (Hebrews 5:12-14). You can easily identify adult spiritual babies because their testimony about GOD is always centered in dependency. "If it had not been for the Lord on my side…" Since they are yet babies they don't know that GOD is waiting for them to grow from dependence to interdependence. That is when the adult child becomes useful to the father to assist him in the family business. Now GOD can depend on us as we depend on HIM.

Single Mothers and Sons

The number 9 means "victory" which represents the victory that we obtain over ourselves. The propensity that we have to sin that once lived within our being has been overcome. Our head or heart is now constantly pointed in the direction of GOD. Once we have overcome ourselves, we must now learn to overcome the sin of the world. This process is symbolically represented by the number 10. This is the place where we would find ourselves if we were the hero in a story of mythology. He goes on a quest to find who he was created to be only to come face to face with a monster that tries to prevent him from getting to where he needs to be. Ultimately, he discovers that the monster was in reality a type of sin or iniquity within himself that he had to overcome in order to be able to overcome the sin of the world.

Once we overcome ourselves and the sin of world, the 0 part of our personality (influences of the world) is added to the 1 and thereby canceled out. This makes us 1 or whole in our mind self, body self, and spirit self. We have fulfilled the command of Hebrews 10:25 to assemble our **selves** together. We no longer have 2 personalities (1 and 0; good and evil). We are no longer double minded or plagued by cognitive dissonance as a result of being complete in Christ yet influenced by the world. We are 1 within ourselves, overcome the influence of the world's sin, and are free from the desire to sin.

We have grown up now spiritually; from duality and conflict in mind, body, and spirit into unity. Now we should understand what "forsake not the assembly of ourselves together" is actually instructing us to do in Hebrews 10:25. The context of the 10th chapter of Hebrews 10 pertains to overcoming the influence of the

Single Mothers and Sons

world to sin. The 25th verse of that chapter is not instructing us to **go** to church as we are taught. It is teaching us that **WE** have a duty to assemble our mind, body and spirit together in unity so that we can **BE** church after we go to church.

The average person that **goes** to church regularly, who says they are born again, and says they love GOD vacillates frequently between living right and doing wrong. This happens because they GO to church but they never learn to BE church; to be 1 with Jesus and to be as He is. Once we become 1 with Jesus, and as we stand next to the 1 and only begotten Son of GOD, the world should **not** be able to tell the difference between us and Him.

This is what the number 11 on the clock face represents; a man who has become 1 in Christ standing next to Jesus, the number 1 Son of GOD. The world won't be able to tell the difference between us and Jesus because the point is for the world to be able see Jesus through us and to have physical evidence that He IS.

Heretofore, we were only positioned in spiritual oneness with Jesus. At this point we are prepared to become physically connected with GOD. Jesus said: "No man comes to the Father but by (or through) me." We have to become as Jesus IS if we hope to become connected and one with GOD or get back up to the number 12 which is in union or eternal perfection with GOD.

Sadly, few of us ever make it to become as Jesus is because we are taught that we can't. Few men ever attain the 15 essential elements of manhood because we are led to believe it is impossible for a man to have the same qualities as Jesus; to be perfect. No one ever

Single Mothers and Sons

rises up to low expectations. Whenever a man does not know he is supposed to obtain something he rarely does. Consequently, women have no knowledge of what a man is supposed to be before they get married. They end up with a man who does not have all that he needs to know or possess in order to be a perfect husband and father. Women learn to tolerate a man for as long as they can and some just divorce him. The man did the best he could but nobody ever told him what he was supposed to know. Nobody told him that he was supposed to have the character and qualities of Jesus before he got married so that he could have the capacity to love his wife like Jesus loves the church.

Although Peter did actually walk on water, most men are told that no man walked on water but Jesus (Matthew 14:28-29). We are given the false illusion that nobody could be as Jesus IS. The primary reason why we must become like Jesus is to convict the world to come to Christ. In order to obtain a conviction in a court of law you must have substantial evidence. In order to convict a person to come to Christ we must have substantial evidence that He IS and that He is indeed the Son of GOD. The world would rather see a sermon than hear one any day. The only way the world can see evidence that Jesus IS, is through us. People of the world should obtain the hope that they too can become as Jesus is by seeing that we are like Him.

Now, there are sciences that we can apply to verify this information but I do not want to make what may already be nerdy and confusing to seem even more complicated. Just know, however, that applying the Theory of Relativity ($e=mc^2$), the Pythagorean Theorem ($a^2+b^2=c^2$), and quantum physics help us understand how a man can become as Jesus is before

Single Mothers and Sons

he reaches 20 years of age. It is actually supposed to happen by the time he is 12 or 13 but certainly by the time he is 14. This is why the Orthodox Jews celebrate their sons reaching manhood at this age with a bar mitzvah. In Africa and other parts of the world a boy's transition into manhood is celebrated at this age with a rite of passage. A boy should be taught or trained by his dad or the elders in his community to obtain the essential qualities of manhood; to become a perfect man, husband, and father before he reaches the age of manhood.

A boy needs both a mother and father to learn to obtain the essential elements of manhood. You see, some of those elements have a feminine quality and character. This is one reason why GOD would not allow Mary to raise Jesus as a single mother. Joseph had decided to leave her because he knew the baby wasn't his but GOD made him go back and raise that boy. A boy learns integrity, excellence, knowledge, bravery, prudence, patience and faithfulness primarily from his father. He learns to be, loyal, honest, selfless, responsible, good, kind, love and blessed primarily from his mother. Without these essential qualities a man will struggle to be the best man that he can be for his wife and family. Hopefully, mom, this book is allowing me to be a type of step daddy to your son and he is learning what he needs to know from me.

Father vs. Daddy

The way we use the word "father" is faulty which prevents us from distinguishing a faithful man from a fool. A man who provided the seed for a child gets credit for being a father on Father's Day even when they never even raised or took care of a child. The word

Single Mothers and Sons

"father" is used in our society to describe a man who guides, guards, and governs; directs, corrects and protects as well as provides and cares for a child. However, that definition more accurately describes a Dad.

A father is actually one who provides the seed for birth. It does not matter whether he raises that child or not, he is a "father" once he provides the seed that conceived the child. A Dad, on the other hand, is a man who provides love along with mental, physical, emotional, and financial support for the child. Dad is the man who is always there with and for the child till the end through thick and thin. It does not matter to a "real" Dad whether or not he provided the seed that fathered the child. He is going to love the child as if it came from his seed anyway. Any male can be a father but only a <u>real</u> man can be a Dad! Every father is not a Dad. Some Dads have never actually fathered a child. But Dads love the children whom they raise and are a daddy to as if they were of their own blood.

Chapter 5
Strive for Victorious Living

"Life is like a university. You don't have to take the classes but you do have to pass the tests."
~ Dr Will

Men can evolve to a higher level of existence once their sacred cows are killed and all of their previous beliefs are challenged for truth. If a recipe is bad, it does not matter how good of a cook you are if you faithfully follow the recipe. The dish will taste bad because the recipe is flawed. Similarly, it does not matter how faithful you are. You won't be blessed if the formula you are faithfully following is faulty. You cannot be blessed while holding on to sacred beliefs when those beliefs you are holding on to are actually preventing you from being blessed.

It is important that family leaders learn to meditate so they reflect on what they have been believing and doing to see if it has actually been leading them to what they really want to do and where they really want to be. Through meditation we can receive knowledge and guidance from our spirit that has a connection to the source of universal knowledge. Your spirit is also the source of energy that animates your body and provides wisdom and knowledge to your brain to direct your body to do what it was created to do. When you get an idea, particularly one that could dramatically change your life financially, it comes from your spirit to your brain. The idea doesn't pop in there out of thin air. Your spirit holds the knowledge of why your family was assembled together and what each member was created to do. It is important, then, for men to

Single Mothers and Sons

receive unfiltered knowledge from their own spirit so that they can communicate with their family effectively and help lead them to do and be what they were created to do and be.

"...the Son of man is come to save that which was lost (Matthew 18:11)."

LOST is an acronym that means: Living Out Side of Truth. Jesus came to save those who are living outside of truth. You are lost when you don't know where you are and can't find where you are supposed to be. You are lost when you don't know the truth about who you are and why you are here. Do you want to know the REAL reason why you cannot find your purpose? It's because you are living outside of truth. You are not where you are supposed to be therefore you cannot find your purpose because it is not in the place where you are. Once you acknowledge the truth about how you got to be where you are it will help you discover where you are supposed to be. Once you get to where you are supposed to be you will find your purpose. In finding your purpose you will discover also that you are not presently who you were created to be. Discovering your true identity will put you on the path to living victoriously.

Once you learn who you are and why you are here your next task is to meditate and get your spirit to reveal the same thing about your wife and children: why did GOD assemble this family collectively and why are they here individually. Knowing what your family was created to do and who they were each created to be will teach you how to lead them to their destiny. The only way a man can achieve this is to overcome himself and overcome the world. That is, having overcome the sin that easily besets him and the temptations of the

Single Mothers and Sons

world. Then, the knowledge he receives from his spirit won't conflict with knowledge in his brain. Being victorious over himself and the world and will make communicating with his spirit easier and more clearer.

"...whatsoever is born of GOD overcomes the world: and this is the victory that overcomes the world, even our faith (1 John 5:4)."

"But thanks be to GOD which gives us the victory through our Lord Jesus Christ (1 Corinthians 15:57)."

GOD provided a man with the particular wife and children he has for a reason. The people GOD placed in his life are there to assist him in completing the purpose for which he was created. His family members are resources and assets that he needs to achieve glory in the sight of GOD. The only way he can achieve glory or significance in a biblical context is to complete and fulfill the purpose for which he was given birth. As he fulfills his purpose, he must assist his family members in completing the purpose for which they were born as well. The way GOD measures the stature of a man is by how well he leads his family into their destiny.

A father or dad is the governing authority in a child's life. He is responsible for doing 12 things for a child to prepare them for presentation to the Heavenly Father before they reach the age of 12: guide, guard, govern, direct, correct, protect, comfort, encourage, warn, impact, inform, and instruct. Instruct (in/struck) means to strike or forge the heart and lead them to overcome the natural urge to sin and conform unto righteousness. This is why the word cautions fathers to not provoke your children to wrath. A child has to know you love him for instruction (in/struck/tion) to work otherwise it will feel like a fight.

Single Mothers and Sons

Achieving Universal Significance

There is a difference between being special, purposeful, and significant. Everyone was born with a purpose. Everyone is special because each person, like a snowflake, is uniquely made. No one has your same DNA, finger prints, foot prints, retina pattern, vocal pattern, ear pattern, and so on. Those who execute their purpose, sacrificing themselves for the good of mankind as a whole, like Mandela or Dr King, will become significant. Everyone is designed with the potential to do something significant. The earth and the universe have been preprogrammed to assist those who have a heart to sacrifice their lives, like Jesus, for the good of mankind.

Simon Peter went up and drew the net to land full of great fishes; a hundred and fifty and three... (John 21:11)"

Each number in the Bible has a significant or relevant meaning. The universe is built on mathematic principles within a perfect geometric design. Every number that GOD created has a universal purpose and meaning. Jesus promised to make Peter a fisher of men throughout the whole world. The number 153 (1+5+3=9) adds up to the number 9 which represents victory. It is also an allegory for the number of nations, 153, that existed in the world at that time. The scripture is an allegorical picture of Peter going into all nations of the world and drawing men unto Christ Jesus. I provided this example so that you can see how numbers work in the Bible to add greater meaning and reveal a larger significance to every story. Numbers play a significant role in helping us to identify and guiding us into the destiny of our lives.

Single Mothers and Sons

Every person has 3 numbers assigned to their life. Before you were born an allegorical picture of what you were to do here, your purpose, was drawn in Heaven. Understanding how to align the numbers that pertain to your life with their universal purpose gives you access to the knowledge of the universe that will assist you with achieving significance in your life. If you want to be great then follow this universal formula.

Man was created by GOD on the sixth day of creation. The number six, therefore, represents the number of man. Man is born into the world upside down in the symbolic position of a 6. Eight is the number of new beginnings and nine is the number of victory. A child develops in the womb with its head up toward GOD or in a position of victory symbolically represented by the number 9 but then turns its head away from GOD (6) before it enters the world.

The number 9 is also symbolic of a single person. That is, one who has obtained victory over himself or his sin nature which causes him to be at war within himself; knowing that he must do right but sometimes can't stop himself from doing wrong. Whereas he was born upside down, aligned with the number 6, the victorious man stands right side up as a representation of the number 9; a regenerated or victorious man; victorious over himself. The regenerated man is positioned or properly aligned with the universe. In this position he can effectively communicate with his own spirit which is in constant communication with the Spirit of GOD. In that position he can discover why he was born and can learn what he needs to know to responsibly lead his wife and children into their GOD ordained destiny.

Single Mothers and Sons

Once a child enters the world the average parent has to struggle to figure out who they are, what they were meant to be and to raise them properly. A child has to acquire the knowledge that will give him the ability to become who he or she was meant to be. Therefore, each child has to encounter someone in their lives that can help lead them to discover who they are and why they are here. This is why GOD gave children parents and this was GOD's original purpose for education.

You see, GOD intended for education to be a love project; to bring out the best that a child has in them to offer to the world. The word education comes from the Latin word "educare", which means to bring out. Who they are and what they are supposed to do and be is encoded within a child before they were born. It is the parent's job to educate them in an effort to bring out that which they are supposed to deliver to the world. But, the world flipped education and made it a system of putting something into a child instead of bringing something out. It is important that the child has a daddy who has become victorious over himself so that he can hear within his own spirit the direction in which to lead the child. Armed with that knowledge and being at peace with himself a dad can lead (not force) the child to naturally come to the knowledge of his or herself. When a dad has become one with the knowledge of who he is he can then add his life to the child's life, which then helps the child to become what he or she was created to be.

A good dad, whether he is a child's real father or not, always adds to a child's life. Psychologists will tell you that a child's sexual identity, whether male or female, is reinforced by the dad. That is, of course, when he is emotionally available to the child. Likewise, a child's individual personality is reinforced when the dad's life is added to the child's. Again, this only occurs when the dad has achieved victory over himself in life and has turned from being a 6, an upside down man, to become a 9 or a man who is standing upright. The man must achieve victory over himself or become a 9 before he tries to add his life to the child's if the child will have a chance to become what he or she was created to be. That is because any number you add to 9 will come to itself. The child can come to know who he or she is supposed to be more readily when dad has positioned himself where he is supposed to be. When the Prodigal son when awry his father remained where he was supposed to be watching and waiting for his son to come to himself or recognize who he is and where he was supposed to be.

"And when he <u>came to himself</u>, he said... I will arise and go to my father... but when he was yet a great way off, his father saw him, and had compassion, and ran, and fell on his neck, and kissed him (Luke 15:17-20)."

Remember I said each person has 3 single digit numbers assigned to our life when we are born. These numbers, 1 through 9, represent a complete entity. Everything in life is comprised of a trinity or made of 3 main parts. Everything from the human (mind, body and spirit) to the smallest atom (electron, proton and neutron) is comprised of 3 main parts. The three numbers assigned to our life symbolize our identity, personality and destiny.

The destiny number is sometimes called the life number but it is not. Our identity, personality and destiny numbers don't change because they reveal who we are and why we are. The life number is a fourth number that changes depending on where we are on our journey to spiritual maturity. A man must reach the highest number in the series of life numbers which is a 12 but actually goes back to 3 because you add 1+2.

Anyway, I am not going to go into this too deep. There are those who might see this as a type of voodoo. Whenever we are told that something is wicked or evil, we have to first understand that everything was originally made **good**. When GOD created a thing HE always declared it was good. Some things HE created HE declared that they were very good. Since the adversary has no power to create anything on his own he can only take a thing that GOD made good and twist or turn it into something wicked for his purpose.

The word "wicked" comes from the word "twist". Wicker furniture is twisted wood. The wick of a candle is twisted cord. So once we see something that appears to be wicked it is our job to untwist it or turn it back around to discover that which is good. The word "repent" simply means to turn your head from the wickedness of the world, 6, and turn it up toward GOD: 9. GOD provided the science of Bible numerics to give us keys to unlock the knowledge of the universe. The adversary took numerics and devised numerology, turning it into something mysterious and spooky, a type of witchcraft, in order to draw us away from the knowledge of the universe.

The same thing occurred with astronomy. GOD gave us the science of astronomy to help us discover that ALL of the knowledge of the universe is written in the sky. One of the reasons GOD chose Abraham is because his family were star gazers. They knew that the pictures formed in the sky that we call constellations hold the knowledge of the universe (a picture is worth a thousand words) and GOD's plan for mankind or what we call the Bible. Faith comes by hearing and hearing by the word of GOD. Abraham is called the father of faith because he could read and understand the word of GOD as it is written in the sky. If we knew how to read the sky that knowledge would give us power to live free of satanic manipulation. So, satan devised astrology to draw us away from that knowledge and to direct us toward generic nonsense, i.e. horoscope, which is a type of witchcraft whose purpose is to keep us powerless.

The word "horoscope" is comprised of two words: horror and scope. The word horoscope means "to view with fear" which is fueled by superstition. Superstition is a type of witchcraft. The average person who uses daily horoscopes has a fear of the unknown. They are afraid of where life may take them each day so they use the horoscope as a means to see the road ahead, eliminate the unknown, and avoid tragedy. What it does however is rob them of the power to prevent tragedy by being led into their destiny by the Holy Spirit and leads them to unwittingly wander into the devil's territory where there is constant fear and torment.

GOD gave us a means to discover the reason **why** we were born so that we can eliminate the fear of not knowing fulfill the purpose we were sent here to complete. The devil does everything he can to defy the will of GOD so he uses other people to convince you that this knowledge is evil. What GOD meant for good the devil twists and makes evil. Whenever he tries to convince you that something is evil your job is to twist it back around to discover the good. If you twist it back and find it to be really evil that means the devil lied and it was already good. His purpose is to distract you

Single Mothers and Sons

from the truth in an effort to prevent you from discovering and completing your assignment. The destiny number along with your inherent knowledge, gifts, talents and abilities provide clues to help you discover the assignment that you were given life to complete.

Now, when a child's identity, personality and destiny numbers are added to the dad's life number that is a 9, the child can come to himself. That is, they can come to know who they are, how they should behave and what they were assigned to do in life. Where the dad is, on his life journey, will have an impact on what the child ends up to doing or becoming in life. If the dad has become a regenerated man or a 9, the child will be able to become whatever he or she was created to become. However, if the dad tries to add his life to the child's life while he is still an unregenerate man or a 6, the child will never come to himself and be what he or she was meant to become. He or she can grow up to be good and do wonderful things but they will never actually be what they were born to become. Whatever the child turns out to be will be impacted by whether or not the dad was able to align his life with his own destiny.

"Now the LORD had said unto Abram, get you out of your country, and from your kindred, and from your father's house, unto a land that I will show you (Genesis 12:1)."

Abraham's father Terah, being grief stricken over the death of his son Haran, refused to continue walking into his destiny where GOD was leading him and his family to go. Since his father could not get over himself and refused to pursue his destiny GOD commanded Abraham to leave his father's house and go into a land

Single Mothers and Sons

that HE would show him. In effect, GOD was saying: I am going to be your ABBA or daddy now. I will guide and direct your life and lead you into the destiny that I had planned for you. GOD gave man dominion and authority because HE wants each dad to lead their children into their destiny so that each man can defeat the devil on his own. However, when the purpose and destiny of a child is too important to allow the devil to stop him/her through a dad that refuses to do his job GOD will intervene. This is why mentoring works to help a child become what they were created to do and be.

If the child turns out to be a zero or something other than what GOD meant him or her to be, it will be difficult for the dad to realize his vision for the family. That child will be a drain on the family's finances and will negatively influence other children in the family. The main reasons children are born to parents is for them to educate or bring out of the children who they were coded to be and lead them to do what they were assigned to do so they can help the parents achieve their vision or mission as a family. It is crucial, then, to the family's success that the dad achieve victory over himself and be at peace within himself so the child can have a 9 added to their identity, personality and destiny numbers. Any number you add to nine will come to itself.

"And when he came to himself... (Luke 15:17)."

The Prodigal Son lacked the power to become himself until he "came to himself". Obtaining victory over ourselves will enable us to assist our children in coming to themselves or into who GOD created them to be. We must make the transition from being born in the world upside down as a 6 and reposition ourselves

Single Mothers and Sons

as a 9. Follow the illustration to understand how numbers function. When you add a 9 to any number it comes to itself.

Phenomenon of the Nine

Anything that 9 is added to will return unto itself. Anything that a 6 is added to will become something other than what it was meant to be.

1 + 9 = 10 = 1
2 + 9 = 11 = 2
3 + 9 = 12 = 3
4 + 9 = 13 = 4
5 + 9 = 14 = 5
6 + 9 = 15 = 6
7 + 9 = 16 = 7
8 + 9 = 17 = 8
9 + 9 = 18 = 9
10 + 9 = 19 = 10

Whatever you add 9 to comes to itself. Now, let's see what happens when an unregenerated man, 6, adds his life to a child's life.

1 + 6 = 7 = 0
2 + 6 = 8 = 0
3 + 6 = 9 = 0
4 + 6 = 10 = 1
5 + 6 = 11 = 2
6 + 6 = 12 = 3
7 + 6 = 13 = 4
8 + 6 = 14 = 5
9 + 6 = 15 = 6
10 + 6 = 16 = 7

We can see immediately that a good third of the children turn out to be nothing and the rest become something other than what they were meant to be.

Single Mothers and Sons

Parents, particularly dad, must prepare themselves to secure the knowledge of their identity, personality and destiny so they can become victorious over the forces in their own nature that prevent them from recognizing who they really are and what they were meant to be and do. Dads must become victorious over themselves in order to prepare their children to become victorious. When we have not come into the knowledge of who we were created to be, it is impossible to lead our children to become who they were created to be. We must already be what we expect our children to become.

Men who were not prepared for victory by their natural father must make GOD the Father their "abba" or Daddy Father. In HIM is the victory that overcomes the world through faith. Through HIS Son, GOD can lead you to the knowledge of who HE created you to be. Like the prodigal son came to himself and returned to his natural father, we must return to the Heavenly Father and obtain victory over ourselves and the world through Christ. If we assign and align our lives with the heavenly Father we can come to our self and then we can properly prepare our children for victory. When men clothe ourselves in victory we can cover our children with victorious lives and that will prepare them to leave home as young adults dressed to the 9s.

When a child is linked to a victorious daddy he or she has a much better opportunity to come to become what GOD created him or her to be. When the child grows into the person and does the thing that they were created do, the child brings glory to the dad. The child, then, can assist the dad to do for the family what he was created to do. People of old world heritage understood this principle and practiced it. This is one

Single Mothers and Sons

of the reasons their businesses were always called whomever and son.

Now, the same numerical principle applies to a man's wife. When a woman is married to a victorious man, she can come to be and do what GOD intended her to be and do. Then, she can assist her husband to do and be what GOD created him to do and be. The wife, however, is most critical to the man's success because she will bear the seeds of his children. Therefore, a man must be sure he marries the right woman and a woman must ensure that she marries a man who can "appreciate" her or increase her value.

This may come as a surprise but a man cannot receive the knowledge he needs to select the right woman until he is single. The word single in this context means to be whole within one's self and connected or one with GOD. If you want to know if a person is eligible to be married all you have to do is check to see if they are single. A person who is not single is not ready to be married. A person who gets married that is not single will not make a marriage. He or she will only make a mess. In time, the issues related to a man's lack of singleness will prevent him and his spouse from becoming one. They will have difficulty cleaving to one another or becoming one in body and soul. Couples who cannot cleave to each other eventually leave each other.

"...while men slept his enemy came and sowed tares among the wheat and went his way. But when the blade was sprung up, and brought forth fruit, then appeared the tares also (Matthew 13:25-26)."

Once a man is single and has received the knowledge of the type of woman will make him a good wife, he will suddenly discover several options in his presence. He will come in contact with several women that are endued with the gifts, talents and abilities that could help him achieve his created purpose. All he has to do then is make a selection from the options that are available. Be advised, my brothers, that the adversary will be placing women in your path at that time also. He will present you with women who look good to you but are not good for you.

"Whoso finds a wife finds a good thing, and obtains favor of the LORD (Proverbs 18:22)."

Notice the word does not say he who finds a woman finds a good thing. It says he who finds a wife. Every man is not qualified to be a husband and every woman is not prepared to be a wife. Every woman who appears goodly is not godly. A lot of women who are blessed with beauty of face and booty can't cook, won't clean and don't do dishes. Select the one who looks good who also knows how to handle domestic responsibilities and who will not cause you to compromise your beliefs, goals and aspirations to be with her. A woman that you have to compromise to be with will turn you away from your destiny. It is critical for a man to marry the right woman. Then he can produce the right children to assist him in achieving his created purpose and fulfilling the vision that GOD established for his life, his family and the individual lives of its members.

Lead Your Family to Discover their Gifts

"And when they were come into the house, they saw the young child with Mary his mother and fell down and worshiped him: and when they had opened their treasures, they presented unto him gifts: gold and frankincense; and myrrh (Matthew 2:11)."

Single Mothers and Sons

A man must meditate or communicate with his spirit in order to discover the things hidden within his family that he needs to fulfill the vision for his family. It is important that every father and husband teaches his family how to do this as well. Each child is born with a treasure chest of gifts, talents, knowledge and abilities buried inside of them. You have to teach your children to find them, mine them, and market them and somebody will pay you for them.

When leading children to commune with their spirit they must be taught that there are 5 voices that they have to contend with and help them understand how to identify which voice they will receive proper knowledge for their lives from: the voice of our mind, the voice of our body, the voice of our spirit, the voice of GOD and the voice of the adversary. The only two voices that will lead you into the knowledge of your identity and destiny are the voice of your spirit and the voice of GOD. The voice of the adversary, of course, will try to lead you away from that knowledge and will use the voices of your own mind and body to help him do it. First, know that your body does speak to you. Every time you get hungry that is your body telling you to give it something to eat. Second, the mind controls the body and causes it to act. The unregenerated nature of a man is centered in his mind. This is what a man who wants to be upright or victorious must overcome and make holy and acceptable to GOD; the mind of his spirit.

The mind must be renewed so that the body will submit and be acceptable to do what the man was created to do. When the mind is unregenerated or has not been renewed the adversary will manipulate it to get you to lead your body to do what he wants you to

Single Mothers and Sons

do. If you have ever heard the voice of GOD, satan will try to speak as if he is GOD. The only way to really know the difference is by reading the word of GOD. The voice of GOD will always be consistent with the words of the Bible. The voice of the adversary will always be contrary to the words of the Bible. If you are unregenerated, even though you know what the Bible says, the adversary can lead you to do wrong although you know that it is not right.

The key to being victorious then is in knowing the word of GOD, knowing how to recognize the voice of GOD and knowing how to recognize the voice of your spirit. The voice of your spirit receives instruction from the Spirit of GOD. The rare times that you will hear GOD's voice is when you happen to tune into their conversation. Most of the time whatever the voice of GOD said to your spirit will be transmitted to your brain by your spirit. The voice of your spirit sounds like your own voice. You will be able to hear that voice communicating to your body and brain.

If your mind is not regenerated, you will hear your mind making arguments as to why it cannot do what the voice of your spirit is leading it to do. So, in order to effectively communicate to his family on the outside a man must be at peace or without communication conflicts on the inside. Once he leads the family to become conflict free, they can grow to do and be what they were created to do and be and they will discover their hidden knowledge, gifts, talents and abilities.

If a man teaches his family to meditate and commune with their spirit the treasure chest of their hearts will open up to reveal their gifts. Our gifts lead us to good success on earth. Good success, completing that which GOD sent you here to do, gives both you and GOD glory. So, your gifts not only lead you to success on earth they also reserve a room for you in heaven.

Victorious Living Leads to Fulfillment

The world's economic system is designed for a person to decide what they want to do or be. Then we go to college to learn how to do or be what we decided to do or be. As a result of following the world's system, 80% of all working people expend one third of their life in a career or vocation that they don't enjoy. That is, they do not experience fulfillment in what they do every day for at least 8 hours a day. Some of these people may be successful. However, there is a difference between being successful and being fulfilled. People who are successful and famous often struggle to feel fulfilled.

The main reason people do not feel fulfilled is because they know they are not doing what they really want to do. They have a yearning inside of them to do something else, something that will make a difference. Many of these people have fought to climb the ladder of success only to reach the top and find that their ladder was leaning against the wrong building. At the time they are supposed to be celebrating success they feel trapped. Having invested all the time, money and energy in pursuit of their career, they feel they have no choice but to continue in it. However, they do have a choice. They can begin to pursue the thing that they really want to do.

The thing that is causing the yearning inside of them to do something different is their spirit. Their spirit knows why they are here, what they are supposed to do, and is trying to lead them to do it. However, their own mind and educational training fights against them. This is why it is important for a man to teach his children to meditate or communicate with their spirit at a young age. It will provide their young mind and body with a connection to their spirit. Then, their spirit can influence them to pick a college education or career that is commensurate with what they were created to do or be. Having a connection with the knowledge of their spirit will make it more difficult to be led astray or into pursuing a career that will make them miserable. When the time comes to make a career decision their spirit will help lead them to make the right decision.

Once a person begins doing that which they were sent here to do, the treasure of their heart opens up. GOD then adds power to the gifts, talents, knowledge and abilities that they have inside of them. These gifts are made available to help the person complete the thing that GOD sent them here to do and to meet their needs: financial, family, physical, emotional, etc. The provisions you need to complete the vision that was established for your life will always be supplied because provision is only given in support of the vision that GOD has for your life.

When we are not pursuing the vision, there is no need to supply the provisions. We may chose a career that we think will provide the best job or that we might like to do. However, if it is not in line with what GOD sent us here to do, we will not have power added to our knowledge, gifts, talents and abilities. If you are not using them in some way to pursue your career, they will lie there dormant until something provokes you in a way that draws them out.

As each member of a family begins operating in their created purpose they will begin to receive the provisions that were set aside for their lives. The entire

Single Mothers and Sons

family begins to become both enriched and fulfilled. They are doing something their heart desires and they are reaping the rewards of doing it. It is crucial, then, for a man to teach his children the word of GOD while they are young. This will help them to eliminate many of the starts, fits and failings of life.

"...I know him that he will command his children and his household after him and they shall keep the way of the LORD... (Genesis 18:19)"

GOD made Abraham the father of many nations for two reasons. The first was because he was a faithful man. The second was because GOD knew Abraham would teach his children. The thing that GOD wants from the union of a man and woman is godly children. A child who is trained to be godly will grow up to do that which they were created to do. A faithful man will teach his children to be faithful also by the example that he sets before them. Any man who teaches his children to be faithful will become great, mighty and blessed in his life and through his wife. He can't help it; it will just happen.

"Seeing that Abraham shall surely become a great and mighty nation and all the nations of the earth shall be blessed in him. For I know him, that he will command his children and his household after him and they shall keep the way of the Lord, to do justice and judgment; that the Lord may bring upon Abraham that which he hath spoken of him (Genesis 18:18-19)."

In order to be an effective leader, a man has to be willing to be a servant. Men have a responsibility to both lead and serve their family in the ways of GOD. The way GOD leads a man into HIS ways is by effectively communicating to him that which HE wants him to do. The way that a man leads his family into his

Single Mothers and Sons

vision is by effectively communicating with them. A man communicates with his family when he talks to and listens to them. He communicates effectively when what she says matches up or is consistent with everything that she does.

Establish Order and Consistency in the Family

Men must establish order and consistency in the family to eliminate chaos and confusion in the home. Children need order, consistency and discipline in the home in order to feel secure. Contrary to popular belief, children love discipline. It makes life seem fair and it makes them feel that someone cares about what they do. Children also love order and consistency because it makes life easier for them. Order and consistency sets boundaries for children and allows them to know what to do and what to expect on a daily basis. When children don't know what to do or what to expect from their parents, they become frustrated and hard to contain. They lose respect for their parent's guidance and begin to follow their own guidance or that of their friends.

Therefore, a man must establish the order of the family. The father must be the Chief Executive Officer (CEO) of the family. He oversees the family operation, makes the decisions and sees that they are carried out. A man's three main objectives in leading his family as its CEO is to keep his wife and children: on the path of righteousness, headed toward completing the vision and within budget. The mother is the Chief Operations Officer (COO) of the family. She helps design the plan of operation to achieve the family's vision in conjunction with the CEO, runs the day to day activities and implements the decisions of the CEO.

Single Mothers and Sons

The children are the staff that help complete the tasks, assigned by the COO, which will fulfill the intent of the decisions of the CEO.

If a man is trying to run the day to day operation of the family, he is out of order. If a wife is trying to make decisions and oversee the operation of the family, the man is out of order. If the children are trying to circumvent the directives of the mother by going to the father, they are out of order 9 times out of 10 because the father is out of order. If the father countermands a directive given by the mother without a closed door discussion with her, he is out of order. These are basic things in a family that maintain order, which are based upon proper division of effort and common courtesy. However, the father sets the tone for order in the family by keeping himself in order at all times. Whenever anything is out of order in the home it is because the man is out of order or is not doing his job properly.

Learn to Communicate in Love

Communication often breaks down in a family when a man is overbearing, inconsistent and acts as if he never makes mistakes. Men who make the best fathers are those who remember how it was to be a child. A man has to control his desire to dominate his family. When he leads them to be who they are, they will be who they are supposed to become.

Everyone makes mistakes and nobody knows this better than children. No one knows better that they made a mistake than the person who made it. A man's job is not necessarily to point out the mistakes children make, but to point out how not to make it again. When a man acts as if every mistake a child makes is the end

Single Mothers and Sons

of the world, they will not learn or grow. The child becomes emotionally paralyzed. And as the child observes the father making mistakes (and believe me they will) they will grow to resent and lose respect for him.

Therefore, a father has to learn to communicate with his family in love. Communicating in love will allow him to correct and discipline his family in a manner that will foster growth and reduce the need, over time, for correction and discipline. The children will learn and yearn to do what is right out of love and respect for a dad who consistently strives to do what is right and who treats them right. This is why knowing how to communicate effectively with one's family is so important. This is also why providing a stress free atmosphere in which to communicate is important. Family meetings are the best way to communicate with the family in love.

During a family meeting, each person gets a chance to express themselves fully without interruption. The only interruption that should be allowed is in the form of a question that will allow for clarification or to gain a better understanding. Questions should not be used to make the person think their position is not valid or to throw them off track. Each member of the family must be an active listener while other members are talking.

Remember, whatever the person speaking feels is real to them. It may not seem like a big deal to you but it is a big deal to them. Each member has to learn to respect how other members feel. There are other rules that must be established for the meetings such as no one gets to talk out of turn, no yelling, loud talking, arguing, name calling, bickering. Dad must control the meeting, acknowledge each speaker and be the referee unless he is the subject of the complaint. In that case, mom becomes the referee. All issues concerning the operation of the family should be discussed. All problems and complaints about the operation of the family should be addressed.

The vision, mission and goals of the family are reviewed and/or revised at the meeting. Any mid course corrections that must be made and the reasons for the corrections are announced. All family members who have achieved any goals or milestones are acknowledged, celebrated and rewarded at the meeting. The dad must constantly reinforce in his family that the goals attained are only plateaus not the summit. New goals and levels of achievement are set as the former ones are attained. Everyone is reminded to support everyone else in the attainment of their goals and aspirations. The children must understand that their competition is not their peers within the family, but their peers outside the family. Every man who learns to overcome the world, overcome himself, and govern his family properly can achieve victorious living.

Chapter 6
Overcoming Obstacles

"For whatsoever is born of GOD overcomes the world: and this is the victory that overcomes the world, even our faith. Who is he that overcomes the world, but he that believes that Jesus is the Son of GOD (1 John 5:4-5)?"

Everyone has obstacles that we have to overcome in our lives. These obstacles are barriers that prevent us from executing our created purpose and achieving the goals and aspirations we have set for ourselves. Sadly, most of the obstacles that we have to overcome are barriers that we either put in place ourselves or walls that we refuse to cross over. The boundaries for what we would achieve, be or do may have been set for us as youngsters. We may have had a dream to attain a professional occupation only to have someone tell us that we could never be or do that. Instead of being more determined to achieve that goal, most of us gave up and decided to set our sights on something else. Others embarked on a quest toward a particular goal only to discover that it was very tough to achieve so they gave up. They put aside the pursuit of their created purpose, lofty ideas and high aspirations and decided to accept that which everyone else who they grew up around expected to achieve.

The Nike Corporation has a slogan designed to motivate the viewer to achieve their peak athletic potential by challenging them to "Just Do It". Although their real goal is to seduce us to buy sneakers, their ad is a model for the type of attitude we must adopt in order to overcome life's barriers. Whenever we want to do certain things or achieve certain goals, there is going to be barriers that we must fight through or obstacles to overcome in order to get there. If that goal is something a lot of other people want to achieve, such as winning the Super Bowl, we will have to invest a lot of time, energy, blood, sweat and even some tears to overcome competitive resistance. There may be a lot we will have to fight through to do what we want to do, but the only way to get through it is "Just Do It".

Many of us know that we can do or be whatever we want to do or be yet we never come close to living up to our potential. We have heard the clarion call to "Just Do It". We know that there is really nothing stopping us from achieving the goals that we set for ourselves even many years ago. Yet, we never take the steps or do the things necessary to get started. We usually bind the thought or inhibit the process by making some excuse that usually begins with "I would've, could've or should've" followed by "but". Someone may ask "Why didn't you go to law school, for example. The usual response is, "I would've, but..." So, have you even looked into getting in yet? "Well, I would've, could've or should've, but..." A big "but" is a dream killer. Too many people delude themselves into believing that they want to be successful however they sit around on their "buts" and do nothing except talk about doing something. When these guys don't achieve any level of success they always look for some "other" person to blame for their shortfall. If we REALLY want to achieve success we have to get our buts out of the way otherwise they will crush all of our goals, dreams and aspirations.

Single Mothers and Sons

Get your "BUT" out of the way!

My greatest personal enemy to success is not my greatest mortal enemy or an enemy outside of me. My greatest enemy to success is the inner me, the enemy inside of me or the in-a-me. It's the enemy inside of me telling me that I cannot be what I want to be. It's the in-a-me leading me to procrastinate and fail to do what I am supposed to do. I have to find a way to overcome the in-a-me that keeps me sitting in front of the TV when I know I should be doing something else. I must find a way to deal with the enemy inside of me that provides me with excuses not to do that which I know I can and should do. I have to kick every "but" that gets in my face immediately. Something inside of me must change or I will keep creating obstacles to my own success.

The first obstacle that we have to overcome for success after our self imposed limitations is a lack of relationship with GOD. Without coming to the knowledge of who you are and what you can do by faith, it is difficult to achieve and retain success. When a man does not have GOD in his life, it leaves a lot of room for buts to live in him. Having the knowledge of who we are, whose we are, what we have, and what we can do make us eligible to access to the power of GOD. This power enables us to do **all** things (Philippians 4:13). Things that once seemed impossible are possible with the power of GOD working in us and for us. Matthew 19:26 says, "With men this is impossible but with GOD all things are possible." A relationship with GOD produces the faith to remove the fear and doubt of those buts. When faith comes in the "buts" have to leave.

Single Mothers and Sons

"If any man has ears to hear, let him hear (Mark 4:23)."

"But blessed are your eyes, for they see: and your ears, for they hear (Matthew 13:16)."

Jesus healed a lot of blind, deaf, crippled, and demon possessed men. I had to ask GOD why were there so many men in disabled condition in the region where Jesus grew up? HE showed me that the physical condition of men reveal the spiritual condition of a region. Being collectively blind, deaf, cripple, and possessed is an indication of Spiritual blindness and deafness in men. Those with spiritual eyes opened can see that a principality level demon had taken over and usurped the authority of the men in that region for many years. Thus, their women were plagued with incurable issues, their boys were under demonic possession, and their girls were dying for seemingly no reason. Mark 9:24 indicates the men in that region had lost all power to wage a spiritual battle over that demon and win.

"And straightway the father of the child cried out, and said with tears, Lord, I believe; help you mine unbelief."

Principality and powers demons are very defiant and have no respect for male authority so they take it from every man who is not spiritually strong enough to stop them. Under the law of Natural Selection a man who cannot defend his authority has no right to have any. Men whose eyes are open can see that we have a generation or two of young people in America that are under demonic influence. They have no respect for male authority therefore they engage in acts of civil defiance. Men act as if they have no power or authority to bring their sons and daughters back into godly

Single Mothers and Sons

order. That is because although many men regularly attend church they have allowed themselves to become spiritually deaf and blind. They have allowed preachers to make them believe that only they can hear from GOD. Therefore, the men of GOD are unable to see and hear what the spirit of GOD is saying to them to defeat this demon for their family.

The power of GOD to face down demons already resides in you. You just need to recognize that the power to fight demonic forces and win comes by combining faith with hearing and understanding the word of GOD. You must also realize Hebrews 4:2 says that faith is not profitable or does not become powerful unless it is mixed with the word of GOD. Epoxy is a type of glue with two ingredients that have no power to glue anything together alone. But mix the ingredients it becomes one of the most powerful adhesives in the world. Faith has no power to produce unless it is mixed with the word of GOD. Fighting with the left/right combination of faith and the word of GOD gives us the opportunity to retake our spiritual authority and recover the territory that the demon has stolen.

If you want to access the power of GOD to help you get your demon out of the way, you must confess your sins before GOD. Don't try fighting the devil while you still have some of his pie crumbs on your mouth. This is important because Revelation 12:10 says that satan, like a prosecutor, is the accuser of the brothers; accusing you before GOD day and night. However, it doesn't say that he is a false accuser. You know there are things that you did. So, when you confess your sins, you have a chance to make a plea bargain before trial. It is crucial that you confess to GOD before the adversary can accuse you before HIM. If you confess while on the witness stand, the case is closed and satan gets to recommend sentence. If you confess before the trial, Jesus the Wonderful Counselor; our Public Defender, gets to recommend your sentence. Since the wages of sin is death something in your life has to die. And since Jesus wouldn't recommend that you die your car that was working well might suddenly die.

As we get closer with GOD, we will begin to discover the things in ourselves that keep us from achieving success. Light will be shined on the dark rooms of our hearts and reveal things that we did not know were hidden there. All the little slights, hurts and rebukes that we received from our relatives and friends are brought to our remembrance. We will realize that we played the tapes of those hurts, rebukes and slights in our minds and rehearsed them with our mouths every time we thought of achieving our dream. The negative self-talk that we engage in produce would haves, could haves, should haves and the buts in our lives. Coming to the realization that it is our own selves that is keeping us from doing what we want to do will teach us to overcome our psychological obstacles (which is actually satanic torment) and use our spiritual power and authority to chase the demons away.

Achieve Peace with GOD and Self

"Not forsaking the assembling of our**SELVES** together (Hebrews 10:25a)"

Man is a tri-part being with 3 selves (spirit self, mind self, and body self) that struggle against each other for supremacy. It is crucial for men, to separate ourselves from sin, to bring our SELVES together or in agreement with the word of GOD so that we can have internal peace and so that GOD can trust us with HIS power. Every man needs inner peace to overcome sin and the obstacles in his world. Jesus said "These things I have spoken unto you, that in me you might have peace. In the world you shall have tribulation: but be of good cheer, I have overcome the world (John 16:33)." As we go through trials, tribulations and face the obstacles of life, how we do it determines how we come through it. If we can resist the devil's pressure in peace, we will come out like pure gold. By contrast, if we try to relieve ourselves of the pressure by giving others grief, we will continue to remain in satan's hold.

Again, most of the obstacles that we face are self imposed due to the sin that lies hidden within. We become enemies to ourselves as we are driven by various lusts and desires living inside of us to do things that are detrimental to our own well being. The temptation to satisfy lust and desire is the result of a basic instinct to conform our outward behavior to align with our inner nature. Defects of our inner nature degrade our inhibitions over time and manifest themselves in various forms of lust. Sometimes they manifest at an early age and sometimes later in life. In order to effectively eliminate these obstacles we must be fully aware that they are there and if not eliminated we will cause ourselves trouble.

The 5 greatest self imposed obstacles that every man must overcome are: religion, poverty, mediocrity, himself, and a false self image. Men who delude themselves into thinking they are someone or something they are not have difficulty becoming who they were created to be. There is great wealth connected to the man GOD created you to be. When a man cannot figure out who he is or is comfortable pretending to be someone else he never reaches his

Single Mothers and Sons

GOD ordained destiny where the wealth is located and it causes him to languish in poverty and mediocrity. When a man knows that he is powerful but religion and societal pressure leads him to pretend that he is not power this too will cause him to languish in poverty and mediocrity. Traditional religious doctrine teaches humility in a way that makes people believe it is shameful for them to think highly of their self. The Apostle Paul, however, does not teach us to NOT think highly of our self. He warned against thinking MORE highly of our self than we ought to think; meaning that we should not delude our self into thinking we are something that we are not. There is no Bible prohibition against being who you really are, my brothers, and feeling great about it.

"For I say, through the grace given unto me to every man that is among you not to think of himself **more** highly than he ought to think (Romans 12:3)."

We have to guard ourselves against traditional religious doctrine because it can make us like hamsters on a wheel running after an illusion that we cannot see and will never catch. Religious men, because of false teaching, create a false self image based on religious piety which prevents them from growing into the man GOD created them to be. Their true identity and the things they really want to do through religion are attainable through the truth of the word of GOD. But religion makes truth largely unavailable particularly when the truth conflicts with religious doctrine. They are conditioned to fight to hold on to doctrine so they never get to have the things their religion promises to produce. They see their preacher prospering in those promises but they never stop to ask why it is happening for him and not for them.

Single Mothers and Sons

The most difficult of the 5 obstacles to overcome is our self. Proverbs 4:23 says to guard your heart with all diligence because out of it flows the issues (ish you) of life. Most of the "ish" you are going through is due to what has been coming out of you. Proverbs 23:7 says that as a man thinks in his heart so is he which sounds a lot like Rene Descartes who said I think therefore I am. The way life has been treating you is due in part to who you are. Who you are is a direct result of how you think.

Some men do not think highly of themselves so they have a very high level of low self esteem. They need an excuse for the reason they are low or mediocre performers so they find some person or group to project the hate they feel for themselves on to. They would really like to take themselves out but they are too cowardly to do that so they terrorize their wives, children or "other" people just so they can feel powerful.

Ultimately, it is our responsibility to assemble or get our selves together in order to have peace with our selves and to protect our hearts from the temptation of lust and sin entering in. Various issues arise that become obstacles in our lives because of what is in our own heart. These issues arise to alert us, by the grace of GOD, that there is something in our heart that we have to do something about. To keep ourselves from going through issues and facing unnecessary obstacles we have to guard our hearts. The best way to guard our heart is by completing the perfection and purification process to purge our self of the iniquities within us. Secondly, we guard what comes into our hearts by restricting what we see, hear and say.

Single Mothers and Sons

Every man, at some time, will reach a point of incompetence; the obstacle of a lack of knowledge. Our family will be faced with a problem or issue where we literally have no clue as to what to do. Some guys look at me like I have two heads when I tell them that to avoid being paralyzed by this obstacle every man needs knowledge in several areas before he is qualified to get married and lead a family. Every man that is eligible to get married is not qualified. In order to qualify we must have knowledge in the following areas: spiritual, social (who knows who), legal, history, medicine, political, and financial. You don't have to be an expert on anything but you have to know just enough about everything to piss off your friends. If your family has a problem, the solution will reside in one of these areas.

History is one of the more critical areas of knowledge but it is the one that we avoid most. History helps us to obtain a greater understanding on how things are and why. The number one question that men get from our children for which we often have no answer is: why! As family leaders men must understand how the condition of the country, people, families, the economy, etc came to be. History contains stories of opportunity and opposition. It is a record of how people who faced the same experiences prevailed and why some failed. A couple of books on history that would be good to have in your library are: Lessons of History and Lessons on Philosophy by Will Durant.

Many men find themselves trapped behind the obstacle of lack of knowledge and most women have never seen a true renaissance man that is protean in nature because we fell for the meme: nobody likes anybody who knows everything. The dichotomy here is women don't like it when they have to depend on a

Single Mothers and Sons

man who doesn't have and doesn't know how to find the answers to their family's problems. This is one of the things that cause women to begin contemplating divorce. The position of husband is an appointed position. Your wife could have appointed any man to that position but she gave it to you. If you fail to live up to what she expects she will lose faith in you. Expectation is the foundation of faith. Once women lose faith they become disappointed. Once women become disappointed they will dismiss you from your appointment.

As society was being dumbed down steadily, we willfully joined the band of know nothings thus we learned to do nothing therefore in a downturned economy we have nothing. Suddenly, have entered an era where everyone wants to be wealthy but we can't because we know nothing about history, politics, money, business, and finances. Being misguided socially created another obstacle to success for us in 3 areas: mindset, skill set, and environment. Poverty and wealthy are not states of money they are states of mind. In order to become and remain wealthy a man has to develop a wealthy mindset. Acquiring wealth demands that you have a marketable skill more than a marketable product. If you know something everyone else doesn't and if you can do something better than everyone else can, you have a skill that can pay the bills. As a result of choosing to know nothing we find ourselves with a desire to be wealthy but surrounded by people who also know nothing and living in an area that is depressed economically. Men who are wealthy have the right mindset, a good skill set, and they positioned themselves in an environment conducive to success.

Guarding Your Heart
The three gates through which either good or evil can enter into a man's heart are: the eyes, the ears, and the mouth. Good or evil can enter into our hearts by what we see, what we hear (Ecclesiastes 1:8) and what we say (Matthew 15:11). The only way the adversary learns how to influence a man or entice him to sin is by observing the things he looks at, the things he listens to and listening to the things he says. The adversary knows that the eyes and ears are never satisfied with just seeing and hearing because we will begin to talk about whatever we see or hear. The adversary can lure us into sin because we will, eventually, begin to do the things we have been talking about.

There is a 7 step process that leads to a breakdown of church going men's inhibition to sin and causes iniquity to develop in their heart. Those steps are: observation, stimulation, admiration, experimentation, participation, consummation, and reprobation. Just in case you are cherry picking chapters or didn't start reading from the beginning you will find each of these steps explained fully in Chapter 1.

Men are more motivated or stimulated to act on whatever we visualize. Pornography is a booming industry because it appeals to a man's basic instinct to gratify his sexual lusts through the eyes. Therefore, a man has to guard his heart from having to deal with the issues of life by turning the eye gate to his heart away from things that could lead him into sin.

As we travel along the path that GOD established for our lives, we will encounter obstacles. The adversary will kick things in our path designed to cause us to trip and fall. He will place things along our path designed to capture our attention and cause us to deviate off course. The devil knows what he can use to draw you off the path of righteousness by simply learning what you like to look at. This gives him an idea of what force is living inside of you that will work to lead you off course. You know this is easy for the devil to do. If you look to the left while walking or driving you will tend to drift to the left. Since men are easily distracted by sexy objects the devil can use one to lead us off course. The path of righteousness is a straight and narrow path that is surrounded by areas of sin. As you deviate off course you move from righteousness into sin. The further you move off the path of righteousness the deeper you go into sin. The more you deviate the more you become deviant. This is another reason the scripture warns you:

"Let your eyes look right on and let your eyelids look straight before you. Ponder the path of your feet and let all your ways be established. Turn not to the right hand or to the left: remove your foot from evil (Proverbs 4:25-27)."

Although the adversary places his share of obstacles in our path those obstacles are still self imposed because satan can only do to you whatever you allow him to do. He can only use the iniquity and sin hidden inside you to lead you to do what they predispose us to do. GOD knows the devil uses our sin and iniquity to gain and maintain a stronghold over HIS people. This is why HE sent Jesus who said:

"The Spirit of the Lord is upon me, because HE has anointed me to preach the gospel to the poor; HE has sent me to heal the brokenhearted, to preach deliverance to the captives, and recovering of sight to

Single Mothers and Sons

the blind, to set at liberty them that are bruised... (Luke 4:18)"

We have become poor, blind, bound, bruised and captive mourners as a result of allowing ourselves to be under satan's authority. GOD gave us the authority to dominate him. Yet, we chose to allow him to dominate us. Ephesians 4:27 says "Neither give place to the devil" which reveals that we have both the authority to give him place in our lives and to take away any place that we had previously given him.

Men must ensure that we have peace with our selves, with GOD, and with our family. When we are at peace with GOD we are free of sin and in right standing with HIM. When we are at peace with ourselves and our family GOD can enter into that environment and bring the power for prosperity. This power covers every area of your life to free you from every yoke of bondage. We have a power available to us to overcome a lack of knowledge, emotional stress, persecution, spiritual blindness, and every kind of abuse. We have the power to make ourselves free. GOD has made this power available to you but it only works in the lives of men who at peace.

Once we finally recognize just how much power GOD has made available we will stop acting pitiful and become powerful. Once we finally realize that we have all the power of heaven and earth residing within us we will stop letting the devil defeat us. You have GOD in you (John 17:23). You have Jesus in you (Colossians 1:26). You have the Holy Spirit in you (Romans 8:11). You have the anointing or the power of GOD in you (1 John 2:27). You have the Kingdom of GOD in you (Luke 17:21). So with all that power living in you, my brother, WHO is preventing you from doing, having and being what you want? With all of that POWER living IN us what MORE do we need GOD to do for us?

1 Corinthians 4:20 says "the Kingdom of GOD comes NOT in word but in **POWER**". We have to STOP living like we are powerless when GOD has ALREADY made us powerful. GOD has given us a super advantage over the devil and has made us **all** powerful. Yet, through religion we have allowed him to make us disadvantaged (one who has had their advantage taken) thus we have been living like we are poor and pitiful rather than rich and powerful. Jesus is King of Kings therefore every man is supposed to be a King ruling over the Kingdom of GOD on earth.

Everyone will go through trials and tests in life and have to overcome obstacles. The state in which we go through and overcome will determine the results we achieve. We endure the trials and overcome the obstacles in peace with GOD and man, but we have to turn hell upside down in the process. Those who overcome the world have learned to put the fire of hell out in their lives. They live in a type of peace that passes all understanding of those who watch them do it. Men who overcome the world turn their test into a testimony. Men who do not overcome the world just turn their test into the "moanies". Rather than being winners they become whiners.

What to do in the Mean Time

While we are enduring persecution, trials and tests it gets so hard at times that some of us begin to feel that GOD is being mean to us. Like Jesus on the cross, we feel like crying out "My GOD, my GOD, why have you forsaken me"! This period of pain, between going through and coming out of persecution, trials and tests is what I call "the mean time".

As we are working to come completely through persecution, trials and tests while fighting to not give up, cave in or quit, in the mean time we must know what to do. The word "mean" in one sense of this context denotes an intermediate or middle position of time. In another sense, it conveys a humility or debasement due to physical or spiritual degradation. The purpose in these types of persecution, trials and tests is to prepare you to become who you are supposed to be at you next level of growth; to pressure you to get rid of some of the people, places, activities, and things in your life that you can't take to the next level.

This can be compared to baking a cake. The cake ingredients are first battered or beaten and then subjected to high heat in order for it to rise and become something other than what it was previously. If the mixture is pulled out of the heat before it goes all the way through the baking process, it will fall and never become a cake. You might get to the point where you want someone to help you out of the heat of persecution. A well meaning person may pull you out. However, if you don't go completely through, you will not rise to the next level and you will never grow to be what you were meant to become. Just like a half baked cake your life will be a mess.

There was a little bird that refused to fly south consequently he was having a hard time enduring a very harsh winter. It was too cold to fly and he was starving so he hunted and pecked in the snow for food. Just when he thought he was about to freeze to death a moose came along and took a dump right on top of

Single Mothers and Sons

him. He was feeling even more badly for himself until he realized the moose crap was warming him up. Rejoicing over the prospect that he might yet live the bird began to sing. A wolf, attracted by the bird's song, pulled the bird out of the crap and ate him. The moral to the story is everyone who takes a dump on you is not your enemy and everyone who pulls you out of crap is not your friend.

It seems like a mean thing for one person to dump on another. However, mean things occur in the times of transition from one level to another. A seed needs to be buried alone in the dirt and in the dark so that it can grow to be what it was created to become. In the mean time, it is covered in fertilizer (or excrement) while it is being transformed into a flower. Then, it has to push up through the pressure or weight of the dirt and crap that was dumped on it in order to rise to the top and reveal what it has become to the world. When someone attacks us for no reason it seems like a mean thing for them to do. No one likes having dirt kicked on them. No one likes it when they are dumped on for seemingly no reason. However, we can rejoice once we recognize that the mean time is the place of transition from feeling sorrowful to being successful.

In the mean time it is hard to remain with GOD because we feel like HE has left us. We question within our hearts "How could GOD allow the devil and his disciples to throw dirt and dump on HIS faithful servant like this?" The mean time is when we begin to shift the blame for what we are going through on to GOD and accuse HIM of being unfair. However, GOD is the one who sends someone with the water of the word to show you what you need to be cleansed of in order to live or remain at your next level of growth. It seems like a mean thing to pour water on top of your dump and dirt because that makes you look like a muddy mess. Yet, the water also makes it easier to push through the dirt in order to reveal what you have become to the world. What do we do in the mean time? The ultimate goal of persecution is to try your faith in an effort to choke the word out of you (Mark 4:14-20). Therefore, we stay in the word, stay with GOD and maintain the proper attitude. Then, HE can lead you to be what we were meant to become before the foundation of the world.

Obstacles to Financial Breakthrough

In Acts 1:3 **after** His resurrection Jesus spent **40 days** teaching His disciples about the Kingdom of GOD. He did not spend time teaching them about building a church, salvation, resurrection, or how to get into heaven. Their questions to Him in Acts 1:6 reveal that in spite of everything He had been teaching they were still thinking that the coming of the Kingdom of GOD had to do with a military solution to Roman oppression. Jesus was teaching them about a new level of prosperity and power that He had delivered which they could use to end their own oppression. But, they just could not give up their old religious teachings based on old Jewish tradition. They were still stuck in their belief that He was going to do for them what He had just spent 40 days teaching them that they would be empowered to do for themselves. This is the reason Jesus executed plan B and called the Apostle Paul.

The reason Christian church is not working today is because rather than being established on what Jesus was teaching the disciples set up a Christian religious doctrine that was simply a modified version of old

Single Mothers and Sons

Jewish doctrine and tradition. Jesus said that He came to preach the gospel to the poor. The main struggle among GOD's people today as it was back then is financial. The teachings they receive on how to prosper through tithing is not working because it is based on old Jewish tradition. Jesus introduced a new economic system better than tithing that He would use to empower and prosper His people. That economic system is what Jesus called the Kingdom of GOD.

GOD's people are not being led to follow GOD's will through Jesus' New Testament teachings therefore they are constantly searching for ways to open the windows of heaven and have the Old Testament promise in Malachi chapter 3 poured out on them. They use scriptures like a ring of keys trying one after another hoping to find one that will finally open up the window but none of them work. In Matthew 16:19 Jesus said He will give you the keys **OF** the Kingdom so you can bind and loose (lock and unlock) things in heaven and earth. Jesus has already given you the key but religious doctrine has led you away from the knowledge of where and how to use it.

If someone gave you a key to a safe deposit box with a million dollars in it but you don't know what bank to go to is that key any value to you? Even with the keys of the Kingdom described in the Bible, old religious tradition and false teaching on what the Kingdom of GOD really is has prevented us from finding out where the metaphoric bank is. Therefore, we have not been able to access the funds. If you really want to experience the promise of prosperity rather than be victimized by the power of fake prophesy you have to discard all of the doctrine being taught currently because it is all a cleverly crafted lie.

Single Mothers and Sons

The truth is the Kingdom of Heaven is the place where GOD resides and the Kingdom of GOD is the economic system the Kingdom of Heaven operates on. The Kingdom of GOD is the system that GOD uses to distribute wealth and provision to HIS children on earth. America is the place where we reside. Capitalism is the economic system that America operates on and produces various avenues of revenue for her citizens to tap into.

Matthew 18:18-20 reveals one of the keys of the Kingdom of GOD is power. That is, power that we receive through partnership by being in agreement with GOD, the earth, and with each other. The universe is set up to reward cooperation but not competition. Mark 11:24-26 reveals two other keys of the Kingdom: faith and forgiveness. You must live peaceably with all people especially your spouse or it will automatically lead to poverty. Then, Matthew 11:12 says the Kingdom of GOD is taken possession of by force which means power or virtue. The virtuous take it or enter into the Kingdom of GOD by the force of virtue. In Matthew 6:33, Jesus didn't say to seek Him or GOD first. He said seek the Kingdom of GOD first. However, without the virtue or power of His righteousness you cannot access the Kingdom's treasury room.

"For where your treasure is there will your **heart** be also (Matthew 6:21)."

"If you love me, keep my commandments (John 14:15)."

The 10 commandments are the Kingdom of GOD keys for integrity. They lead us to remain one with or in righteousness with GOD. See Exodus 20:3-17 and Deuteronomy 5:6-21. This means that you can't have anything in your heart that is offensive to GOD such as anger, bitterness, strife, malice, deceit, racism, sexism, political rancor, etc. Finally, In His Sermon on the Mount, Matthew 5:3-10, Jesus listed the remaining keys, things that we must **BE**, in order to unlock the Kingdom of GOD: poor in spirit, mournful, meek, merciful, a peacemaker, reviled and persecuted, with a hunger and thirst for righteousness.

"...the mystery which has been hid from ages and generations is now made manifest to HIS saints: to whom GOD would make known what is the riches of the glory of this mystery among the Gentiles; which is **Christ in you**, the hope of glory (Colossians 1:26-27)."

There is a single key to unlock the Kingdom of GOD and that key is called righteousness. However, there are several teeth that must be cut onto the key in order for it to open the lock. The mystery of the key's teeth is revealed in the list of the keys above to be the character qualities and attributes of Jesus Christ. If you desire to open the treasury of Heaven, the glorious riches of the Kingdom of GOD, you must have Christ or the character qualities and attributes of Jesus **in** your heart; for where your treasure is there will be your heart also.

This may seem impossible for men to do but with GOD **ALL** things are possible. Once you put complete the purification and perfection process you will find all the things that are unrighteous has been purged from you. And if you have been perfected in the measure of the stature of the **fullness** of Christ, you will find the key within you to unlock the Kingdom of GOD all shiny and new that has been hanging up just waiting for you. Your mom used to put the house key around your neck so that you wouldn't lose it. GOD put the key **IN** you so the devil can't steal it from you and so that you can't lose it to him.

Say "so what" to your past

There are people over forty years old that are still being affected by things that happened to them in their childhood. There are men who were abandoned by their fathers that are still dealing with issues related to their fathers not being there. There are adult men who were sexually abused as children who are still emotionally disturbed as a result of that abuse. I know a guy who is nearly 65 years old that is still upset with his mother over spankings that he got as a child, which he believes he didn't deserve. When I observe middle aged people who are mentally and emotionally vexed over things that happened to them as a child, my visceral reaction is to say: "So what, that happened to you as a child! When are you going to get over it?"

Everyone has had something happen to them as a child that could have left them scarred emotionally. Some people allow it to scar them and some people do not. Why is it that some people cannot move on? Emotionally they never grow up therefore they remain the same age psychologically they were at the time they were scarred. I am a compassionate person and I can be touched with the feeling of their infirmities. I was abandoned by my father and abused as a child myself. I allowed it to bother me too until I was about 24 years old and married with three sons. As I was talking with GOD and feeling sorry for myself one day for not knowing what to do with my 3 boys because my father didn't show me, GOD said "He is not your father, I AM". That jerked the slack out of my back. My mind was immediately enlightened and the way I approached life suddenly changed. From that day my mindset has been to say to myself "so what" your father abandoned you. "So what" you were abused. Those things are something that happened to you. They are not who you are!

Life is now much easier to matriculate through and I have become successful because my mindset was changed through revelation. I could now see that it was not in my best interest to turn the things people did to me into an indictment against myself. I could now see that people who would hurt, harm or abuse others need help themselves. It became clear to me that hurting people hurt people. They need to relieve their hidden hurts so they do things to pass the pain they feel on to someone else. Now I understand the things other people try to do to me is not my problem, it is their problem. They were once prey and their pain turn them into a predator. When people are angry with me due to no fault on my part, I say "so what". I simply leave them alone and never allow their problem to become my problem. They are going to stress themselves out, become sick, and die early. I refuse to let them cause me to die early with them.

It is tough sometimes to just move past people and leave them to their own circumstances. They only strike out at me because I am in their presence. When they see me living free, being who I am and doing what GOD would have me to do, they become angry because my presence reminds them of how inadequate they are. The best thing I can do for both them and me is to get out of their sight. I have learned to keep my edge and retain the ability to win because I learned to say "so what". So what, that person is angry with me. I didn't do anything but be who GOD created me to be and they

Single Mothers and Sons

got offended. It is not my problem that they are offended, it is their problem. The attitude of "so what" guarantees me victory over the obstacles of past personal pains, former sins, and other people's problems.

The adversary uses the sins of our past to try to control our future. He will try to convince you that GOD never loved you because of things that happened to you or that he could never love you because of things you have done in your past. It does not matter how major or minor your sins were, he will try to use them against you. The devil is a sneaky character who does not have the courage to attack you from the front. So he will attack your from the back. This is why he always goes back to the past to condemn you. This is why he leads his preachers to use the Old Testament to deceive you. He wants to keep you constantly looking back so that you will be of no value to the future. Once the future arrives you will still be looking back at the past. This is one of the reasons why GOD said it is not good for man to be alone.

Ephesians 6 describes how GOD has given us a suit of armor to protect us from the attacks of the adversary. Notice the armor only covers the front of the body. The reason it only covers the front is because GOD does not intend for us to retreat when we're under attack (Psalm 78:9) and GOD intended for you to have a spouse with their suit of armor standing with you back to back. This is why submitting "one to another" in Ephesians 5 is important. When you are standing back to back you cover his back and he covers yours; you submit to him and he submits to you. When you are suited in GOD's armor with a spouse wearing theirs and covering you

Single Mothers and Sons

there is nothing the devil and his demons can do to defeat you.

The adversary believes he has the right to attack you because of the sins you committed. He lays your sins out before you to justify or convince you that you deserve to be attacked or punished. Don't fall for that trick! Whenever he attacks, you have to fight back. When you advance to thwart the devil's attack, he will throw your sins on the ground in front of you like land mines to stop your advance. But you have to keep going because moving forward will place your sins behind you. The devil can no longer use them now to control you. Since your sins are now behind you, you must never retreat. Once you retreat you will step back over or backslide into the sins you had already overcome so then you will have to fight to overcome them again. The problem with backsliding is each time the sins get more difficult to overcome.

There are other reasons why you should never retreat in the face of satanic attack. First, the protective armor does not cover your back. If you retreat, you lose the power to be protected by someone else with GOD's armor and the devil will kick you square up in your back side. Second, running from the adversary gives him the authority to influence and control your life. When you give the devil authority over your life you also yield authority over your children and your wife. Third, if you turn your back and run, you will deprive your help meet of the ability to do her GOD ordained job; protect your head and cover your back. Fourth, you will be leading your wife back into view of your sins. If you go back into sin it forces her to make a choice: to either sin with you or leave you.

Single Mothers and Sons

The term help meet in Hebrew means "a proper, suitable or fit helper". Your wife is a helper, given by GOD, who is proper, suitable and fit for you. Your wife was made suitable, proper and fit to help you through the challenges you will face, with respect to the purpose or call GOD placed on your life. She is ordained to protect your head by pushing you forward closer to GOD and at the same time protecting your back by repelling the enemy's attacks on her family. In the process, she helps you to get over or overcome your sins, thus, removing them from before your eyes. She protects your back by putting on her armor and placing her back to yours. Once the adversary tries to attack you from the back she is there to help fight him off.

Now, many men get frustrated because they believe their wives never forgive them of their sins and never let them forget. Each time they have an argument she tries to throw every one of them in his face. Understand what I am about to say from this perspective: Whatever is wrong with the wife is a result of something that is wrong in the husband. The reason it is easy for a wife to remember all of her husband's sins is because **he** hasn't moved very far away from them. He has stepped past his sins so that they are no longer before his eyes. But, since he has not moved very far away from his sins, while the two of them are positioned back to back, they are still before her eyes. Therefore, a man cannot be satisfied with just getting past his sins. He has to move far away from them to protect his wife from having to continually look upon his sins.

The Bible describes a virtuous woman as a crown to her husband. The word virtue in Greek means "strength, power or moral energy". A virtuous wife

Single Mothers and Sons

crowns her husband's head with the strength to face the devil and his sins, the power to overcome them, and the moral energy to endure. A man without sin is honorable before GOD and other men. Therefore, a virtuous woman also brings her man honor. Don't deprive yourself of the gifts, talents and abilities that GOD placed in your wife. Don't refuse to allow your wife to assist you because you think you know it all or because you don't want to appear to be henpecked. You have to say to yourself: "So what! I don't care how it looks to some fool. I have to utilize my wife to her maximum capability which includes helping me." Besides, there's nothing wrong with being henpecked when you are pecked by a good hen.

Leading a woman into spiritual battle requires love. Leadership is a love project wherein the heart of a man must contain the courage, candor, and commitment to face the enemy, endure to the end, and win. You cannot lead men into war and ask them to fight for you unless they know you love them. The character, candor, and commitment (C^3) that directs a man's conduct therefore comes from his center; his heart. Psalms and Proverbs were placed in the center of the Bible to show us GOD's C^3. They teach us the wisdom GOD uses to guide HIS life so that we can learn to be as HE is, shape our conduct, and translate GOD's C^3 into $C4$; the dynamic power to create great change in the earth and to fight the devil and win. Here's a quiet secret: women were born with this power. GOD gave it to them to use to help their husband. Whenever she sees her man exercising his power she will naturally unleash hers on his behalf.

I like to compare the attitude of "so what" to the type of attitude that a defensive back (DB) in the game of

Single Mothers and Sons

football has to have. Most DB's have to overcome physical discrepancies and a lack of knowledge on every play. They normally play at a great disadvantage because the receivers are usually bigger, stronger and/or faster. Plus the receiver knows where he is going whereas the DB doesn't. To overcome a difference in physical size, strength and lack of knowledge the DB has to counter his disadvantage by using three things: power, position and pain.

The DB has to use power to jam the receiver, break up the timing between him and the quarterback or destroy his rhythm. He will use position to negate the receiver's speed, lock him against the sideline or stay between him and the ball. Or, if you are from the Darrel Green school of single coverage, you position yourself ahead of the receiver so you can see the quarterback, the ball and the receiver at all times. Finally, the DB will use pain to make the receiver think more about where he is at all times instead of concentrating on catching the ball.

The DB is one of the toughest guys on the team because he has developed an attitude of "so what". You can see this clearly in a guy like Richard Sherman. He has the attitude of "so what, this receiver or running back is bigger, stronger or faster than me. I am going to stop him anyway. I am going to control his actions and make him do what I want him to do. He may be bigger, stronger or faster on the outside, but so what! I am bigger, faster and stronger on the inside. Regardless of what my disadvantages are I will win because I want to win more than he does. By the end of the first quarter, he will know that I am the man who will impact his longevity in the league and that I have the power to cancel his contract!"

Single Mothers and Sons

Whenever men are competing for a job, promotion, contract or position, we have to take on the attitude of the defensive back and say "so what". The person we are competing with may be bigger, stronger and faster outside; so what. I am bigger, faster and stronger on the inside. The person may have more experience and education; so what. They may be a Rhodes Scholar and have a lot of book smarts, but I am a "road" scholar because I have a lot of street smarts. When you are sitting in front of decision makers, you have to make them believe the only reason they were born was to give you that job, promotion, contract or position. You have to have the confidence and courage to give them an offer they can't refuse. Look that person in the eye and say: I know you are looking for a person with certain qualifications or skills but I will show you that you don't need a person like that. Give me 30 days working for free and I will prove that you need a person like me!

Chapter 7
A Call to Leadership

"A successful man finds the right place for himself but a successful leader finds the right place for others."
~ **John C. Maxwell**

The role of husband and father is the ultimate call to leadership. The need for competent male leadership in the modern family world-wide is compelling. To competently lead a family there are certain things a man must BE, KNOW and DO in order for a family to successfully achieve its goals and for each family member to reach their GOD ordained destiny. The stature of a man can be measured by how he leads his children to reach their destiny and his wife into the completion and fulfillment of her created purpose. Good leaders lead with the heart of a servant and lead as they would want to be led. Every man has a duty to provide leadership for his family. He cannot pass that responsibility off to his wife. If he believes that he is not responsible enough to lead a family, he must find a way to become response able. This chapter is for men who understand the importance of providing competent leadership for their family.

Jesus is the perfect example to use as a leadership icon for men because of the way in which he conducted himself as a leader and how his followers conducted themselves in His absence. The word says in Colossians 1:18 that He is preeminent or the first example for us in all things. As such, Jesus is a living example of what every leader should be, know and do. He is a larger than life illustration of the principles that leaders should embody more than just employ. The biblical account of how He guided, guarded and governed or directed, corrected and protected His disciples reminds us of the factors a husband and father must consider before taking actions that will affect his family. Jesus' personal manner of leading each disciple provides an example of how men should be flexible in the way they lead each member of their family.

The Leadership Challenge

Men must be able to encourage, empower and inspire their family members to reach their GOD ordained destiny, achieve their family goals and attain their individual personal goals. Most people in the family will go along with the program and do what is expected. However, there will be some who are resistant to the process. Pursuting the family's vision may seem simple to us, but it may be against one or more of our family member's natural will to do. They will say "I don't see why I have to go through this or why I have to do that." It is at times like these when you will need good leadership skills. The essence of quality family leadership is having the ability to encourage and empower people to do things that may be beyond their natural will to do; to lead them to want to do what you would have them to do. Leadership inspires others to give of their time, talent and substance for the greater good of the family and being willing to sacrifice what they want for themselves.

Although some men seem to have a natural ability to lead, most leadership skills do not come naturally. They are learned through study and experience. This chapter will share insight into the leadership challenges other men have faced in dealing with their family members. To make good decisions and take proper actions you must understand some of the challenges you will have to deal with. Once you have a clear picture of the types of challenges you will face you can prepare to handle them when they arise in your family.

Teenagers can be a walking leadership challenge. The tension and stress a parent feels as a result of raising teenagers is natural. It is a natural result of a young person moving toward maturity and reaching for autonomy. If you are going through this with a teen it may sound cruel for you to know that GOD programmed that tension to be there. The teenager has grown to an age where he or she is getting ready to be released from his or her parent's authority. The stress and tension a parent feels is the catalyst that is needed to cause them to fly away. It is the same type of stress and tension a bow has to go through in order cause an arrow to fly. The parent is a type of bow, the child is the arrow and GOD is the archer. If the child has been pointed in the right direction as she was growing up, whenever she flies away, she will go the right way.

"As arrows are in the hand of a mighty man; so are children of the youth. Happy is the man that has his quiver full of them: they shall speak [contend] with the enemies in the gate (Psalm 127:4-5)."

When the child is young and not ready to fly away, he rests comfortably in the parent and does whatever the parent tells him to. Once the child is almost ready to fly away, his head rises up and he begins to think and do for himself independent of the parent. This causes stress and tension for the parent and the child begins to pull away. This situation is in GOD's hands. HE is the archer. GOD is pulling the parent away from the child so HE can cause the child to go in the direction

Single Mothers and Sons

HE wants him or her to go. It's the parent's responsibility then, as the bow, to handle as much tension as they can so the child can go far and high once they fly.

You see, a father is like a caretaker or gardener for GOD. He is to take care of the little flowers that GOD planted in his life. However, the flowers he was given charge over were not intended to be planted in his garden for the rest of their lives. He is only to take care of them until they are ready to be replanted where they were created to be. The parent must let them go to do and be what they were created to do and be. Some parents cannot seem to let go and allow their children to grow, so GOD set the tension to pull them out.

We must remember then that when the tension comes, GOD put a program in the child to cause them to pull away from the parent at a certain point in their maturity so the child will go in the direction HE created him or her to go. The average parent wants to keep their child or arrow pointed down in a safe direction. That is, so the child cannot "go off" and hurt himself or somebody else but doing that restricts the child's chances of success. GOD programmed every child for success therefore the parental bow must allow their little arrow to be aimed high toward the sky be released in the direction he was created to go (Jeremiah 1:5). It is a scary thing for a dad to let his little arrows go without knowing what will happen or where they will land. Yet, he knows the child cannot stay home forever. Therefore, a dad must make sure the child is taught to depend on GOD for guidance and direction. This way, once the child has left home, he or she will not depart from that teaching. The whole purpose of a **pare**nt is to **pre**pare a child to make the transition from the care, guidance, and direction of the natural father to the Heavenly Father. When it is time to hand the child over, the dad then must let go and trust GOD to guide, guard and govern; direct, correct and protect his child.

The Prodigal Father

"...A certain man had two sons: And the younger of them said to his father, Father, give me the portion of goods that falls to me. And he divided unto them his living. And not many days after the younger son gathered all together and took his journey into a far country and there wasted his substance with riotous living. And when he had spent all, there arose a mighty famine in that land; and he began to be in want. And he went and joined himself to a citizen of that country; and he sent him into his fields to feed swine. And he would have filled his belly with the husks that the swine did eat: and no man gave unto him. And when he came to himself, he said, how many hired servants of my father's have bread enough to spare and I perish with hunger. I will arise and go to my father and will say into him, father I have sinned against heaven and before you. And am no more worthy to be called your son: make me as one of your servants... (Luke 15:11-19)."

This story is called "the Prodigal Son", by Bible scholars however the story is actually more about the father than it is the son and should therefore be called "the Prodigal Dad". The word prodigal describes a man who spends money freely and recklessly. If we examine the actions of the father closely, we will see that the son is a reflection of the father. The son wasted his money riotously or extravagantly because that is the example

Single Mothers and Sons

of living and spending that he observed from his daddy. The problem with a son observing the error of his father is the son will always commit that same error but on a more destructive level.

When the son returned home his father began to heap material things on him lavishly. He gave him shoes, a metaphoric pair of $250 Jordan's, which were expensive in that day. The robe can be compared to a custom made designer suit. The ring was a type of credit card that allowed him to have access to all of his dad's money and make purchases freely. Then, the prodigal father threw his son an extravagant party. The fatted calf was usually only served to dignitaries and honored guests because it was expensive.

"Now his elder son was in the **field** and as he came and drew nigh to the house he heard music and dancing. And he called one of the servants and asked what these things meant. And he said unto him, your brother is come; and your father has killed the fatted calf, because he has received him safe and sound (Luke 15:25-27)."

There is a principle that occurs in the Bible repeatedly as an observation rather than expression wherein a good father hides his life in the life of his son so that to know the son is to know the father. We don't need to be told much about the father if we are told all about the son. Observing the behavior of the elder brother also provides some insight into the heart of the prodigal father. Notice in the previous verses it says: "A certain man had **two** sons... and he divided unto **them** his living." When the father gave the younger son a portion of his living, he gave the elder son his portion also. So now look at where the elder son was before he came to the house.

Single Mothers and Sons

"Now his elder son was in the **field**..."

"Now the serpent was more subtle than any beast of the **field**... (Genesis 3:1)"

Preachers and Bible scholars give the impression that the elder brother was working hard plowing a corn field or something before he came to the house. However, the word "field" is not referring to a piece of farmland. In Hebrew the word field (sadeh) means in the "wild". To farm boys it means going to the city or to an area of the city that we might call the red light district. There was the Garden of Eden or GOD's oasis and then there was the field which was satan's territory. The field is the place outside of the Garden where Cain killed Able (Genesis 4:8). Pay attention the next time teachers send a note home requesting permission to take your child on a "field" trip. Anyway... now look at the elder brother's attitude. His mouth reveals what he has in his heart.

"And he was **angry** and would not go in: therefore came his father out and entreated him. And he answering said to his father, lo, these many years do I serve you, neither transgressed I at any time your commandment: and yet you never gave me a kid, that I might make merry with my friends: But as soon as this your son was come, which has devoured your living with **harlots**, you have killed for him the fatted calf. And he said to him, son, you are ever with me and all that I have is yours (Luke 15:28-31)."

The elder son was angry enough to kill his brother like Cain killed Able because he began to feel like his father favored the younger brother over him. When people are angry they say things that later they say that they didn't mean to say. In some ways they are just trying to make an excuse for expressing how they really

Single Mothers and Sons

felt. But in some ways they are right that they didn't **mean** to say what they said because it exposed what they were holding in their heart all along. The elder brother was supposed to be nowhere near where the young brother had been. So, how did **he** know the younger brother spent his money on "harlots"? You see, thieves think everybody steal, liars think everybody lie, and men who like hoes think everybody goes to strip clubs.

Accusing the brother of spending his money on harlots reveals what he had been doing in the field. Wherever satan or a satanic spirit is located you will find illicit sexual activity with it. The elder brother was obviously feeling guilty about something since he didn't just go into the house himself to see what was going on. When I had snuck away from the house for a few hours instead of just walking in I would ask one of my brothers: Is mama home? I wanted to know if she had been looking for me so I could have an excuse for why I was missing ready. So now the father had to soothe the evil that was brewing in his heart against the father and his brother in a similar manner as GOD attempted to soothe Cain.

"And the LORD said unto Cain, why are you wroth and why is your countenance fallen? If you do well, shall you not be accepted (Genesis 4:6-7)?"

I used this story because the sons presented a leadership challenge to their father. Cain presented a leadership challenge to GOD. Sooner or later every son develops the gumption to make a demand of their dad. It may be for more money, autonomy or responsibility but there is a point in every son's life where he will take a stand with his father. This is natural and should be expected. Whenever a son takes a stand, the dad must

Single Mothers and Sons

be prepared to yield to their demand (within limits of course) or he will inhibit the child's mental, emotional and perhaps spiritual growth. Men must learn to yield to their son's desire and may have to drive him to leave home while keeping his room ready in the event of his return (mama's do this by nature). Birds know when it's time to make their babies go. Dads have to know when it is time to make his son go.

Family members present natural leadership challenges to fathers and the devil presents spiritual challenges to make it hard for him to lead his family the way GOD would want them to be led. The only way a father can effectively lead a child to be who they were created to be is by going to GOD to find out what HE wants him to do with the child. Then he has to guide the child into being and doing what they were created to be and do.

A man fulfills his parental purpose more effectively when he functions as the child's dad more than as their father. Men who try to forcefully assert their authority as a child's father are usually the ones who forget to be their dad. Earthly fathers have a desire to make the child into the image of what <u>they</u> would like them to be rather than helping them to develop into the image and likeness of what GOD created them to be. A man who supplied the seed to birth a child is called "father" even when he only planted the seed and walked away. Then, there are men who do not physically walk away from their children. While they remain in the home as father they don't serve their children as dad because they make themselves emotionally unavailable. Any man can father a child but every man can't be a dad. Being a dad is hard work that takes real patience, unconditional love and the intestinal fortitude to face the adversities that come with raising a child.

"...if any provide not for his own, and especially for those of his own house, he has denied the faith, and is worse than an infidel (1 Timothy 5:8)."

A man must know that there is a difference between being a father and a daddy in order for him to properly raise and nurture children. Men have a responsibility to provide nurturing and mentor leadership for a child. If a young girl is to maintain her virginity into her twenties, she needs a dad that gives her strong emotional support. He has to be there when she needs the ear, arm or embrace of a man that unconditionally loves her. The presence of a dad in a young man's life helps him become secure in the knowledge of himself, his manhood and the knowledge that he is responsible for protecting the virtue of young women.

Raising children is a leadership challenge that every man who has given birth to a child must stand up and face. The way GOD measures the stature of a father is in whether or not he led his wife and children onto the path of their divine destiny. A husband and/or dad is responsible for what the people he is given charge over do or don't do. It does not take a special type of man to lead his family to fulfill their created purpose. It simply takes a man who has obtained victory over himself and who will yield himself to selflessly serve his family.

Leadership Defined

Leadership is the process of influencing your family to accomplish the family mission and reach their GOD ordained destiny by providing purpose, direction and motivation.

Single Mothers and Sons

Purpose gives the family reasons why they should do things that seems difficult to them. Men must establish priorities, explain the importance of completing the family's mission and focus family members on the tasks at hand so they will function in a timely, efficient and disciplined manner. It's not enough to just do what needs to be done; doing it <u>when</u> it needs to be done is just as important.

Direction gives the family an orientation to the things that need to be accomplished based on the priorities and standards defined by the family's vision, mission or goals. When men reinforce priorities and standards it will give the children order. Order is a key element, along with discipline and consistency, in leading, serving, and maintaining a family.

Motivation is similar to inspiration. It gives a family member the internal drive to do everything they are capable of doing to complete their mission. It also causes family members to use their initiative when they see the need for action. Men motivate their family members by caring for them. A good leader challenges his family to complete their goals and objectives as quickly as possible and encourages them to take on all of the responsibility they can handle through leading by example. Jesus always instructed His disciples to follow Him; to do what He did.

"And He said unto them, follow me and I will make you fishers of men (Matthew 4:19)." "And as He passed by, He saw Levi the son of Alphaeus sitting at the receipt of custom and said unto him follow me (Mark 2:14)." "The day following Jesus would go forth unto Galilee and found Philip and said unto him follow me (John 1:43)."

Single Mothers and Sons

The Factors of Leadership

There are four major factors of leadership. These factors are always present and they affect the actions a man should take and when he or she should take them. The factors of leadership are: the led, the leader, the situation and communications.

The Led is the people whom you are responsible for leading. All family members should not be led the same way. A man must correctly assess each of his family member's competence, motivation and commitment so that he can take the proper leadership actions with them at the correct time. He must create a relationship with each individual that motivates them to actively participate in the family's mission, accomplish their goals, and complete their tasks because they want to not because they have to. The key ingredients involved in developing this relationship are trust, respect and confidence.

The Leader, of course, is you. A family leader must have an honest understanding of who he is, what he knows and what he can do. Men must know their strengths, weaknesses, capabilities and limitations in order for them to control and discipline themselves to lead their family effectively. Men must also continually monitor their actions to ensure each family member is treated with dignity and respect.

The Situation is always different. Even the same circumstance can be different in another situation. Leadership actions that work in one situation may not work in another. To determine the best leadership action to take, first consider the situation and the resources available to help you handle it. Then consider the family member's level of competence, motivation and commitment to doing what needs to be done. The situation also includes the timing of actions. Family leaders must be skilled in identifying and thinking through the situation so that he or she can take the right action at the right time.

Now, what if you take the wrong action? It happens. We all make mistakes. Analyze the situation again, take quick corrective action and move on. Learn from your mistakes and consult with others so you can learn from theirs. Also, learn to humble yourself and apologize to your family members when you make a mistake that affects them. Even a two year old knows when dad made a mistake that affected them. They need an apology too.

Communications in this context is the exchange of information and ideas from one person to another. Effective communication occurs when your family understands exactly what you are trying to tell them and when you understand precisely what they are trying to tell you. When we want to communicate a thought, idea or feeling, we normally think of doing it orally, in writing, through physical actions or a combination of these. Public speaking experts report that when communicating only 7% of what the listener hears comes from our words. 38% of the message they receive is deduced from our tone of voice and 55% is interpreted from body language. So, a leader must be aware that his ability to communicate effectively will not be based solely on the words he says. How he said those words will be more important than what he said. A leader must also be aware that he communicates standards of behavior and performance by his personal example and through the behaviors he ignores or rewards in those he is leading.

Single Mothers and Sons

There is a phenomenon that occurs in communications where what I think I thought I said is not what you think I thought I meant. There is another phenomenon likened to it known as the whisper effect. That is when you whisper something to one person and have them whisper that message to another. This is repeated until the message is exchanged between ten people. Invariably, the message is dramatically altered at the end from what it was at the beginning. Leaders must be aware of these two phenomena in communications and guard against them. Precious time and resources can be wasted and hurt feelings can be avoided when we take time to make sure that we are clearly understood. Develop ways of making sure those you are talking to or depend on to relay your message actually understand what you are saying. Be sure your messengers don't develop the habit thinking they know what you intended to say. Finding a polite way of getting them to repeat your message back to you is the best way to be sure that you are understood.

The way you communicate in different situations is important to effective leadership. Your choice of words, tone of voice and physical actions will also affect your family member's ability or willingness to follow your lead. Leadership is more than setting the proper example. The ability to say the correct thing, at the appropriate moment and in the right way is also an important part of leadership.

You may have noticed that communication breaks down between two people often times, not because of what was said, but because of how it was said. A person could say "You look nice", but the tone voice or inflection on certain words will make that phrase turn from complimentary to critical. If you have ever played

Single Mothers and Sons

with a puppy, you know that puppies respond to the tone of your voice more often than to what you are actually saying. You can pet puppies and speak in a very pleasant tone of voice, while actually calling them dirty little mutts. Yet, they will roll around and wag their tails as if you are saying something nice.

It is possible, therefore, to be critical of those you are leading and make them happy to receive the criticism. We can learn how to be critical without being confrontational by becoming skillful at being tactful. Tact is the ability to tell a man to go to hell and make him feel happy to be on his way. Most people go through life trying to avoid confrontation. It is an unpleasant experience that we would rather not deal with.

One of the pitfalls of leadership arises due to delaying correction that would resolve a problem just to avoid a confrontation. Without confrontation there can be no resolution. When the person is finally confronted it usually occurs at a point of anger and much more damage is done after there is a big blow up. Men must learn to tactfully correct the people they are leading at the appropriate time before there is a need to confront. The person should walk away knowing they were just reprimanded while feeling good about their ability to make the necessary adjustments. The confrontational approach should only be used after attempts to tactfully correct have failed.

"And when they were come to Capernaum, they that received tribute money [taxes] came to Peter and said, does not your master pay tribute? He said, yes. And when he was come into the house Jesus prevented him saying, what think you Simon, of whom do the kings of the earth take custom or tribute, of their own children

Single Mothers and Sons

or of strangers? Peter said to Him, of strangers. Jesus said to him, then the children are free. Notwithstanding, lest we should offend them, you go to the sea and cast an hook and take up the fish that first comes up; and when you have opened his mouth, you shall find a piece of money: that take and give unto them for me and for you (Matthew 17:24-27)."

In this situation, Jesus tactfully corrects Peter's behavior and teaches him how to deal with this circumstance in the future. Contrary to popular belief, Jesus and the disciples were not poor. They had plenty of money. If it wouldn't take us too far off point, I'd show you that Jesus wore designer clothes. When Peter came into the house the scripture says Jesus prevented or stopped him. Stopped him from what? Jesus stopped him from going into the treasury to get money to pay the taxes. He first made Peter realize it was unfair that they had to pay taxes out of the money they collected for ministry while children of the king could go free. At the same time, He taught him not to offend the laws of men. So, Jesus taught Peter how to depend on the grace of GOD to pay his taxes.

Jesus made this correction a pleasurable experience by providing enough for Peter to pay his taxes as well. Paying taxes from the treasury could have drained them of money they would need for other things. Knowing He wouldn't be around for long, Jesus had to teach Peter how to handle this requirement while He was gone. Knowing Peter was sensitive to correction, Jesus corrected him in a tactful manner which left him feeling happy in the end.

The Principles of Leadership

The 8 principles of leadership are excellent guidelines and provide the cornerstone for all parental action. They are universal and represent fundamental truths that have stood the test of time. Family leaders can use these principles to assess themselves and develop a plan of action to improve their ability to lead.

Know yourself and seek self improvement. Knowing yourself allows you to assess of your strengths and weaknesses. Seeking self improvement means continually developing your strengths and working to overcome your weaknesses. This will increase your competence and the confidence your family members will have in your ability to lead.

Be spiritually proficient. This means you have done or are doing all that you expect your family members to do in the sight of GOD. You are active in study and obedient to the word. Men must do all things to a standard that is higher than merely what is required to provide an example of excellence to their children.

Seek responsibility and take responsibility for your actions. The fact that you decided to get married and/or have children demonstrates that you seek responsibility. But some men may need to develop the fortitude to take responsibility for their actions. They may still be tempted to make excuses when they did not perform well or do what they were supposed to. Your family wants you to take the leadership initiative within the home. When you see something that needs to be done, do it. If you make a mistake, your family will find out about it. If you discover that you made a mistake before your family does inform them of your error and what you plan to do to correct it. This will teach them to do the same.

Make sound timely decisions. A husband and father must be able to rapidly assess situations and make sound decisions. Indecisive leaders create hesitancy, loss of confidence and confusion. This could lead to a loss of opportunity, a lack of resources, and even a loss of life. A husband and father must be able to anticipate and reason under the most trying conditions and quickly decide what actions to take. Therefore, men must prepare for emergencies in advance by developing a crisis management plan. This is done by thinking of everything that can go wrong and devising a plan to handle them. A crisis management plan that is financed, reviewed and well rehearsed (like a fire drill) will eliminate hesitancy, confusion and unsound or untimely decisions during an emergency.

Set the example. Your family members want and need you to be a role model. This is a heavy responsibility, but you have no choice. No aspect of family leadership is more powerful. If you expect courage, competence and commitment from your family, you must model them first. Your family members will imitate your behavior. You must be doing what you require of them. Your personal example will affect those you are leading more than any amount of motivation or inspiration. The example you set helps to develop and direct your family's attitude and actions.

Know your family members and look out for their well-being. Personal problems impact personal, professional, and academic performance. A husband and father must be close enough to his family

Single Mothers and Sons

emotionally to discover why they are having a hard time. You will need to recognize something is wrong without being told, lead them to open up to you, and find out what you can do to help them overcome whatever obstacle they are facing. Commit a time to actively listen to them and their concerns. Every child needs their dad to do three things for them: stop for them, talk to them, and touch them. When dads show genuine concern for their kids they learn to trust and respect him as a leader. Telling your family that you care about them will have no meaning unless they consistently see you demonstrating care.

Keep your family informed. The average person does their best when they have the information they need to do what needs to be done. A person can become discouraged when they do not. Children need to have order and consistency in their lives. They need to know what to expect from day to day. The more things change the less happy they will be. Keep your family members informed on activities and special events that you have planned for them and especially on changes that will happen from the normal daily routine. This will help them make decisions and execute plans within your intent. Keeping your family members informed enhances their morale and also encourages initiative.

Ensure that your requirements are understood, monitored and accomplished. Your family must understand clearly what you expect from them. They need to understand what must be done, when it must be done and if there is a certain order in which things must be done. Monitoring their progress lets you know if they understand what needs to be done. It shows your interest in their success and provides emphasis that the job they are doing is important. Over emphasis on accomplishment causes resentment and under emphasis leads to frustration.

Leadership Attributes

Leadership attributes define what a man must be, know and do in order to effectively lead. He must learn what a leader must be, know and do in order to lead his family effectively in all situations.

BE - your capacity to lead flows through your individual beliefs, values and character. Your ability to inspire family members to do the right thing, even things they may not think they are capable of doing, is influenced by the example you set.

Beliefs and values have great power. They can motivate your family to do or not do what you expect of them. Respected men of strong and honorable character are able to influence the beliefs and values of others. Some people who learn of their ability to influence others become corrupt and eventually abuse it. As a servant to your family before GOD, you must be ever mindful not to abuse your power over those you lead.

Fundamental to what leaders must BE is morally strong, courageous enough to make hard decisions, and consistent in all that they do. This will give your family members the will to complete their family mission and achieve their goals.

A man must strive to be who GOD created him to be. In our society, we focus on doing what we want to do more than being who GOD created us to be. We have become in effect human doings more than human beings. Whenever we greet someone we say "How do you do or how are you doing?" One of the first questions we ask a person that we just met is "What do you do?" We never think to ask how do you **be** or what were you created to be? Their being is much more valuable to the world than whatever they are doing.

KNOW - to be an effective leader you must know how the four factors of leadership affect each other and what your family members must endure in order to do whatever you ask them to do. You must be a student of human nature and most of all, you must be keenly aware of your own strengths and weaknesses.

Caring for a family not only requires you to be competent but also a confident leader. You must know the word of GOD and be able to share the appropriate word at the appropriate time. You must be able to operate independently within the scope of the vision for your family and be willing to give of yourself, your time and resources to ensure each of your family members' success. A dad must know how to help an ordinary individual make the transition to become an extraordinary person. You do this by caring for your wife and children, building trust, suppressing the potential for negative behavior and bringing out the potential for excellence. Ultimately you have to teach your family to be wise and live their lives by the word of GOD in your absence so that they will make wise decisions whenever you are not around.

DO - as stated earlier, you must provide purpose, direction and motivation to help your family members complete the family mission and reach their GOD ordained destiny. Purpose gives your family a reason why they should do what is required. Direction shows them what must be done. Motivation gives them the will or internal drive to do it.

Single Mothers and Sons

Some people say that behavior is more believable than words. Your behavior sets the example for your family members. Saying all the right words and having all the right values and knowledge will have no meaning if they are not reinforced by your actions. Your actions are what your family will follow. Your actions give life to purpose, direction and motivation for your children. Children are more likely to do what you do than what you say. They would rather see a sermon than hear one. Your actions will help to see some of your family members through trying circumstances they might otherwise be unwilling to go through. Your actions will demonstrate to them why it is important. Positive actions always inspire others to follow.

Take a look at how a father's faithfulness to GOD inspired his son to become faithful to him even unto death. I'm going to chop up the verses to make a long story short so please read Genesis 22:1-12 in its entirety to get the full story.

"And it came to pass... that GOD did tempt Abraham, and said unto him... take now your son, your only son Isaac, whom you love... and offer him... for a burnt offering upon one of the mountains which I will tell you of. And Abraham rose up early in the morning... and took... Isaac his son... the wood for the burnt offering, and rose up, and went to the place of which GOD had told him...

And Abraham took the wood of the burnt offering, and laid it upon Isaac his son; and he took the fire in his hand, and a knife... and Isaac spoke to Abraham his father, and said, my father... behold the fire and the wood: but where is the lamb for a burnt offering? And

Single Mothers and Sons

Abraham said, my son, GOD will provide himself a lamb for a burnt offering...

And they came to the place which GOD had told him of; and Abraham built an altar there, and laid the wood in order, and bound Isaac his son, and laid him on the altar upon the wood. And Abraham stretched forth his hand, and took the knife to slay his son.

And the angel of the LORD called to him out of heaven and said... lay not your hand upon the lad, neither do you anything to him: for now I know that you fear GOD, seeing you have not withheld your son, your only son from ME."

This story is actually an allegory of the relationship between GOD and HIS only son Jesus who was faithful to His DAD unto death. Remember, Abraham was already 100 years old before Isaac was conceived. If you know how to count time chronologically in the Bible you will see that Isaac was about 33 years old at the time Abraham was ready to sacrifice his life. Therefore, Isaac was a young man that was strong enough to overpower his 133 year old dad and save his self from being sacrificed. Yet, he was faithful and obedient to be sacrificed for his dad whom he could clearly see was being faithful and obedient to GOD.

Abraham's faithfulness to the word of GOD didn't permit him to see any risk in losing his son. GOD had promised that through Isaac he would become the father of many nations. So, if he did sacrifice his son, GOD would have to bring him back to life. The moral to the story is when we are faithful and obedient to GOD and we love our children they will be faithful and obedient to us even unto death. Of course you'd never want him to do it but wouldn't it be great to know that your son would be willing to die for you.

Single Mothers and Sons

Leadership Styles

Leadership style is the personal manner and approach of leading. Style is the way leaders directly interact with those being led. Men who are effective leaders are flexible in the way they interact with their family members. They deal with different family members differently, changing the way they interact as the person or the situation changes. Your manner and approach of leading will obviously depend on your training, education, experience and view of the world. You have to be yourself, yet flexible enough to adjust to the people and the situations.

For years, when people talked about leadership styles, they expounded on two extremes: an autocratic style and a democratic style. Autocratic leaders use their legitimate authority as a husband and father and the power of their position to get results while democratic leaders use their personality to persuade and involve their family in solving problems and making decisions. This fails to consider the possibility of a leader using different styles and being flexible enough to be autocratic at times and democratic at other times or to combine the two styles sometimes.

There are three basic styles of leadership: directing, participating, and delegating.

Directing Style - a dad is using the directing style when he tells a child what he wants done, how he wants it done, where he wants it done and when he wants it done. Then he monitors closely to ensure the directions are followed. This style is clearly appropriate in many situations. When time is short and you alone know what needs to be done and how to do it, this style is the quickest way to get the job done. When leading a child who lacks experience or experience at doing what you need them to do, you will need to direct their behavior using this style. They will not resent your close scrutiny. You will actually be giving them what they need and want. Asking inexperienced family members to solve complex problems would be frustrating for them. It could cause them to shut down due to feeling overwhelmed and nothing will get done.

Participating Style - a leader is using the participating style when he involves the person being led in deciding what to do and how to do it. If the person being led has some competence and supports your goals, allowing him to participate in deciding how to get the job done can be powerful in building a strong team. Participation will build confidence and increase your family's support for the final plan if they help develop the plan.

You will be faced with situations that will require you to switch styles of leadership. It is important, therefore, that you know your kids well and their level of competence in every area. Remember, each style of leadership will involve some amount of directing. The objective of using the participating style is to develop competence in your children to the point where they can begin to operate on their own, make decisions and implement your directives in your absence. The more you can teach them by directing and develop their decision making skills through participating the quicker you can prepare them to move on to the next style of leadership, which is delegating.

Delegating style - a dad uses the delegating style when he gives problem solving and decision making authority to an individual member of the family. This style is appropriate when dealing with young adults who support your goals and are competent and motivated to perform the task. Some things are appropriate to delegate and others are not. The key is to provide the training and responsibility necessary to increase the family member's problem solving potential. Always be mindful of their competence, experience and proficiency as you determine what problems they should solve. Even the most competent family member likes to know what he or she has been assigned to do is important. Checking periodically on what they are doing lets them know that you are interested in the outcome of their work and will provide you with an opportunity to deliver help and guidance when needed. This will help them learn to solve problems more efficiently. It will also help them become comfortable with the delegating style of leadership more quickly. My daughter's favorite phrase from the time she turned 3 was: "I can do it!"

Choosing a Style

Choosing the correct style of leadership requires leaders to understand the four factors of leadership. He must size up the family as a unit, know each member and examine every situation carefully in order to choose the right style. Every style is not going to work in every family or with every family member in every situation. Therefore, it is important for a man to know what he wants to accomplish in the situation and select the style that will give him the desired result.

A parent must be aware, particularly with teenagers, that each child has an individual personality as well as a group personality. This is true within the family group dynamic as well as within their peer group. If you want to correct the behavior of your child as an individual, you must take them out of the group to correct them in order to be effective. Trying to correct the child within the group will lead to other communication problems later not only with that child but with other members of the group as well. This is true whether in a group of family members or peers. The group will be forced to chose sides and/or make value judgments on your actions as a leader. There are exceptions to every rule. Correcting a child in the presence of his or her siblings, for example, at times will serve as a method of directing and protecting the other children. Being careful to avoid embarrassing a child as you are correcting them, in most cases, will make them easier to lead later.

Each person responds to different leadership styles at different times in their personal and professional growth. As people and situations change or as new tasks are required you will need to be flexible in the leadership style you use. Even though you successfully used the delegating leadership style with a family member, you may need to temporarily return to the directing style of leadership if you give him an unfamiliar or a new task. Since the child is unfamiliar with the new task you will need to tell him what to do and how to do it. As they gain competence, confidence and motivation in this new task you can shift your style again to the participating or delegating style. Assessing the leadership needs of the person being led will allow you to determine what leadership style to use.

Chapter 8
Executive Decision Making

"Quick decisions are unsafe decisions."
~ Sophocles

Anytime you are leading a family and you don't have an answer it's a problem. In order to solve the problem, just like in math, you must use the proper formula or apply the proper solution. Then, you will eliminate the problem by finding the correct answer. The only correct answer to 2+2 is 4. You can get to 4 other ways but the only correct answer to 2+2 is 4.

Decision making for a family is largely an exercise in problem solving. Families normally run on autopilot once its operation has been established. Whenever a problem arises the family stops running normally and will look to the leader to make a decision and solve the problem with the correct answer in a quick or timely manner. Men who don't know how to make decisions for their family in a timely manner are going to have problems. You can produce the right answer but if it was not timely the crisis may be over but you didn't solve the problem. It is crucial to the proper functioning of a family that men learn the process of making decisions so that they can produce the right answer for the present situation at the right time.

Each day of your life you are faced with situations that demand a decision before you can get where you are going or finish what you are doing. Some decisions are minor such as what to have for lunch or where and other decisions are critical such as whom to marry. The decisions you make today will have either a positive or negative impact on your life tomorrow. If you decide to eat pizza for lunch every day, it will have an impact on your heath over time. If you decide to marry a lady who is crazy, you could find yourself in a hostage situation tomorrow. You are currently in the situation that you find yourself in today because of decisions you made yesterday.

We are all products of the things we have been thinking, believing, saying and deciding. If I find the type of woman I have been looking for and decide to approach her today, I could be living with the girl of my dreams tomorrow. When I decide not to go to work today it may cause me to lose my job tomorrow. My decision not to go to work today may deprive my family of what they need tomorrow. A family is a corporate entity. The head of a family is an executive position; Chief Executive Officer. A family CEO must make executive decisions daily that produce the results for himself and his family that he needs to achieve.

Unless you have some type of guidance any decision that you make can have the potential of being a good decision or a bad one. We will never know whether a decision was a good decision or a bad one until we actually see the end result. In situations where we do not really know what to decide, many of us become paralyzed. We put off making a decision until we get to the point where we must decide. Then, we usually make a decision that is intended to be safe, which is actually equivalent to not making one at all. That decision, generally, will not produce the result you actually need. Procrastination in decision making can also cause men to make decisions that fall on one of the two extremes of our spectrum of choices. We may decide to do nothing and hope it goes away or to do a little of everything we can think of and stand hopeful that something in that mix will work.

The Decision Making Process

The decision making process can be simple. However, pressure from outside forces can make it seem complicated. There are right decisions for every situation as well as wrong ones. The right decision can usually be found in the center of your being or within your own spirit. Wrong decisions normally originate in the realm of common sense, conventional wisdom, opinion, media memes and in the doctrine of the infamous "they". The problem with "they" is they always have something to say but they are rarely right.

Your senses were designed to help you make physical contact with a material world not to help you make decisions. You can make decisions using conventional wisdom but that is not wise either. Your family members were all designed to be unique and produce a unique impact on the world. If you decide that it is wise to follow convention, you will trap yourself and family in the circle where you'll receive the same mediocre and unsatisfactory results that everyone else in the convention always get.

"I was almost in all evil in the midst of the congregation and assembly (Proverbs 5:14)."

The word convention in Hebrew (mowed or ya' ad) means the same thing as the word congregation. If we follow conventional wisdom it will position us in the congregation and we could find our self in the midst of all evil or a bad decision. The word congregation describes a group of people that are hanging around doing nothing. Civil law recognizes that when people hang around in a big group doing nothing it usually

Single Mothers and Sons

leads to trouble so congregating is unlawful in most states. The reason evil is associated with a congregation in the Bible is because GOD's first command to man was "be fruitful". People in congregations usually produce nothing, get into the habit of murmuring and complaining, and generally become unfruitful thus violating GOD's command. When we fail to produce it puts us in a congregation of evil because evil is simply doing the opposite of that which GOD has commanded us to do.

Common sense, conventional wisdom, opinion, etc press for your attention during the decision making process to coax you into utilizing one of them. The one we chose most often when we don't know what to do is conventional wisdom because that's what "everybody says" we should do. Then we are left confused as to why we didn't get a breakthrough.

The decisions you make will invariably be according to or influenced by the norms within the various value systems that you govern your personal, professional and spiritual life by. Pressure to conform to group values or peer norms such as religion, gender, profession and so on may lead you to place more of a premium on those relationships than with your family. The key to making good decisions for a family is by eliminating the influence of all other value systems from your decision making process except that which conforms to the vision and direction that GOD has planned for your life. Failing to do so will allow all the other value systems to seemingly close in on you and cause your values, direction and vision to be squeezed out. Thus, you will make decisions that will not bring about a result that will benefit your family.

Single Mothers and Sons

Everyday life decisions are influenced by values that you adhere to or govern your life by in your zeal to follow ordinances and laws. Some people hate littering for example. They would never toss trash on the ground and they detest those who do. Then, there are values you ascribe to that were established by the founders of our nation. Social, political or fraternal organizations to which we pledge loyalty have value systems that can impact our decisions. The professions you and I spend most of our waking hours pursuing have institutional value systems upon which we build our career and professional reputations. The values of our friends and associates have tremendous influence on our decision making. What they think is important to us, so their value system impacts our decisions on the homes we buy, the areas in which we buy, the cars we drive, the clothes we wear, the places we vacation and so on. Value judgments we've placed on others and the judgments they've placed on us effect how we decide to conduct ourselves relative to those judgments.

Traditions, along with religious ordinances and laws, affect the decisions made for the family at certain times of the year. At Christmas time, for example, we may decide to spend money we don't have on things that our family really doesn't need. Superstitious values are strong enough to create a direct conflict between belief in the power of GOD versus belief in the power of superstitions. Finally, our own personal value system that we established for our own lives and families can figure greatly in the way we formulate decisions. All of these value systems can create pressure for men to make decisions based on flawed opinions and bad information.

Single Mothers and Sons

This only pertains, of course, to those who have not learned how to glean guidance from their own spirit as a guide for their lives. External value systems lead you to lean on forces and sources outside of yourself when the guidance and influence you need to direct your life is already inside of you. Your spirit knows why you are here, what you were sent here to do and can lead you to be and do your best you. GOD has established values in your spirit and in the word that will direct your decisions in accordance with HIS vision and purpose for your life.

To prevent yourself from succumbing to the pressure of external value systems at critical decision points, you must learn to allow your conscience, which is the voice of our spirit, to dominate the decision making process. Before I fully recognized that I was allowing the voice of my spirit to guide me, I was making great decisions and getting fast promotions. People wanted to learn how to do what I was doing would ask me how did I know what to do. The only answer I could give them back then was: "I don't know; I just knew."

Your own spirit has the answer to **all** things. It has been in communication with the Holy Spirit and can direct your decisions to conform to the will of GOD for your life. Your spirit will help relieve the pressure from the margins or outside forces and increase your internal power during the times you decide to go against organizational and professional values. While most people will go along to get along simply because "everybody else does it", you will realize you can't because of your conscience. When you are faced with temptation to use your position as family leader to make things easy for yourself, for example, the voice of your spirit will remind you of the need to earn the trust and confidence of your family. It will convict you to gain the trust and confidence of those you love by demonstrating consistent and honorable values, morals and character. Your own spirit will influence you to make the right decisions.

Practical Decision Making

While some are experienced in being led by the spirit, there are those of us who still feel the need to have more practical points on which to operate in making decisions. This is not a bad thing for those who have not yet learned to be led by their spirit. In fact, it is good for a leader to know his or her limitations and to seek guidance that is appropriate to their situation. The following, therefore, is a practical process for making decisions that is useful until you learn to be led by your spirit:

Identify the decision point - isolate the decision that must be made, the problem or situation it will address and the point when the decision must be implemented for it to be timely.

List your options - be cognizant of the pressures that will be exerted from the value systems at the margins to be included on the list. Try to exclude those early in order to avoid confusion or conflict during the analysis phase of the process.

Analyze your options - make sure each option under consideration is consistent with the vision and direction GOD has established for your life and the problem you are trying to solve.

Recognize every option selected will produce intended and unintended consequences. Try to advance each option in your mind and project it as far ahead as you can to see what results it will produce. Purchasing a new refrigerator on credit today, for instance, may lead to bankruptcy tomorrow if you lose your job. Consider the unintended consequences of your decision and make a plan to deal with those consequences as if they might happen tomorrow.

Avoid paralysis of analysis. Analyzing our options can become confusing and overwhelming at times. Some of us shut down at this point and decide to do nothing hoping the situation will go away. Take your time doing the analysis one option at a time. However, you must be productive and keep moving toward a final conclusion. Proper analysis will produce a sound decision, but it must be timely in order to provide an effective solution. Some men make a decision matrix listing each possible decision for the situation, its pros and cons, and consequences.

Make a selection. The right decision will be a one that solves the problem, advances your vision and places your family's needs ahead of your own.

Implement the decision in a timely manner.

Evaluate the decision to determine if it is leading to the desired result and if it keeps you operating in the economic system of the kingdom of GOD instead of the system of credit. Anytime you recognize the decision is not leading to the desired result, you must immediately go back to the list of options and start over.

Finally, there may be times during the decision making process when you will be faced with situations that will force you to deal with ethical dilemmas. That is, when you have to choose between two alternatives that are equally offensive to GOD and to your own moral principles and values and you become stuck between the proverbial rock and hard place. Times like these measure your mettle and test your character to see if you have integrity. Integrity is character that has withstood a test. An integrity test is designed to see if you will remain connected to or one with GOD in the face of an ethical dilemma.

Your character (which is who you are when no one else is watching) is proven whenever you decide to follow your spirit and operate in the system of GOD's Kingdom when it would be easier to operate in the system of the world. Remember, the system of GOD is set up to make a way out of no way. When your back is against the wall with no means of escape a door can be made in that same wall that didn't exist before for you to run through. Commit to consistently follow your conscience and you will be supplied with whatever you need.

"Delight yourself also in the Lord; and HE shall give you the desires of your heart. Commit your way unto the Lord; trust also in HIM; and HE shall bring it to pass. And HE shall bring forth your righteousness as the light and your judgment as the noonday. Rest in the Lord and wait patiently for HIM: fret not yourself because of him who prospers in his [evil] way, because of the man who brings wicked devices to pass. Cease from anger and forsake wrath: fret not yourself in any wise to do evil. For evil doers shall be cut off: but those that wait upon the Lord, they shall inherit the earth (Psalm 37:4-9)."

Decide to allow your Spirit to be your Guide

While there is no safe position in the world, there is a safe position in life. The only safe position in life is in the word and the will of GOD. The will of GOD is the straight and narrow path that was established for each of our lives. Surrounding that path is a field of unknown dangers. We have to avoid making decisions in life that will have us hanging on the edge of the path of life because it could lead to destruction or failure to fulfill your vision. Allowing yourself to be guided by your spirit and your vision in the decision making process will keep you from making decisions that boarder on the edge of disaster. If you divide the books of Psalms and Proverbs into 30 sections and read one section every day, the Spirit of GOD will help your spirit use the word of GOD to make decisions that will guide you on the path to fulfilling your vision. That path will lead you to peace, safety, joy and prosperity as well as lead your family to become wealthy.

Everything that happens in our lives, whether good or bad, is the result of decisions that we've made. Many of us think that when another person does something bad to us it was their fault. On the contrary, it was actually our fault for placing ourselves in that position. The reality is, we made the decisions that led us into the position to have something bad done to us. Your spirit is constantly trying to lead you out of danger but more often than not you ignore its instructions and walk into danger anyway. If I chose not to take heed to the leading of my spirit, then I chose danger over safety. A man may rob me one night, for instance, while I was walking home. The man was wrong for robbing me but it was my fault that he had the opportunity to do it. Had I not made the decision to be there or chose that route to walk, the robbery would not have happened when and where it did. Each one of us has to take responsibility for the things that occur in our lives as a result of the decisions we've made. We must learn to make proper decisions by always

Single Mothers and Sons

listening to that "something" from our spirit (that told me to or told me not to) for the positive experiences of life to begin to outweigh the bad ones.

Our spirit tries to protect us all regardless of whether we are good or bad from hurt, harm and danger. We know in our hearts that this is true because we have all had that experience where we felt "something" on the inside directing us. After an event happens we say "something told me to or something told me not to". The something inside of you telling you what to do or not to do was the Holy Spirit communicating to your spirit. Then your spirit sends those instructions to your brain. Your spirit is a powerful internal force that will not only protect you but also lead and guide you into all truth pertaining to your life. If you want to the knowledge on anything to be clear in your mind, the Holy Spirit will lead and guide your spirit into all truth.

"Howbeit when He, the Spirit of Truth is come, He will guide you into **all** truth; for He shall not speak of Himself; but whatsoever He shall hear, that shall He speak; and He will **show** you things to come (John 16:13)."

"But the Comforter, which is the Holy Ghost, whom the Father will send in my name, he shall teach you **all** things and bring **all** things to your remembrance, whatsoever I have said unto you (John 14:26)."

"But the anointing [Spirit of GOD] which you have received of Him abides in you and you need not that **any** man teach you: but as the same anointing teaches you of **all** things and is truth and is no lie and even as it has taught you, you shall abide in Him (1 John 2:27)."

Single Mothers and Sons
Good Decision Making Prevents Decay

Men do not get very much instruction on how to fulfill their roles as husbands, fathers, and leaders. Many men did not have a father or role model in the home to teach or show them how to be a man. The same is true for many women. Their mothers did not have husbands so they didn't have an example in the home to teach them how to love, respect and relate to a man. So we struggle in these roles deciding to do whatever we think is best. This often leads us into conflict over whether to do what is right or that which is wrong, but expedient. It is of paramount importance to our family's future that we always find a way to do what's right, to do it because it's right and then do it right the first time. This is important is because everything must be used the right way and treated properly or it will eventually become rotten or bring destructive results.

Anything that is not used the way it was intended to be used will rot. Whenever your body, marriage, family, finances and so on are not used the way they were designed by GOD to be used, they will rot. One of the laws of thermal dynamics, entropy, dictates that anything left to itself tends to breakdown. Have you ever noticed that when a house is occupied it tends to thrive but a house that is left empty rapidly deteriorates?

Everything must be used for what it was intended to be used for or it will begin to breakdown or rot. If an apple is taken off a tree once it becomes ripe and eaten, it will be used for what it was intended. Therefore, it will benefit the one who used it the way it was supposed to be used. However, if you take that same apple, place it on a counter and never eat it, it will

Single Mothers and Sons

eventually spoil or become rotten. Then, someone will have to come along to kill the bugs and clean up the mess after it damages the counter and stinks up the room.

Jesus had to come along to clean up the mess that Adam made. Have you ever wondered why Jesus died such a painful death? We understand that He had to die for our sins but why couldn't he have had a heart attack or just died peacefully in His sleep? Why did He have to endure all of that pain before He died?

There is a universal law called "the Law of Excruciation". This law dictates that whatever created an imbalance in the earth, that thing or a like thing has to suffer the consequences of correcting the imbalance. Adam was a man so in order for Jesus to correct what Adam had done He had to come as a man. He had to become the last Adam and suffer the consequences required to fix the imbalance that the first Adam created. The imbalance Adam created was due to sin. Wherever sin occurs pain is associated with it. Adam's sin produced an enormous amount of pain. Sin has a debt that must be paid (the wages of sin is death) and pain does as well. The pain of sin must be reconciled along with the debt of sin. Sin can be redeemed with blood but pain must be requited with pain. Therefore, in taking on Adam's debt of sin Jesus had to pay for the pain he created by enduring an excruciating amount of pain.

A man that decides to marry a woman who has been made imbalanced by another man has to submit himself to the law of excruciation. He must love her enough to suffer the pain of correcting the imbalance that the other man created. This is one of the reasons GOD instructed men to love our wife as Christ loved

Single Mothers and Sons

the church **(Ephesians 5:25)**. Jesus sacrificed His life to heal, restore, and empower His bride the church. A man must sacrifice himself to heal, restore, and empower his wife. If he doesn't understand that he has to endure the pain of healing her pain, he will only cause her more pain when he leaves her. Don't start the process if you are not strong enough to finish it.

A man must learn to utilize their family properly or another man will have to come along and clean up the damage he caused. When a wife is not utilized the way she is supposed to be by her husband, she will become rotten. When a child is not utilized the way he or she is supposed to be by the parents, the child will become rotten. When money is not used the way it is supposed to be by the family, it will become rotten. You name the thing; whatever is not used the way it was designed to be used becomes rotten. Cars and clothes that are used or to create a false impression of wealth breakdown, wear out or become rotten quicker than cars and clothes that are used for transportation and protection. Even our own body when not used properly will wear out, break down or rot quicker than it should have when it is misused. This is why so many men are clocking out in their 40's and 50's

While you are seeking, searching or trying to make a decision your spirit is always there waiting to lead you into the right thing to do. It always knows what you need and can always show you where to find it. Men who have not learned to listen to their spirit will find that most times they seek an answer from GOD that answer never comes. This happens when you want an answer that can only be given to one who is in proper position with himself and in proper covenant with GOD. GOD won't give you an inheritance that only

Single Mothers and Sons

belongs to HIS legal heirs. Once you become a legal heir, then you will also have a **right** to have your prayer answered in accordance with GOD's will and timing and in accordance with your ability to hear the answer.

"He that has ears to hear, let him hear (Matthew 11:15)."

The sons of rich men are sometimes not included as heirs in their father's will. This occurs often times because the son is not making decisions in accordance with his father's will. The same thing happens with unsaved men. They are not making decisions in accordance with the Heavenly Father's will. Consequently, they are not included in their Father's will as legal heirs to HIS fortune. Since they refuse to act in accordance with GOD's will, they are excluded from HIS inheritance. GOD requires men to be saved by the blood of Jesus before we can receive HIS inheritance. So, GOD, by the Holy Spirit tries to talk to each of us and guide us into repentance. HE may give men who refuse to repent a few bones from the table of HIS heirs to demonstrate HIS love. But they can't fully partake of the inheritance until they repent, overcome the world and become a legal heir. Until they decide to follow GOD's will, HE has to cut them out of HIS will.

There was a four hundred year period before Jesus was born in which all communication from GOD with the children of Israel was cut off. GOD still loved and cared for HIS people. However, they decided not to listen to HIM or HIS prophets. So GOD decided to not speak to them until the people turned their hearts back toward HIM without being called. Before Jesus' ministry began, there were enough people who were ready to hear from GOD. So HE sent John the Baptist to urge the people to receive water baptism as an outward demonstration of an inward repentance. Many people heard John's preaching, they knew he had to be a prophet of GOD and decided to repent. Others heard the same words at the same time, yet decided not to repent. Similarly, there are people who hear the gospel of Jesus and decide to turn toward GOD. Still there are others who hear the same gospel but decide to turn away from GOD.

"For this is good and acceptable in the sight of GOD our Savior; who will have all men to be saved and to come unto the knowledge of the truth (1 Timothy 4:3-4)."

The Holy Spirit will only lead you and guide you into the truth of what GOD has planned for your life. If you are seeking guidance on something that takes you out of the will of GOD for your life and family, the Holy Spirit will not get involved in that. He will remain silent except to lead you back in the right direction. Now, he will lead you into desires that you have in addition to the mission which GOD sent you here to do, but never in place of it. Therefore, to be led into all truth, you have to allow yourself to be used in the manner in which GOD created you to be used. If you do not, you will simply be placed on the metaphoric shelf to rot.

This is the only real reason that some of us end up in jail. We refused to allow ourselves to be used the way GOD intended for us to be used. As I stated earlier, anything that is not used properly will become rotten. Since we did not allow ourselves to be used properly by GOD we became rotten. Some were not used properly by our parents and became rotten. Some were not used in a proper manner by our friends and became rotten.

Single Mothers and Sons

Others were not used properly as a spouse, parent or child by our family and became rotten. A barrel of ripe apples is not a suitable place for a rotten apple because it will cause the other apples to rot. The only suitable place for a person who has become rotten is a jail cell. There, he or she cannot cause others in the barrel of life to become rotten. So he or she must be removed and placed in a bin with other rotten apples. This is not meant to be a knock on my brothers and sisters who are incarcerated. That is something that happened to you. It is not who you are! You can repent and become who GOD created you to be too!

The way for you to keep from turning rotten and be a productive member of society, is to allow yourself to be used by GOD. GOD will, then, reveal the vision that HE has for your life and lead, guide and direct you to fulfill it. Any man leading a family must lead in accordance with the vision that GOD has for his life or that family will become rotten. A man who tries to lead without a vision will soon find that he has no followers. Those whom he is leading will begin to show signs of becoming rotten. "Where there is no vision the people perish (Proverbs 29:18a)." Instead of leading the family to follow him to success he will ultimately find himself walking alone.

Make Sound Timely Decisions

A sound decision is one that yields the following results: 1) glorifies GOD; 2) advances HIS vision for our lives; and 3) places our family's needs ahead of our own. A decision is timely when it satisfies a requirement, addresses a need and is executed at the proper time. My son is scheduled to play in a championship football game, but he needs cleats because he lost them. If I decide to buy him cleats after the game, that decision was not timely. There are times when we must go to our spirit for guidance on a decision we are struggling to make. The decision is timely if it is executed when the answer is received. The Spirit of GOD is omniscient, so HE will provide your spirit with the answer at the time it needs to be implemented. If you receive an answer and decide to execute the instruction at a time that you feel is right, it becomes an untimely decision.

As a parent, you will have the responsibility to teach and train your children to make sound timely decisions. The only way they will fully understand why you make the decisions you make, once you teach them, is to allow them to make decisions themselves. Your children will never really understand how to do make good decisions until they are allowed to make them. In order to feel like they are part of the family team, have some input into the decisions made in the home or some control over their own destiny, your wife and children need a chance to make decisions for the family on their own. In every case where it does not make a difference you should allow them to have their way. If the decision they make is one that will break the budget or pull you off track from a certain goal, you will have to override their decision. However, you must teach them **why** you have to do that and encourage them to make another choice. This will train them to make sound decisions for their families once they marry or for themselves if something happens to you.

The decisions a man makes will affect the long term growth or health of his family. Abraham's father, for example, made a decision that could have affected the long term financial health of his family, except he had a faithful son. Each person in the Bible who did what GOD directed him to do was highly blessed financially. GOD ordained or equipped them with everything they needed to do what HE called them to do. GOD supplies all of your needs so that seeking your needs won't be a distraction from doing what HE called you to do. In the fulfillment of your purpose for HIM, GOD provides you with personal fulfillment. That is where all of your physical, financial, family and social needs are met.

Now, when I decide to not answer the call of GOD, which is HIS plan A, I miss the move of GOD. My decision, then, forces GOD to use plan B. In Matthew 22:14, Jesus said "For many are called, but few are chosen." That is because GOD calls many people but few of us decide to go. If GOD has to use plan B, it forces HIM to take me through my purpose either the long way or the hard way. When I resist HIS efforts to execute plan B, HIS plans will no longer include me. Therefore, GOD has to call up a plan B free agent to replace me. Jesus' disciples could not understand what He called them to do so He called the Apostle Paul. GOD's plans will be carried out, but I will be left out. Consequently, I will forfeit the blessings or provisions associated with obeying the call and my family will be deprived.

The best decision a man could make after making the decision to follow the word and the will of GOD is to decide to live life in one take. That is because whenever you make a mistake you'll have to do a retake. Pain is created with a mistake so pain will be experienced with the retake. You will know you are blessed if you get an opportunity to do a retake after you have made a mistake. It would be less painful if we lived life in one take but you learn valuable lessons in the retake after a

Single Mothers and Sons

mistake. Steve Harvey being invited to host Miss Universe again is proof that those who are blessed get an opportunity to do a retake even after they have made a colossal mistake. GOD will always be there to lift you back up when you fall. When you are blessed the only way that you will stay down is if you lay down.

Determine to Stay Focused

In Genesis 3:9, after Adam had sinned, GOD asked him... "Where are you?" GOD is omniscient so HE was not asking Adam where he was located. GOD knew where Adam was. GOD was asking Adam, in effect, "Do you know where you R?" because Adam had made a conscious decision to step outside of the will of GOD for his life.

You see, Adam knew full well he had sinned. He made a conscious decision to do it. However, once he came to the reality of the consequence of what he had done, Adam was ashamed and hid in the bushes. GOD came to talk with him to see if he understood the full impact of what he had done. Adam made a decision that was not within the boundaries GOD had established for him and his wife. Therefore, that decision took him out of the area of protection, prosperity and peace or the Garden of Eden. Adam might have thought he could knowingly make a bad decision and just continue to move forward with his life, but GOD showed him it was not that simple. The decision he made caused him to move froward, not forward. As a result, his family had to move out of the garden of grace into a field of tribulation.

The world is in its current state because fathers and husbands have made decisions for their lives and did not understand how their decisions would also affect

Single Mothers and Sons

their family's life. A lack of knowledge on proper decision making started as far back as Adam. Eve was deceived, but Adam made a decision. Eve slipped into sin whereas Adam fell (1 Timothy 2:14). I suspect, and this is pure speculation on my part, that Adam made the decision to eat the fruit because he did not want to lose Eve. Once the adversary tricked Eve into committing sin, she became his possession. In a way I can understand why Adam made the decision he made. Eve was the best thing GOD had made and he loved her. She was the result of some of GOD's best work so she must have been beautifully built, with a gorgeous body and she was running around naked too! Come on, man! I wouldn't have wanted to give her up either. So he decided forfeit dominion over the whole earth just to keep Eve.

Now, if you look at the ethical dilemma Adam faced logically he should have asked GOD what to do about this. GOD had made Adam the CEO over the earth. HE walked and talked with Adam all the time. If Adam had asked GOD what to do, GOD may have given him an exact duplicate of her and let the first Eve go or HE could have done something to redeem her. GOD would have led Adam into making the right decision. However, he chose to make a decision under pressure from the adversary instead of taking the situation before GOD.

Making decisions in haste and without consulting your spirit keeps you in a position where you should be going forward, but instead you are "going off". Most of us become frustrated and angry when things do not go right. Some of us decide to commit crimes to compensate for other bad decisions. We make those kinds of decisions out of frustration from not knowing what else to do. It makes "sense" that this bad decision may provide temporary relief from the other bad decision. The end result, however, is we usually end up in deeper trouble when we make decisions based on our senses, and sometimes common sense, rather than our spirit.

The adversary applies this pressure to your life to force you to move froward toward him, instead of forward toward GOD. He distracts (dis/track) you to get you to stop looking forward and look towards him. The adversary and his disciples will pull you off course before you even realize that you have gone off. As soon as you go off, you begin to lose. This is the reason the word of GOD teaches you to look not to the left or to the right, but straight ahead. This is the reason you cannot just cruse through life, you have to press through it.

"Let your eyes look right on and let your eyelids look straight before you. Ponder the path of your feet and let all your ways be established [by the word]. Turn not to the right hand nor to the left: remove your foot from evil (Proverbs 4:25-27)."

Every day of life brings you and me to a point where decisions must be made. The decisions we make today will have either a positive or negative impact on our lives tomorrow. Unless we have spiritual guidance, any decision we make can potentially be a bad one. We should understand, therefore, that allowing our spirit and the word of GOD to influence our decision making will lead us to achieve more positive results than negative ones. The word and the Spirit of GOD will guide you into all truth.

Making unsound and untimely decisions for the family is worse than making no decision at all. Over time the family will begin to reject a man's leadership because he will appear to be weak and indecisive. Therefore, a man has to make sound timely decisions in order to retain respect as the CEO of his family. Again, the way to be sure the decisions we make are sound and timely is to rely on the word and your spirit for the answers. Then, do what it says when it says it.

Chapter 9
Family Relationships

"Likewise, you husbands, dwell with them according to knowledge, giving honor unto the wife, as unto the weaker vessel and as being heirs together of the grace of life; that your prayers be not hindered."
~ 1 Peter 3:7

Men must learn how to properly live with and relate to our family in order to keep them in the grace of GOD. Traditional religious teaching has the definitions of grace and mercy twisted to conceal the power in grace that GOD has made available to us. They say that grace is the "unmerited favor of GOD." The truth is mercy is the unmerited favor. Whenever you are in need of mercy it is because you are guilty. You did something you knew that you were not supposed to and now the punishment is about to come down. Therefore, you plea or beg for mercy to escape the level of punishment that you know you deserve. GOD does you an unmerited favor or shows you mercy by not giving you a sentence that is commensurate with the act committed. Grace is the power of GOD operating on behalf of the believer. GOD has given us the authority, as a part of our inheritance as HIS children, to come BODLY to the Throne of Grace to find help in the time of need. Our Heavenly Daddy uses HIS power on our behalf when we need HIM to simply because we are HIS children. Grace is not given as a favor that we don't deserve it is given out of love from the heart of a father to his children. Men need the grace of GOD in order to lead, guide, and protect their family.

Single Mothers and Sons

What is the Importance of the Woman in the Family?

1 Peter 3:7 instructs men, as husbands, that we must learn how to live with our wives according to knowledge in order to have grace, GOD's power, operating on our behalf. When a husband knows how to honor his wife and lead her to enter into the power of agreement with him there will be nothing (with the grace of GOD) that they will not be able to achieve.

Women are critical to the spiritual health of a family and vital to the completion or fulfillment of the family's vision, mission or purpose. The woman was designed by GOD to be a life giver. Everything that is birthed into the earth is birthed through a woman. If children are going to be birthed into the family, they must come through a woman. If the man's vision for his family is going to manifest in the earth, he has to make sure it is received and conceived by his wife. The husband has to explain the vision to his wife in a way that causes her to receive it in her heart and conceive it in her mind. GOD spoke HIS vision to mother earth and she brought forth life. The Holy Spirit spoke the vision of the Savior to Mary and she gave him life. A husband has to speak the vision of the family to his wife in a way that will convince her to give it life. If the wife conceives the vision in her mind, she can deliver it through her body. While the husband is responsible for guiding the family's vision, the wife is responsible for giving birth to it and helping it to grow. This is why GOD birthed the vision HE had for the redemption of mankind through a woman.

"... the angel Gabriel was sent from GOD unto a city of Galilee, named Nazareth, to a virgin espoused to a man whose name was Joseph, of the house of David

Single Mothers and Sons

and the virgin's name was Mary. And the angel came in unto her and said, hail, you that are highly favored, the Lord is with you: blessed are you among women. And when she saw him, she was troubled at his saying and cast in her mind what manner of salutation this should be. And the angel said unto her, fear not, Mary: for you have found favor with GOD. And, behold, you shall conceive in your womb and bring forth a son and shall call His name Jesus. He shall be great and shall be called the Son of the Highest: and the Lord GOD shall give to Him the throne of His father David... And Mary said, Behold the handmaid of the Lord; be it unto me according to your word (Luke 1:26-38)."

A woman was chosen to receive, conceive and give birth to the vision GOD had for HIS family which HE planned to bring forth through HIS Son. The angel explained to Mary what GOD's vision was in a manner in which she could receive it and conceive it therefore she delivered it. The ministry of Jesus would not have been birthed into the earth had it not been for a woman. Joseph had nothing to do with Jesus being birthed into the earth. The transaction occurred between GOD and Mary. Joseph was responsible for guiding Jesus' growth to maturity. However, Mary was responsible for giving HIM birth.

As a result of the transaction that occurred in the Garden of Eden, GOD has given men the power to protect women from satanic influence and HE gave women the power to protect men from satanic attack. As a consequence of not understanding how critical women are to the plan of GOD for the family, men seem to aid the adversary with his plan to inhibit the power of women to do her job of stopping him from defeating men. It is satanic attack on the mind of men

Single Mothers and Sons

that causes them to think a woman can't do a man's job. In the church, for example, the men think that a woman is not supposed to preach. Yet, if it had not been for a woman who gave birth to a male preacher, who first took him to church, who first taught him how to pray, and first made him read the Bible, his ministry would not have been born. If it had not been for his mother or grandmother who fought the devil to save his life, he might not have lived to lead a ministry. It is ridiculous to say that a woman should not preach. Women are life givers. They give birth to ministry as well as everything else in the earth. Even the earth itself, we call mother. Adam was birthed out of mother earth. A woman, then, ought to be able to do whatever she gave birth to.

Due to historically chauvinistic interpretations of scripture some women have a problem with the Bible because of the way they believe it describes a woman in relationship to a man. For example, 1 Peter 3:1 says, "Likewise, you wives be in subjection to your own husbands..." Many women who read this may feel that they don't want to hear anything else the Bible has to say. However, if they would not stop at the first sentence and continue to read through verse seven, they will begin to see that GOD holds the woman in high esteem and has given her a great responsibility. GOD's will is for the woman be honored within the family.

1 Peter 3:1-7 comes out of the context of Genesis 3:16, in which Eve was deceived. Even though she was deceived and did sin, the fall of mankind was **not** charged by GOD to Eve. Men charge Eve with the fall of man but GOD charged the fall of man to Adam. As a result of her sin, however, GOD charged Eve with an

Single Mothers and Sons

awesome responsibility: to stand as a moral fixture between man and the devil, to be the guardian of the moral conscience of the world, and to whup the devil and keep him off her family. Basically HE was charging her to never let the adversary influence her, her husband or children again.

GOD would never give you a mission to complete without equipping you to do it. Therefore, one of the two weapons of warfare that GOD gave women to defeat the adversary is unconditional love. In Genesis 3:15, GOD told the adversary, "And I will put enmity [intense ill will] between you and the woman..." The woman was made the mortal enemy of the adversary and charged her to wage war against him. That is why in days past there was always a mother, grandmother, great auntie or some other woman who was whuppin' the devil and keeping him off the family! She was ordained and equipped by GOD to do it. Do you remember how some men used to call their wives a battleaxe or a ball and chain? Well, battleaxes and ball and chains are weapons of war. Some are pretty and ornate while some are primitive and rough, but they both get the job done!

While a woman has the ability to fight against the devil and win, she also has the ability to influence the heart (or nature) of her husband. Through the power of love, she can lead him away from sin, push him toward GOD and to teach the children to love. If a man is the head of the family, the woman is surely its heart. The main thing that GOD desires from the union of a man and woman are children with good heads and good hearts.

GOD made woman to dress and adorn man like a crown; to make him feel better and look stronger. A crown is supposed to be worn in a prominent position on the man's head and should be adorned with his finest jewels. A woman should not have anything to do with a man who is not willing to place her in a prominent position in his life or adorn her with his finest jewels. The thing that makes a king different from an ordinary man is his crown. The thing that makes a great man different from an ordinary man is a virtuous woman. Just as a good crown protects a man's head, a good wife protects her husband. She brings honor to him by exemplifying the crowning qualities of womanhood: a devotional spirit, modesty, liberality, wisdom and virtue.

"For a man indeed ought not to cover his head, forasmuch as he is the image and glory of GOD: but the woman is the glory of the man. For the man is not of the woman; but the woman of the man. Neither was the man created for the woman; but the woman for the man. For this cause ought the woman to have power on her head because of the [fallen] angels (1 Corinthians 11:7-10)."

Submission vs. Subjection

"Submitting yourselves one to another in the fear of GOD (Ephesians 5:21)."

GOD gives a husband, as the designated leader of the family, a wife. Her job is to help her husband meet his responsibility to complete the vision or mission for the family established by GOD. Therefore, the Bible describes the wife as a help meet instead of a help mate. It is important for a husband to have a wife with the gifts, talent and abilities that complement the gifts, talent and abilities he has to assist him in completing his GOD given assignment. A wife, in effect, is equipment or equipped with what the man needs to do his job. Any man can select a mate but it is hard to find a wife who is meet. That is, suitable, proper and fit for him as it pertains to what GOD sent him here to do. A mate could help you get along in life, but a meet will help you get ahead! You can achieve success with a mate but you will achieve glory with a meet. A husband and wife who are "meet" for each other are more likely to achieve victory in life, successfully realize the vision they establish for their family, and receive glory in heaven.

Notice the scripture above says "Submitting yourselves one to another..." Do you see it does **not** say that the wife is supposed to submit herself to her husband? It states that the husband and the wife are to submit themselves to one another. Both the husband and the wife are to submit to each other, if their union is going to work. She does not just submit to him. He must **also** submit to her so that neither of them are superior to the other. However, one is in subordination to the other simply because one has to be the leader or there will be confusion, inaction and stagnation in their growth and progress toward the vision of the family. The reason most of us have a problem with words like submission and subordination is because we have assigned negative social and political connotations to these words. We don't really know what they mean so they create problems. Therefore, we must break them down syllabically.

The word subordination is composed of the prefix "sub" which means under, the base word "ordain" means to empower or equip. The suffix "tion" means act or process. The word subordination then means the act or process of equipping under. Subordination in the

Single Mothers and Sons

Bible context is the act of empowering or equipping by putting on or getting under.

"For as many of you as have been baptized into Christ have put on Christ (Galatians 3:27)."

We put on Christ to equip or empower Jesus to do His work in the earth through us. When a wife places herself in subordination to her husband, she gets under him or puts him on like she is wearing a jacket. When a jacket is not being worn it is lifeless and just hangs or lies around. While a jacket is being worn it has life, power and strength. It can to what it was designed to do which is to cover and protect. It can also turn, move and do everything it needs to do to execute its mission. Take the jacket off and lay it on the floor, it loses its life, power and strength to do execute its mission. A man is like a jacket. Without a help meet, he lacks the life, power or strength he needs to complete the assignment he was given for his life and family.

"And the rib which the LORD GOD had taken from man made HE a woman and brought her unto the man (Genesis 2:22)."

The word "rib" that Eve was made from in Hebrew is "tsela" which means a beam or subfloor. The woman was designed by GOD to strengthen, gird up, and support her husband. A woman must get under him to push him up or put him on to undergird and equip him with what he needs to execute the vision for their family. The man is equipped or supported when his wife's knowledge, gifts, talent and abilities are added to his. By being submitted to one another and submitted to GOD, it makes the two of them superior to any other couple of the world.

Now, the word submission is a combination of the prefix "sub" and the base word "mission" which of course means job, task or undertaking. "Sub" simply means to be under. To be in submission means to lift up or support another in the completion of their mission. If a husband demands that his wife be in submission to him, he has to provide her with a mission to support; a mission to get under. Why would a woman want to submit to a man who has not given her a vision, goal or aspiration for her to support? Most women have a problem submitting to their husbands today simply because the husband has not given them anything to submit to, a mission to get under or any reason to submit! Brothers, there is no reason to follow a man that isn't going anywhere. A woman can't be a help meet to a man who hasn't given her anything to help with.

"Likewise, you wives, be in subjection to your **own** husbands; that, if any obey not the word, they also may without the word be won by the conversation of the wives (1 Peter 3:1)."

The other problem that a good number of women have in submitting to their husbands is due to the emotion that accompanies the words submit and submission or because of how hearing those words being used makes a woman feel. When the word submit is used in the context of marriage today to most women it feels like the word subject. The word subject is comprised of the prefix "sub" and the base word "ject", which means to throw; that is, to throw under. To be subject, in most women's minds means to throw one's self under their husband and allow themselves to be walked on.

The definition of the word subject, in the context of 1 Peter 3:1, means that a woman must be amenable to carrying the burden of helping to execute, direct, and guide the vision of her **OWN** husband. This instruction was given because many wives are more apt to help carry the vision of their preacher or employer than for their husband. Peter is teaching here that the preacher's wife has a husband and the boss's wife has a husband. Therefore, every wife has a duty to submit to her **own** husband. She must be amenable to his guidance and direction but she must never allow herself to become subject to him in terms of being walked on. The same is true for a man. He must submit himself to his wife as his queen but he must never become her subject.

Every family body, just like every physical body, must have a head. The word "head" in this context means leader or guide. Jesus is the head of the church and Christians are the body. The head of the church gives guidance and direction to the body. The husband is the head of the family and the wife is the body of the family. Just as the head gives guidance and direction to the body, the husband gives guidance and direction the wife. The woman is supposed to follow her husband's guidance in the same manner as the church follows Jesus. The husband is supposed to lead his wife in the same manner as Jesus leads the church. No man should marry a woman who is not capable of conforming to Christ like leadership.

A man must die to himself to be married to a woman. A woman must die to herself in order to be resurrected into new life as one with her husband. The primary reason husbands and wives struggle to become one is because one or both refuse to die to their single life and come into harmony or agreement. Either or neither of them want to change and do what is necessary after

Single Mothers and Sons

they <u>get</u> married to **be** married and become one with their spouse.

Take the toilet seat issue as an example. The wife gets furious because the husband refuses to put it down. The husband gets irate when the wife complains because he can't understand what the big deal is: "If she wants the seat down, why can't she just put it down? The issue for her is consideration and an emotional need for her husband to show that he cares about how she feels. Becoming one in marriage does not come without consideration. However, the consideration is not one for the other it is both for each other. The law of averages dictate that if a man just used the facility, odds are his wife will have to use it before he has to again. Therefore, he should put it down for her. The same is true in the wife's case. Once she finishes, she should put it up for him. Dying to one's self is the key to marital unity. Egos must die in order for a marriage to live. Don't expect your mate to have consideration for you. Instead, have consideration for your mate without consideration of what he or she should do in return. This will eliminate most issues that make it difficult for husbands and wives to become one.

"Likewise, you husbands, dwell with them according to knowledge, giving honor to the wife, as unto the weaker vessel and as being heirs together of the grace of life; that your prayers be not hindered (1 Peter 3:7)."

A man who is planning to marry a woman, has to learn to live with her according to knowledge. That knowledge is intimate information specific to her. This means, a man must learn how to live with his wife based on who **she** is not the last chick he was with. The scripture says, in Genesis 2:22, with the rib from the

Single Mothers and Sons

man's side "made" HE the woman. The word **made** in that scripture is translated from the Hebrew word "panah", which means built. The man was created but the woman was built. A woman was built by GOD to be pure power; the power to hold a man up and help carry him into his destiny. Men know innately that anything which is built is created with power. Everything that men build with power we assign a feminine character to it. When we see a powerful sports car, we say "Look at her go; isn't she a beauty". A woman is a powerful high performance vehicle that can take a man anywhere he wants to go as long as he knows how to "handle" her. That is, give her the proper guidance, direction and maintenance. The Bible is the manual that instructs a man on how to handle and maintain the high powered performance vehicle that is a woman.

Every piece of equipment that utilizes or delivers power comes with an instruction manual. It normally states in bold letters on the manual "Read carefully before operating this equipment". It even gives you instructions that appear to be common sense like don't operate an electrical hair dryer while taking a shower. Duh! They do this because they don't want to assume that everyone has common sense. The manufacturer tells you everything you need to know to operate the equipment safely and to keep you from blowing yourself up.

The average man's problem is we usually just start operating the equipment without reading the instructions first. GOD manufactured the woman and the Bible is her instruction manual. It contains her handling and care instructions. Read it and study it carefully, my brothers, then you will know how to operate in marriage correctly and how to keep that powerful piece of equipment from blowing up in your face. If a man does not know how to handle and maintain a woman correctly, she will blow him and their marriage to pieces. You can be the toughest guy on the planet but without knowledge on how to manage a marriage you can be defeated by a woman. Samson was the strongest man in the world. He killed a thousand men with the jawbone of Ass but he was defeated by the woman who slept in his arms. A woman can either make or break you. Therefore, it is imperative to understand how to care for the particular woman that you love, learning how she loves to be loved, before you get married.

The world sets a man up for failure in marriage because he does not need to know anything before he obtains a license for marriage. In order to obtain a licensed to drive he must study a driving manual and take two tests. We fail in life and marriage, not because of what we know, but because of what we don't know. Hosea 4:6 says "My people are destroyed for a lack of knowledge" and most marriages fail for the same reason. A man who does not learn how to build a marriage before he is married will need to retreat. That is, he will have to back up, start over and find a way to get the knowledge he needs. A man who does not read and understand the instruction manual before trying to be married will either become divorced or have to retreat in the form of a separation and start over. There is nothing wrong with launching a tactical retreat to go and get the information you need to prevent making an error. A timeout in football is a tactical retreat wherein the quarterback goes to the coach to get some information he needs to keep from losing some of the yardage he gained. GOD manufactured the institution

Single Mothers and Sons

of marriage. It is important therefore to know what the manufacturer says about it.

The Order of GOD for the Family

"...behold, the angel of the Lord appeared to Joseph in a dream saying, Arise and take the young child and his mother and flee into Egypt and be you there until I bring you word: for Herod will seek the young child to destroy him. When he arose, he took the young child and his mother by night and departed into Egypt... But when Herod was dead, behold, an angel of the Lord appeared in a dream to Joseph in Egypt saying, Arise and take the young child and his mother and go into the land of Israel: for they are dead which sought the young child's life. And he arose and took the young child and his mother and came into the land of Israel (Matthew 2:13-14 & 19-21)."

Here we find something both interesting and strange. Mary was engaged to marry Joseph. Before they came together he discovered she was pregnant with Jesus. In that day, Joseph had a legal right to have Mary stoned to death. Being a just man Joseph decided, instead, to put her away privately. However, an angel appeared to him in a dream and instructed him that it was alright to make Mary his wife. The baby she was about to give birth to was the Son of GOD.

So, we see that Mary gave birth to Jesus but Joseph was not the father. Joseph was Mary's husband but Jesus was Mary's baby. Since Joseph was not Jesus' father, why was GOD telling Joseph what to do with Him? Why didn't HE instruct Mary to take the child into Egypt? The reason is because there is an order of GOD. Instruction, direction, and guidance always comes from the head. The order of GOD is to provide

Single Mothers and Sons

guidance and direction to the family through the husband. Husbands have a responsibility to guide, guard and govern the family or to direct, correct and protect it. The instruction was given to Joseph for the protection of Jesus' life because it was his responsibility to see that Jesus was protected while He was young.

Some women have a problem with the man they marry disciplining her children from a previous marriage. When a man cannot discipline the children it takes away his power to guide, guard and govern his family. He is stripped of his ability to mentor and nurture the children and makes him a non-entity in their lives. In effect, he is the man that is married to mom, not dad. A man whose name is Robert becomes just "Bob" to the children and they are robbed of the benefits of having a dad. This defies the order of GOD for the family. I suggest that if a woman can't trust a man she is about to marry to discipline her children, she should not marry him. She needs to select a man that can be both a husband to her and a dad to her children. Simply selecting a husband for her is selfish and is not fair to the children.

A man is an essential part of a family as the head. Without a man the family becomes like a headless chicken. It is incomplete, won't function properly, and will ultimately cease to live. It will run around crazy for a while but eventually it will fall and die. A man is the head as well as the feet or foundation of the family. The husband gives direction from his position as the foundation or feet. The deeper a foundation is set in the earth, the higher the structure built upon it will be able to rise. The husband also provides wisdom and guidance from his position as the head.

Single Mothers and Sons

The woman is an essential part of a family as the body. She embodies everything in between the head and the feet. The body contains everything that is vital for it to properly live and function. Ergo, the wife contains within her everything that is vital for a family to properly live and function as well. A body can live without feet but it cannot stand. However, a body cannot live without a head and a head cannot live without a body. The head and the body need each other to properly live and function the way GOD designed them. Similarly, the husband and wife need each other in order for their family to live and function the way GOD intended as well.

Contrary to feminist ideology the man **must** function as the head of the family like the head functions on a body. The head of a physical body hold the eyes and brains that provide the body with vision and wisdom. The head sends signals to the body to provide direction. Without the head, the body loses its ability function properly. It may be able to function on its own for a time, but without vision and direction a body will only flounder, not flourish. No one gets through life or achieves success in life alone. Women could have an easier time becoming all they ever wanted to be if they had not allowed feminist ideology to cut the head off their family's body. Our spirit needs a body to have the authority to function in the earth. When a person's brain dies the body ceases to function so the "spirit" of life that animates the body leaves. Doctors can technically keep the body alive by putting it on machines but once the head is dead the body will eventually die too. When a family loses its head it will eventually die or fail to thrive.

Single Mothers and Sons

The Corporate Family

It is the order of GOD that men assume headship of the family. A husband is the Chief Executive Officer (CEO) of the family. Men establish the vision, mission, direction and set policy for the family in conjunction with his wife. A wife is the Chief Operations Officer (COO) of the family. Her job is to put the vision, mission and direction of the family into operation and see that it is birthed or given life. The children are the laborers or the rank and file.

A family is a corporate entity. Therefore, a family must operate like a corporation under a unified vision, mission, objectives and goals in order to be successful. Every Fortune 500 corporation came to be one of the top corporations in the world because they all operate on the principles found in the word of GOD that HE intended families to operate on. I am not saying these corporations are godly. I am saying they all operate on the principles of GOD which will work for anyone who works them. Every principle for organizing the family found in the Bible is exactly what the Fortune 500 use to organize their world-wide corporations. They all hold organizational meetings to guide and direct their members. They conduct financial meetings to decide how their funds will be disbursed. You will find that Jesus did the same thing with His disciples (Luke 10:1-11). If a man is to lead his corporate family to be wealthy he must learn to do what other wealthy corporations do: operate on the principles of GOD.

The man, as CEO of the corporation, must provide his family with a vision or mission. If your wife is cheering for another man on the field, it's because you are not in the game. Anytime the wife appears to be out of order, it is because the husband is out of order. The only reason a woman would work hard to fulfill her preacher's vision is because her husband hasn't given her one to work on. The only reason a wife would try to establish a vision, mission and guidance for the family is because her man wasn't done it. The wife knows inherently that it has to be done and she gets tired of waiting for the husband to do his job. So she moves ahead of her husband in an attempt to motivate him to move. In doing that, she has now reassigned him from the position of husband and CEO and made him one of her children.

There will be a conflict within the family now because, while the husband is acting like a child, he hates being treated like a child. This provides the devil with room to maneuver within and destroy this family because the wife is out of order, taking the lead in the family, which leaves her husband is vulnerable to attack. It is the responsibility of the man to make sure his wife is doing what she is supposed to do and to be where she is supposed to be. He does this by doing what he is supposed to be doing and being where he is supposed to be. If the man is out of order, his wife will move out of position. Then, she will do things, like Eve, that allow the adversary to divide their family.

There a guiding principle that runs throughout the Bible which declares that even though a wife did something she shouldn't have, it is not her fault. The husband is responsible for whatever mistakes she makes. The wife will only make the mistakes her husband allows her to make. If he had been doing his job, she would not have committed the error. This is true about what happened in the garden. Eve ate the forbidden fruit but nothing happened. The world was not changed until Adam ate it too and failed to do what he was supposed to do.

You see, if Adam had been with Eve while she was out looking for food, the adversary would not have had an opportunity to get her alone. Adam was probably like the typical man today who lets his wife go shopping alone while he stays home and watch sports on TV. Adam was probably hanging out watching the reindeer games or something while Eve was out shopping. The adversary had an opportunity to trick her because Adam wasn't with her.

Anything that is wrong with a woman can always be traced back to a man. It may not always be traceable to her husband, but it can be traced to some male. It may have been her father, brother, uncle, an old boyfriend, a former husband, cousin or so on who was the perpetrator of abuse or maltreatment. In some cases a woman will select a man to marry that has some of the same characteristics that her abusers have. Therefore, if the husband finds something wrong with his wife and wants her to change, he must change first. The man must assume responsibility for change in order for her to change.

Taking Responsibility

The world is in its current state because men have failed to take responsibility. Man's irresponsibility started as far back as Adam. In Genesis 3:11, GOD asked Adam if he had eaten any of the fruit that he was commanded not to. He replied, "the woman, you gave me, gave me the fruit and I ate it". In other words, Adam said "It isn't my fault".

You see, Adam never took responsibility for his actions. I wonder what the world would have been like

Single Mothers and Sons

today if he had just taken responsibility for his actions? Man's irresponsibility continues today because he has failed to read and understand the Bible and lead his children to GOD by living his life as an example of Jesus before them. Too many of us have been acting like children ourselves. We do not take responsibility for our own actions. Therefore, we have not been able to teach our children to take responsibility for their actions. A man who still thinks like a child is not mature enough to possess the wisdom and knowledge needed to raise a family. If he wants to lead a family, he has to put away childish things and begin to think like a man.

"When I was a child, I spoke as a child, I understood as a child, I thought as a child: but when I became a man, I put away childish things (1 Corinthians 13:11)."

Too many men, today, are maturing (mentally) later and later in life. Unbeknownst to these men, they are suffering from a mental condition known as "Arrested Development". That is, their bodies have grown to maturity but their minds stopped developing at the natural age of manhood. They had no influence in their lives to help them to continue to mature mentally. As a result, they appear to be men but they act as if they are still 12 years old. A man who is 40 years old physically and 12 years old mentally is classified mentally retarded. Normally, we would provide them with psychiatric treatment and prescribe medication. These men need healing. Yet, they have no idea that they must come in for the cure. The real problem here is a woman will marry one of these guys thinking he is a man when in reality he is only a man sized boy.

A man with the mind of a child has a form of godliness but denies the power thereof. He rejects GOD

Single Mothers and Sons

and the ways of GOD. He thinks like a child, acts like a child and talks like a child. This type of man is easy to identify because he often wears a child's clothes and spends too much time playing video games. There are so many men like this that many children no longer have respect for men. This is partly because they see no difference between men and them. A man with a child-like mind expects to be taken care of and becomes dependent. He looks to get something for nothing because he believes society owes him for being poor or for not having a father. He is selfish, constantly seeks pleasure, wants instant gratification, is reluctant to make a commitment, and truly believes that he should get money for nothing and chicks for free.

A man who suffers from arrested development can be very charming to women, just like a child, because he is really a big kid. Some women are attracted to these men because of their charm and her instinct to nurture. He appears to be someone who **needs** her to take care of him and she is right in her assessment. However, she does not realize that she will grow tired of trying to raise a man sized boy and will start looking for a man who will be a man. By that time it's usually too late because they are already married or have children together. The next woman this man becomes involved with will hear all about how his previous relationship's failure was not his fault. Like most children, this type of man, has an inability to take responsibility. He cannot make the connection between his choices and the effect or consequences of his choices.

One of the reasons Adam failed is because he was born as a man-sized boy. GOD was trying to raise Adam to maturity through giving him a family, but

Single Mothers and Sons

Adam's disobedience cut him off from GOD while he was still immature. Their relationship died or the way they communicated directly ceased to exist. The education and training process GOD was putting Adam through stopped in mid stream. So, he suffered, in effect, from arrested development as well. GOD placed Adam in the garden alone initially to teach him knowledge about the earth and the universe. HE wanted Adam to learn to be responsible for taking care of himself and his environment. Then, GOD gave Adam a wife to teach him how to care for another human being besides himself.

Next, GOD was going to give Adam children so he could understand the actions and decisions that he made in life would impact not only himself but his children as well. He would learn to take authority over his children, protect them from dangers seen and unseen and teach them the ways of GOD. GOD was in the process of teaching Adam that his actions would have far reaching implications for future generations. Unfortunately, Adam disobeyed before GOD could teach him that lesson and his actions have affected mankind unto this present generation. Men must recognize that our actions will have the same affect on future generations of our children. The offenses you commit today will impact your children's children tomorrow.

Growing up into GOD

There are four things that men must learn in order to grow into mental and spiritual maturity and successfully raise their children in a way that will equip them to teach, train and protect future generations.

Single Mothers and Sons

First, men have an obligation to teach children the ways of GOD. If we teach them the ways of GOD, the word promises they will have good success (Joshua 1:8). Second, men must learn to give of themselves to others and chose friends who have chosen to live godly lives. The objective here is to give the children consistent godly role models from whom they can learn to develop a consistent godly lifestyle. Third, men must learn to take authority and dominion over their children and demand obedience. Fourth, men must learn to teach their children through their own lives and through their love not just with their lips.

Children are never going to emulate what they hear you say more than what they see you do. Children learn more about how to live by watching how we live. It is imperative that we already be whatever we expect our children to become. It is by example that our children learn best. However, the lessons they learn when they understand they are being taught out of a motive of love are powerful. It is difficult to lead a person to reconsider the meaning of a Bible verse after grandma taught them what it meant. They don't want to even consider that grandma could have been wrong. The love that was the motivating factor behind the lesson made it have a long lasting effect. So, love as a motive for teaching is powerful. On the other hand, we must teach our children how to live within the will of GOD by repetition. I have been teaching over forty years so I can unequivocally state that teaching is repeating until learning takes place. This is why I have been repeating certain points in this book. So men must consistently teach our children using the most effective tools at our disposal: love, repetition and example.

Single Mothers and Sons

The initial goal in teaching our children the ways of GOD is to set boundaries for them by placing certain restrictions and demanding obedience in order to protect their lives. The first objective in setting boundaries is to remove the gray area that the world has created so they will be able to see the difference between right and wrong, good and evil or life and death. This way, our children will be able to make clear choices that would be beneficial to their lives.

The ultimate goal in teaching our children the ways of GOD is to provide an inheritance of a lifestyle of faith. You see, it is impossible to provide for a child by giving them the natural things of this world such as money, houses, education and so on. These things help provide comfort and security, but they can be lost quickly if the child has not also been taught to live a godly life or if he or she decides to live foolishly. The only way we can truly provide for our children and be sure they know how to live wisely with riches is to train them to live a lifestyle of faith. However, the key is having that lifestyle in us so that we can breathe or inspire it into them rather than simply giving them an example to follow.

Children innately determine their value or self worth based on the amount of love they receive from those whom they love. The average child is motivated by love to take care of themselves. People feel that if nobody cares about them, why should they care about themselves? This is the reason discipline is so important to children. Adults look at me as if I am crazy when I tell them that kids love discipline. You see, children understand that the purest form of love is discipline. They know that whenever their parents truly love them, they will correct them and give them the personal time, attention, and instruction they need.

Kids know that love compels a parent to give of themselves and their time to give their children discipline. We don't spoil children with too much love. We spoil our children by not disciplining them. If we don't discipline children they don't feel loved and will slowly turn rotten. Now, parents must understand that discipline is not the same thing as punishment. Discipline is administered out of love whereas punishment is the product of anger. The motivation to discipline one's self to live godly comes by love not punishment. We were changed and delivered from a life of darkness to light through love. Ergo, our children must be taught and trained through love.

Some men believe they are giving love when they buy their children clothes, food or pay for a place for them to live. That is not love and the children do not perceive that as love. Prison administrators give the inmates clothes, food and a place to stay. Do you think they love the prisoners? No! They are fulfilling an obligation to provide the things necessary for the inmates to sustain a somewhat human existence due to the responsibility they have taken on in keeping them locked up. This is the same reason the government make men who do not love their children pay child support. Government has to force these men to give their children the things they need to maintain a somewhat human existence and to take responsibility for their support. The men pay support, which helps to provide food, clothes, shelter, etc., because they do not want to go to jail. However, it does not mean that they suddenly began to love their children once they put the check in the mail. Giving a child a bunch of things is not giving them love. They need much more than things to feel loved. They need you to give them yourself, your time and the discipline that comes through your teaching.

Finally men, we have a responsibility to love, respect and protect our wives. You have to love her enough to be willing to sacrifice your life for her. You have to be willing to endure the pain that will be required to heal her from the hurt she experienced from past relationships. Communicate constantly with your wife using the five messages that let her hear and feel your love from the heart which are: giving acts of service, spending quality time, saying words of affirmation, giving and receiving gifts, and sharing physical touch (at times other than leading to sex). One of the most important things we can do for our children is to let them see us loving, respecting and protecting our wives. Your children will learn how love and respect their spouse by the example you set. Therefore, pamper your wife and take care of her.

Understand the Female Mind

Most of what women will want to have, do or desire in marriage will be illogical to their husbands. Husbands must remember that when GOD instructs or explains what HE wants or desires a man to do, it will be illogical as well. But, if we just do it, we will achieve miraculous results. If we take the seemingly illogical advice of our wives and just do it, we will achieve miraculous results as well. If you can't see where it will do any harm then it won't.

Men need to understand that GOD created woman to be a little tougher in some areas than we are. The man was created out of dirt whereas the woman was built out of bone. As such, we have a tendency to gravitate toward the dirt. This is why we are logical in problem solving and want to get to the heart of the matter or uncover the root cause. Men have a need to get to the bottom line quickly or back to the dirt. Unfortunately, this accounts for part of the reason why a man could leave home and lay down with some dirty woman who couldn't hold a candle to his wife. He looks for a woman who will let him uncover her bottom quickly.

Many men will go outside of their marriage once they feel that their wives have become a thorn in their side. The reason she becomes a thorn, my brother, is there is something wrong in the marriage and she knows the root of the problem is **in** you. She doesn't know what it is so she tries to go to her roots which means she has to get down inside of you to find it. She is being a prickly thorn because she is trying to get to the bottom of the problem in the marriage from her perspective. Eve was made from a rib that came from the inside of her husband Adam. Ergo, the heart of the matter or root cause of every problem in a marriage for a woman lies on the inside of her husband. This is why she is a thorn in your side, brothers. She is trying to get inside of you to get to the root of it. Her objective is to get into her husband so she can discover what the problem is and try to fix it.

This is why she pokes and prods you to open up to her and let her in. This is why she always asks that question that men hate: "What cha thinkin'"? This is why she always wants to know how you are feeling. She wants to get inside of you! Your biggest problem is you won't let her in. GOD made your wife to be bone of your bone and flesh of your flesh. She is your spiritual protector. She was built from a rib and ribs are designed to protect your vital organs such as the heart, lungs, liver, and so on. Your wife will get under your skin and make you mad to the bone until you allow her to root around inside of you. You have to let her in because she is simply trying to protect your life and your family. So don't go outside of your marriage when your wife is being a pain. Let her get inside of you, she will stop poking, and the pain will stop.

Now, once you let your wife in, be prepared for her to redecorate the place. Once a man gets married on the outside most of us keep our old bachelor pad on the inside. The first thing a woman thinks about when she enters a single man's house is the changes that need to be made. Our favorite musty old couch that we spent many hours sleeping on is the first thing she wants to throw out. To a woman a bed is for sleeping, not a couch. The simple bear cave bachelor pad we retained inside of us will be transformed into a split-level ranch filled with flowers, plants and potpourri.

Men must submit to this change and allow our wives inside to help transform us from the frat boy we used to be into the mature minded married man we need to be. One of the keys to successful leadership is in allowing those who are being led to have input into how they are to be led. A good leader will always be affected, instructed or changed in some way by those he is leading. A husband will become a successful leader for his wife when he allows her to give advice and guidance on how to lead her. In describing how HE will transform HIS people, GOD said HE would "...give them beauty for ashes". When a man allows his wife to help transform him internally, she will give him beauty for ashes externally.

Single Mothers and Sons

A man must remember, then, to listen to his wife. If you are not listening, you are not leading. Listening is important because we are not always right. GOD made woman as a man's help meet; a proper, suitable or fit helper. When HE can't get through to our thick skulls, HE will have an angel go to her so that she can get to us (1 Corinthians 11:8-10). A lot of men don't want to listen to their wives because they think it might make them look henpecked. My brother, there is nothing wrong with being henpecked as long as you are pecked by a good hen! The greatest joy in the world for a man is the love of a good woman. Her price is far above rubies and more precious than gold. The act of showing love and respect for each other will instruct your family and serve to keep them together, strong in love and in the peace of the covenant of GOD.

Chapter 10
Marriage and Sex

"And the Lord caused a deep sleep to fall upon Adam and he slept: and HE took one of his ribs and closed up the flesh instead thereof; And the rib, which the Lord GOD had taken from man, made HE a woman and brought her unto the man. And Adam said, this is now bone of my bones and flesh of my flesh: she shall be called Woman, because she was taken out of Man. Therefore shall a man leave his father and his mother and shall cleave unto his wife: and they shall be one flesh (Genesis 2:21-24)."

Marriage and sex together is an exciting journey that everyone should experience. The time spent together prior to marriage is similar to waiting to get on a roller coaster that you have never ridden before. You are excited while being a little afraid of the unknown. You don't know what is going to happen except that there will be a lot of ups and downs with sudden turns that will jar and throw you about. Once the ride is over, it was so exhilarating that you want to do it again and again. You are shaken, breath taken and a little weak kneed from the ride but it is something that you have got to do again. Marriage and sex were designed by GOD to be something we could not get enough of. HE intended for the love making married couples share to take their breath away, make them shaky and weakened from the experience. GOD wanted sex in marriage to be something people would want to do over and over again so that they would be fruitful and multiply.

Single Mothers and Sons

When addressing the topic of marriage, I believe it is important to inform those who are having sex out of wedlock that they have not really made love yet. They might be living together and engaging in sex regularly. However, they still have experienced the real beauty of love making until they are engaged in the process of making life and making love. Marriage and sex is the process of taking two lives and making one life through making love. In the process of making love, the couple makes one new life from two and produces new life. In the process of making love, the two individuals become one.

Any man who has had sex with a woman knows she has a need to feel the house is secure before she will be comfortable. She needs a sense of security in order to allow herself to come outside of herself and enjoy the experience. If she hears a loud noise, she will want to stop to make sure that she is safe before starting again. Similarly, unless a woman is secure in a marriage relationship, she will never trust a man enough to allow herself to come outside of herself. When a man has not committed to her, a woman is always aware of the possibility that he might leave. She is hypersensitive to the threat of other females capturing him when he is outside of her presence. Therefore, while she may have sex with the man, she doesn't share her deepest intimate self with him. She will try her best to resist the chemical power of love making to prevent herself from fully falling for him because she doesn't trust him. A man has not known the power of making love until he makes love with a woman who completely trusts him.

People look at me strangely when I inform them that marriage is like dying. The couple wears black and white during the wedding ceremony to symbolize death and life respectively. In order for a marriage to be successful, the two individuals have to die to their single lives and be resurrected into new life as one. Couples who don't understand that they will have to die to their former life will not survive in marriage. The more a couple fights to try to resist the change required to become married, the longer it will take to **be** married after they get married. The sooner each individual learns to give up his or her single life (and keep their families out of their business) the quicker they will be married. As single individuals who are married, the couple can only crawl like a caterpillar. Once the individuals are transformed and become one in marriage, they will be able to float like a butterfly.

Contrary to popular belief, two people don't become married when they state their vows. The vows they share are a commitment to one another and a commitment they make to GOD to stay married after they get married. Marriage does not happen at the time the vows are stated. That is only the starting point of the marriage process. Becoming married is actually a process that takes about three to five years to complete depending on the couple. Most marriages fail within the first five years. The first 5 years is a period of struggle wherein the two individuals fight against the process of becoming one because they are afraid to be totally vulnerable. Fear causes them to resist dying to their single lives and transforming into a single new life.

Becoming married is similar to the process a caterpillar goes through to become a butterfly. The cocoon of commitment is very tight initially. As the couple shifts and adjusts in their cocoon, they each must accept a certain amount of discomfort to make the other more comfortable until they are both comfortable. They each of them must get rid of people, places, activities, and things that do not belong in their marriage cocoon. They go through a type of metamorphosis where the two of them transform into something new together that never would have been had they not committed to completing that process. The two individuals are now gone. They have coupled or become one new person.

Sex was given as a gift by GOD to make the process of becoming married easier to bear. Sex is designed by GOD to be a symbiotic dance wherein two individuals float together as they circle each other in a sea of love. Sex was made a pleasurable experience to motivate people to procreate. Sex was provided to make part of the process of becoming one enjoyable or sweet since part of it can also be bitter. When two people complete the process of becoming one, GOD can use them to birth something in the earth that would not have been birthed if they had not come together. The primary thing that is birthed which did not exist before is the marriage itself. Children are only a secondary byproduct. The third thing that would not have been birthed if the couple had not come together is the particular vision or mission that GOD wants to manifest through their marriage.

When two people decide to go into the state of marriage they must know that they will be "marred with age". They must understand that neither of them will be the same as they age. They must figure that both of them will lose their figure. Both of them must know that they will be marred by the scars of life over time as they fight to become one and remain one.

Single Mothers and Sons

Everything that is alive fights to remain alive. Married couples fight in their early years of marriage because they are actually fighting to keep their single lives alive. Each of them will want to retain the things, places, people and activities of their unmarried lives. But they soon find out that it's impossible to hold on to parts of their single lives and remain married. Once they allow their unmarried lives to die gently and be buried, the two can be resurrected into new life in marriage as one. I am stressing this point repeatedly because it is critical to the marriage's survival.

I love to attend weddings where the couple is happy and excited about sharing their lives together. While I am happy for them, I get concerned at times when I know the couple has no knowledge about marriage, what it takes to really **become** married and the strength it will take to stay married. Sometimes, it is hard for me to watch a wedding ceremony, see the couple standing face to face exchanging rings, and not see them as prize fighters standing face to face in a boxing ring. They are very happy that day, but you know the heavy weight bouts are about to begin. So, don't let your wedding ceremony become like the prelude to a prize fight where the contestants agree not to cheat or hit below the belt before they proceed to beat each other senseless. Allow the knowledge in this chapter to prepare you to become married and stay married after you get married.

Choosing the Right Woman

Most of us who are divorced chose to marry a person who looked good, had certain material possessions or both but they were not really the right person. Once the right person crosses our path (and they will because the adversary will point him or her out just to laugh in our face), it will usually be too late. We are usually tied to someone else already who we have probably already discovered is not really the right one.

In the tradition of our society, we determine whether a person will be a suitable mate through the dating process. We use that process to see if we would "love" to live the rest of our lives with that person. Where we have made a mistake in the last four decades is we have been using the dating process to see if we would "love" to have sex with that person. Based on the outcome of the sexual experience we decide if we would "love" to make love to that person for the rest of our lives. Consideration of whether or not we would love to live with that person for the rest of our life rarely enters the picture. Too often people find that they love to make love to person that they hate to live with.

In case you didn't know here is a Muppet news flash. Love is not born out of fornication. Lust is born out of fornication. When we entertain lust before marriage it leads to adultery in marriage. Many people entertain lust before marriage expecting lust to grow into everlasting love in marriage. Over time the intensity of lust wears off and they begin to feel unfulfilled when the "feeling" of love fails to appear. They become lonely in marriage so they step out of the home thinking they are looking for love. In reality, they are looking to satisfy their need for the feeling or intensity of lust. They begin by having emotional affairs, then discreet dates, and end up in adulterous relationships. Once their lust for another person is revealed after they fall into iniquity, their marriage ultimately ends.

A DATE was designed by GOD to be a Divine Appointment To Edify not a doggone appointment to

Single Mothers and Sons

experience one another's flesh. We use a dinner date today as a means of deciding whether or not we want to "eat" or consummate with someone. Words matter so confusing the word dating with the word courting and practicing one thinking that we are doing the other has led to a bunch of failed marriages. We believe that dating is the process where two people try to see if the other would be good to marry. Dating in reality does not begin until <u>after</u> a wedding date has been set. When people announce that they plan to get married but have not set a date for the wedding they are only engaged or espoused to each other. They will not be dating until after they have set and are actually carrying out the plans and actions necessary to stand at the altar on that date. So, dating is an action word. Dating is the process of preparing, moving or proceeding toward a wedding date.

Dating is often confused with courting. Whenever you think about the meaning of the word courting, picture in your mind a court room, a trial, judge, and jury. Courting is a time where two people lift each other up for examination to see if they would be good to marry. Courting is a time of judgment wherein you conduct a trial relationship and at some point you must come up with a verdict based on the evidence. Our family used to be involved in the examination as the jury to help determine the verdict. The problem we have today is the devil has tricked people into believing that nobody should try to judge anybody. And people, especially young people, don't listen to their family members any more. They are more likely to listen to their friends which too often lead them into trouble.

Once the couple is ready to get married a wedding date is set and **then** the dating can begin. Dating

Single Mothers and Sons

should be a time of honest communication and examination of the mission for the marriage. Important decisions on what vision for the marriage will be, how it will operate, who will do what, where and when, and so on after the marriage begins. Dating is not a time for fornication. You must remain sober, not intoxicated by intercourse, so that you can have serious negotiations on how the marriage will work and what you will do with it. Getting married is a business transaction that is very much like forming a new corporation. Getting married is a lifelong commitment and should not be treated lightly. The couple should be working on forming the corporation not fooling around and/or fornicating.

Engaging in sexual activity during the dating process activates hormones that cause our brains to disengage. We become drunk with a chemical cocktail that keeps us from thinking clearly and seeing people as they really are. A decision as important as marriage should never be made while intoxicated or under the influence of intoxicating hormones. A woman must remain sober in order to clearly see if the man is going to love her sincerely. A man should be sober when examining a potential mate to determine whether the woman is willing to trust him completely. He must know whether she will submit to his authority as the leader of their home. He must also know whether or not she will abide by the decisions he makes for the family.

Before a man even begins looking for a mate, he must have some idea of the type of woman who will be meet. That is, he must know what qualities, knowledge, gifts, talents and abilities she must possess that will complement his own in order to help him meet or complete his vision he has for his life and his family.

Single Mothers and Sons

The man has to know where he will be leading his family to go. So, he must also know the type of woman who would be a good help meet to assist him fulfilling the vision he has for their family. Then, he must set out to find the Cinderella, if you will, who will fit his glass slipper and not compromise. If he tries to force fit her foot into his slipper, she may be able to step into marriage with him but they won't be able to walk very far. The fit may look good to him, however, it will be too uncomfortable for her over time and she will scream to get out. Therefore, the man must find the woman who is the perfect fit and who will be able to work and walk comfortably with him in the fulfillment of his vision.

When is it Right to get married

A faithful man should not get married until he has found a virtuous woman. He should not marry any woman until he is sure that he has taken all the necessary precautions, made all the necessary considerations, and that she agrees with his vision for who and what their family will be and do.

Engaging in sex legally should never be a reason for getting married. Sexual compatibility, on the other hand, must be a consideration when deciding whether or not to get married. If the man wants to have sex five times and week and the woman only wants it once a month, sexual incompatibility will lead to fights that can cause the marriage to fail. Men feel rejected and will seek acceptance elsewhere. Sex is an important consideration. However, it should be the last item on the list of considerations as a couple is deciding whether to make a lifelong commitment to one another. A couple does not need to engage in fornication to know if they are compatible sexually. They can discover whether or not they are sexually compatible through conversation.

A person should only get married when they do not have a burning desire to be married. Until a person is happy or fulfilled being single, he or she is not ready to be married. GOD does not refer to a person without a spouse as being single. HE refers to them as being unmarried. Being single is when a person is whole within him or herself and connected or one with GOD. Unless a man is whole within himself and connected or one with GOD and has a woman who is whole and connected or one with GOD, they should not get married. Two half people with problems getting married will not create one whole person or eliminate the problems. Marriage will only unite two half people in one house with a whole group of problems.

What Happens during Sex

The average person can easily engage in premarital sex today because nobody told us there are more consequences associated with it other than unwanted pregnancies or sexually transmitted diseases. However, every act of sexual intercourse changes things in our bodies. We take it very lightly because we do not understand what transpires as we engage in the act of intercourse. You have to know the long term physiological and psychological effects that sex will have on your mind and body. Once you understand the binding impact of sex you will no longer wonder why it is difficult for a person to get over the loss of a lover.

"Unto the woman HE said, I will greatly multiply your sorrow and your conception; in sorrow you shall

Single Mothers and Sons

bring forth children; and your desire shall be to your husband and he shall rule over you (Genesis 3:16)."

When you engage in sex there is a chemical change that takes place in your body and brain. Not only is there an exchange of body fluids, there is also an exchange of 26 powerful hormones. One is called pheromone and another is oxytocin. Pheromone is a powerful attracting chemical. It's the body's natural aphrodisiac that helps make one person become sexually aroused by another. This hormone is passed primarily via one's breath and skin pores through kissing and close physical contact. Oxytocin is a powerful bonding chemical that is also passed through the skin. However, according to Dr Theresa Crenshaw, author of "The Alchemy of Love and Lust" oxytocin is passed primarily through body fluids. Oxytocin is the hormone that is responsible for making it possible for people to cleave to and desire one another.

The exchange of these hormones causes a chemical reaction in the two bodies coming together. Over a period of time this chemical reaction causes the two individual bodies to become one flesh. Since men were designed by GOD to be givers and women receivers, men excrete more oxytocin than women. His oxytocin causes her biorhythm to change to match his and it causes her menstrual cycle, in most cases, to change. In other words, his body chemistry begins to govern hers ("and he shall rule over thee"). This is similar to what occurs when you put two magnets together that are opposites in polarity. In time, one will dominate the other and eventually they will become matched or the same. Some couples are already naturally matched so the bond is created but no noticeable physical changes take place.

Single Mothers and Sons

If the woman's biorhythm does not change to become compatible with the man's, pregnancy may be difficult or she may never conceive with him. Men who have two or more women with whom they frequently have sex will notice that over a period of time all of the women will eventually have the same menstrual cycle. This is why a man can have two or more women pregnant and the children born at practically the same time.

If a woman is having sex with more than one man on a regular basis, she will receive sperm and/or oxytocin from each man. Just as male lions fight for dominance of the pride to ensure their ability to reproduce, according to Dr Robin Baker, author of "Sperm Wars: The Science of Sex", the sperm and hormones from different men fight for dominance in the woman's body. This internal activity can make a woman hyper, overly emotional, aggressive, rebellious and/or combative.

Women receive more oxytocin than they give. Since a man receives only a small amount of this allows most men to be more promiscuous than most women. The woman is chemically conditioned to desire only one man ("and thy desire shall be to thy husband") and is less likely to have more than one partner. That is assuming the effect of the oxytocin has taken place.

The Impact of Sex before Marriage

Sex inside the covenant of marriage, when both parties are complete and fulfilled in GOD and in each other, is a beautiful thing. You have not actually experienced the power in the act of intercourse until you have made love under those conditions. Sex outside of marriage is like fire. Fire is beautiful to gaze upon. It keeps you warm and makes you feel good. But out of a controlled environment fire can be destructive. Sex, by comparison, is also beautiful and makes you feel good and warm. Out of the controlled environment of marriage sex is destructive and somebody usually gets burned. Within the controlled environment of marriage sex is designed by GOD to be highly productive as well as pleasurable.

Sex out of wedlock is a game. The object nature of a game is to produce a winner and a loser. That is, someone wins the grand prize and someone is left with a consolation prize. In the game of sex, a man usually gets to win the grand prize of a woman's virginity and/or virtue. The woman is usually left where she needs to be consoled, left alone with a child, or just left.

Men must realize that the unmarried woman is not open game. GOD sees her exactly the same way he sees the married woman. She is holy and sanctified before HIM and a man cannot touch her unless it is in the institution of marriage. The breakdown of the American family can be traced back to the early sixties when we decided to forego marital relationships for free sex. The breakdown of the family in our society today is a direct consequence of that decision.

Too many adults and youth get caught up in the sex game based on the belief that we have to gain experience in order to learn. We are misled by the fallacy that experience is the best teacher. The truth is wisdom is the best teacher. Wisdom will teach you to not do something whereas experience will teach you that you shouldn't have done it. Operating in wisdom will help you save yourself from the pain and emotional anguish that you would have had to endure in order to gain the experience.

Single Mothers and Sons

When two people engage in sex they initiate a process that the Bible calls "cleaving" that will cause them to be chemically bonded or become one flesh. Once they "cleave" together and become one flesh separation becomes very difficult. Genesis 2:24 says "Therefore shall a man leave his father and his mother and shall cleave unto his wife: and they shall be one flesh." One flesh cannot become two individuals again unless they are ripped apart once the partners have cleaved. Ripped apart is how long term couples feel when they separate. Therefore, a man and woman cleaving unto one another is not some symbolic biblical mumble jumble. It is a real bond is created when two people have sex and a real scar is produced after they break up.

The word "cleave" means to unite with or to stick to like glue. Once two people become one flesh they are like two pieces of paper glued together. It is very difficult to completely separate two pieces of paper that have been strongly glued together for a long time. Any attempt to separate them will result in two "raggedy" pieces of paper. After couples separate they still have pieces of the other person stuck to them. It becomes difficult, then, to cleave to a new mate because you will always have pieces of the former mate stuck on you and stuck between you.

A man experiences emotional distress due to separation but not as intensely as a woman feels it. I am referring to real men not man-sized boys because they sometimes respond as a child would be expected to if his mommy left him. The emotional effect on a woman can range from mild distress to the extreme equivalent of postpartum depression. One of the reasons this occurs in women is due to a loss of

Single Mothers and Sons

oxytocin from her body. She begins to experience withdrawal symptoms as her body detoxifies from his hormone. This process can actually take up to two years to complete. The longer she experiences the withdrawal process, the less her desire for that man will be. A woman may be assured the process is complete by a change in her menstrual cycle. That is assuming there was an initial change. Another way to be assured is if she sees her former mate and wonders what it was she saw in him in the first place.

When couples separate there is a tearing of the flesh from one flesh back into two individuals. This tearing is similar to the tearing of the flesh that a mother experiences during child birth. It is often a traumatic and emotional experience, which under any other circumstance would cause people to bond together. This is why people who break up often get back together. Physical and emotional bonds are hard to break and the process of breaking up is difficult to complete. Unrelated people who experience a plane crash, war or hostage situation together, for example, develop a lifelong bond or kinship with one another. The physical and emotional struggle of child birth helps create a strong bond between the mother and the child. Once the child (who has the mother's biorhythm) is born, one flesh becomes two individuals.

When a man has an orgasm or kisses his wife, he is actually cleaving or breathing new life into her. He is placing into her his emotions or the way he feels, his intellect or the way he thinks and his will or what he wants. As the wife receives from her husband, she also gives the hormones to him that imparts her will, intellect and emotions through her breath, saliva and vaginal fluids. These hormones, over time, have the effect of assisting the two individuals to think, feel and desire in compatible ways. This is what GOD was describing when HE said the two shall be as "one flesh". HE wasn't saying they would be one physical body rather they would become one in physical nature. She will become as he is and vice versa.

The suggestion that the wife also passes hormones into the husband might seem confusing to some. However, it is quite simple when you think about it. As a man ejaculates the seminal fluid is blown through the prostate gland by muscular contractions with the assistance of air. It works basically the same way as squeezing an aspirator. If you had water in an aspirator, there would naturally be air in there also. As you squeeze the water out, air will come out as well. At this point the aspirator is depressed. Once you release it, air will rush back in and any fluid that the opening of the aspirator is in contact with will come in too until the bulb of the aspirator is filled. Once a man ejaculates it is like the bulb of the aspirator has been depressed. Air and the fluids will come out. Air and any fluids that the opening of the penis is in contact with gets collected and travels back up through it. The wife's hormones are drawn into the man's body and begin to engraft a part of her into him.

Why is Sex so Pleasurable if it is so Forbidden?

The act of sex is only forbidden before marriage for reasons previously discussed. Sex is designed to provide intense pleasure, but its primary purpose is to create life. The pleasure one derives from the act of sex can cause one to desire it more than they desire to obey the word of GOD. The act may indeed become a substitute for worshiping GOD for some. As a husband becomes skilled in administering intense sexual pleasure, his wife begins to reverence him and allows him to have complete power over her. Whenever the desire for intense sexual activity becomes out of balance in a person's life it makes his or her life disorganized and leads to a type of perversion. It may cause a man's wife to unconsciously view his penis as a type of shrine or alter at which she kneels to worship.

A man is anointed from his waist to mid-thigh. That is where the center of his power is located. The male sexual organs comprise a trinity: one penis plus two testicles. It can easily be perverted into a type of god for him or his mate. This is why it is easy for a man to get some women to take communion with it. A baby receives its blood type and the life of its flesh through the sperm of its father. "For the life of the flesh is in the blood... (Leviticus 71:11a)." Sperm is essentially blood. When a woman orally copulates she takes the flesh and blood of a man into her mouth as if she is taking communion. The word "testicle" is a combination of the words "testament" and "oracle". The word testament means a covenant or an expression of conviction. The word oracle means a shrine in which a deity reveals hidden knowledge or the divine purpose through. The male sexual organs were designed by GOD to be used to cement a covenant relationship between a husband and wife through which HE could produce offspring to reveal or execute HIS divine plan and purpose.

There is a thin membrane covering a woman's vagina called the hymen. There is no medical reason for this membrane to be there. However, the presence of it means the woman is still a virgin. On the first occasion of intercourse the membrane is severed and a small

Single Mothers and Sons

amount of blood is produced. A covenant with GOD is always cut in blood. GOD placed the hymen across the entrance to a woman's vagina because HE intended the first act of intercourse after marriage to be a type of blood covenant that is cut between a husband, a wife and HIM. A man is playing with GOD when he engages in intercourse with a woman to whom he is not married.

In the same manner as a man's reproductive organ represents a trinity, a woman's reproductive organ also represents a trinity. Just as some women can get carried away with penis worship, men can lose control of their brain function over vagina worship. This may seem silly, but we will recognize how it can easily occur once we realize that GOD left us a reflection of the love and beauty in HIS plan of redemption for mankind in the body of the woman. Sex or the act of intercourse was designed by GOD to be a good thing. However, the adversary tricked us into believing it was a bad thing, never touch or look down there, because he didn't want us to discover how the plan of salvation for man was designed in our bodies.

The vagina was designed by GOD to represent the three types of places of worship: the tabernacle, synagogue and church. These places of worship were designed to be levels of a passageway to lead us to GOD, into one refuge or into new life as one in Christ Jesus. In the woman's reproductive organ there are three chambers with each one representing a place of worship and an area of the tabernacle: outer court, inner court and the Holy of Holies. Every spirit of man was born of GOD in heaven and sent through a passageway into the earth. Just as there is a trinity of worship chambers designed to lead us to GOD, there is

Single Mothers and Sons

a trinity of chambers that ushered us away from HIM in heaven, into the earth. Those three chambers are symbolic of the three chambers of the woman's reproductive organ.

The three chambers of a woman's reproductive organ are: the womb, the cervix and the vagina. The passageway to GOD is the same as the passageway from GOD, only it's reversed. The womb represents the Holy of Holies or the temple. The cervix represents the inner court or the synagogue. And the vagina represents the outer court or the tabernacle. A child starts in heaven with GOD, is placed in the womb, and passes through the cervix and out of the vagina. Man enters the outer court of the tabernacle, passes through the inner court and goes into the Holy of Holies to get to GOD.

Neither men nor women seem to understand the power that GOD has placed in them that is located between their waist and middle thigh. The man has the power to deliver the seed of blood or life into the womb. This is the reason the blood type of the child is the same as the father not the mother. The woman has the power to deliver life out of the womb. The three elements or trinity of a man's reproductive system represents the triune GOD Head or the initiator of life. The three elements or trinity of the woman's reproductive system represents the temple of GOD wherein we go to be born again or receive new life. The hood over the entrance to a woman's reproductive system or the labia is a representation of the door of the temple that was covered with a doubled over curtain made of goat's skins.

"And you shall make curtains of goats' hair to be a covering upon the tabernacle... and shall double the

Single Mothers and Sons

sixth curtain in the forefront of the tabernacle (Exodus 26:7-9)."

When a man enters a virgin through intercourse, his action is symbolic of a priest going behind the veil of the temple to make a covenant sacrifice. The husband goes in behind the veil of his wife's reproductive system, blood is shed and a covenant between the man and woman is cut. This shedding of blood enters the couple into a blood covenant with GOD as well. GOD hates divorce because it breaks that commitment to and blood covenant with HIM. The consummation of the marriage covenant, as the man enters the woman, is also symbolic of a priest entering into the tabernacle to atone for the sins of other men. The other men's sins that a husband must atone for or actually be cleansed of, is his father's, his father's father, and for every man that had sex with his wife before him. This is critical!

If a man has been before GOD and purged himself of the iniquities of his father's sins before he enters the woman, he can produce a godly child. What GOD wants more than anything else from the union of a man and a woman are godly children. However, in order to obtain a godly seed, the man must first be cleansed of all unrighteousness and have a good relationship with GOD before he enters into or goes behind the veil of a woman's reproductive organ, if he expects to produce godly children. If he is not cleansed of his iniquities, the man will defile both his wife and his children.

"Know you not that you are the temple of GOD and that the Spirit of GOD dwells in you? If any man defile the temple of GOD, him shall GOD destroy, for the temple of GOD is holy, which temple you are (1 Corinthians 3:16-17)."

Single Mothers and Sons

Our bodies were prepared by GOD from the foundation of the world to be HIS temple and a habitation for the Holy Spirit. It matters greatly to GOD what we do with this temple. This is why Every time a man enters a woman it is symbolic of Jesus entering into a holy temple to receive the atonement of men's sins. New life is produced after atonement. A woman has to experience pain, shed blood and take on water 12 times a year to cleans her temple of sin and keep it perfect in the sight of GOD. The number 12 in the Bible is the number of eternal perfection. A woman's body is a symbolic representation of the body of Christ. Jesus' suffering on the cross is symbolic of the suffering a woman has to endure each month as a result of Eve's sin. The pain she has to experience giving birth is symbolic of the pain Jesus endured on the cross in order to give birth to the church. The water and blood that was shed from His side is emblematic of the water and blood a woman sheds as she gives birth and menstruates. There is a lot more that I can share about this but I will save it for a grown men's conference. Some of what I shared already may be too much for boys to understand.

Chapter 11
How to Find a Virtuous Woman

"The world and all things in it are valuable but the most valuable thing in the world is a virtuous woman."
~ **Muhammad**

A venerably wise person once asked the question "Who can find a virtuous woman because her price is far above rubies." The implication to the question is that a virtuous woman is hard to find because she is rare and that rarity gives her an expensive quality not found in most women. The word virtuous means one who possesses strength, power, and moral excellence, which lead to purpose, provision, protection, and peace. A virtuous woman is hard to find but a faithful man must do all that he can and spend all he has to find her. A virtuous woman is essential to the success of a faithful man. Every superman needs a super woman and every man who wants to be King needs a Coretta Scott.

You will Know Her when You See Her
The virtuous woman, like the faithful man, has characteristics and qualities that identify her as such. Above all of her other qualities a virtuous woman is trustworthy. The heart of her husband safely trusts in her so much that he will have no need to seduce other women. A virtuous woman will do good, not evil, to her husband all the days of her life. Whatever she wants in terms of clothing, jewelry, etc, she will work to get them on her own and may not necessarily depend on him to provide them. At the same time, a virtuous woman is a good home maker. When money is tight,

for example, she can make a good meal out of seemingly nothing. She rises very early each morning to prepare meals for her family and shares with the neighbors who are needy.

A virtuous woman understands how to utilize her creative ability to earn the money to purchase a home and decorate it. She won't just give herself to any man to because she knows how to protect her virtue. She also exercises to take care of her body and keep herself healthy. A virtuous woman does not have low self-esteem, understands her personal value, and will retain her virtue in the light as well as the dark.

The virtuous woman is a star. The reason her is compared to the price of a ruby is because a Star Ruby is a rare precious stone. When you look at it through a jeweler's lens you will be able to clearly see that it has six perfect points of light. However, the six points of light that you see are only the end. There are also six perfect points at the beginning. Six plus six is twelve or the Bible number of "eternal perfection". A virtuous woman's beginning is perfect as well as her end just like the points of light in a Star Ruby. This is why her light shines brightly in the light as well as the dark. She retains her virtue during the day and she keeps her virtue at night.

The other character quality that makes a virtuous woman easier to identify is she works hard, extends herself to help the poor, and is never worried about her children being without provision. The clothing she wears is always elegant not revealing and the material and colors resemble that which a queen would wear. As a result of the way the virtuous woman carries herself, her husband is known and respected throughout in their city. Simply because he chose her to be his wife he is counted and consulted as a wise man among the city leaders.

The average woman of virtue is enterprising and knows how to bring wealth to her household. She keeps herself busy with the business affairs of her husband, in charitable causes, and the care of her home. Her words are full of wisdom, grace, and compassion. Therefore, her children call her blessed and her husband also praises her. Many women have learned to act virtuous and get treated as such but a true woman of virtue out shines them all.

The Value of Virtue

The favor that some women receive because of their external beauty can make a woman appear to be virtuous when she actually is not. The way a man can test a woman of true virtue is to give her something to do. The work of her hands will reveal if she has the favor of GOD. The virtuous woman possesses strength, power, and moral excellence. Therefore, a true woman of virtue has the anointing to make something out of what appears to be nothing and riches, honor, and glory always come as the reward for her work.

Every woman should strive to be a woman of virtue. Every woman should receive the same honor and respect. One thing that women must understand about men is that every man wants a virtuous woman whether he deserves her or knows how to care for her or not. The unfaithful man who is determined to capture a virtuous woman will sleep with a bunch of women who will allow him to until he finds the one with true virtue. Women who pretend to be virtuous will get used by an unfaithful man until he finds the true woman of virtue. Then they will just get left.

Single Mothers and Sons

The virtuous woman sees herself as having value so she retains her virtue. She won't let anybody touch her or handle her who is not her husband. Retaining her virtue will make the men that she allows in her life see her as special. Men never put value on anything they have no knowledge of or can just use for sex. Rather than having sex virtuous women lead the men they are interested in into intimate conversation. Virtuous women want to talk to a man to discover what is in his mind. Women who have sex with a man too quickly never get to intimacy. Once she has sex with him, he will feel like he doesn't have to talk anymore until he wants more sex. A man has to be made to recognize that a woman has value before they have sex. If he really recognizes her value, he will treat her like she is special and not lead her into sex until they are married. He will be sure to capture the heart of her mind before another man asks for her hand.

Like any other hot commodity on the market a woman's value has nothing to do with what it cost to create her. Her value has to do with what a man is willing to sacrifice to marry her. It may have cost only $10 in canvass and paint to create the Mona Lisa but she is worth 700 million because a man is willing to sacrifice millions to get her. The water and dirt required to assemble a woman's body may only cost $7. However, her price becomes far above rubies when that is the price the faithful man who recognizes her value is willing to pay. Price is never an issue when a quality product is being presented. Jesus was willing to sacrifice His whole life to redeem his wife. When a man finds a virtuous woman he won't get her unless he is willing to sacrifice all of his possessions and part of his life to make her a part of his.

Single Mothers and Sons

A man who recognizes that a woman is valuable will understand that she is also value able. That is, she has the inherent gift, talent or ability to add to or increase his value. Once he has appraised her value, if he is a really sharp businessman, he will immediately move to appreciate it. To appreciate means to increase in value. In other words, he will want to show her that in return for adding value to him, he will add value to her. He will try to do something for her or offer her a proposal which leads her to see that partnering with him will be beneficial to her as well.

The faithful man will recognize a virtuous woman immediately. He already understands that a real king is recognized by his crown. GOD created the woman to be like the crown of a king. A faithful man understands this and will be willing to place her in a prominent position in his life to cover and protect his head. GOD made the woman to dress and adorn the man like a crown; to make him feel better and look stronger. A crown is supposed to be positioned to protect the man's head and should be adorned with his finest jewels. A woman should not have anything to do with a man, then, who is not willing to place her in a prominent position in his life and who is not willing to adorn her with his finest jewels.

The thing that makes a king different from an ordinary man is his crown. The thing that makes a great man different from an ordinary man is a virtuous woman. A good crown protects a man's head and a good woman protects her man. She brings honor to him by exemplifying the crowning qualities of womanhood which are: a devotional spirit, modesty, liberality, wisdom and virtue.

Single Mothers and Sons

They say that behind every great man is a good woman. I say behind every man who thinks he's great is a woman rolling her eyes. But seriously, when you examine the lives of the great men of history you will see that what they were able to accomplish is largely attributable to the woman in their lives. No ordinary man could ever become great without the help of a good woman. GOD created virtuous women for the purpose of helping good men become great.

Barack Obama shared an interesting story that illustrates this point. He said that he and Michelle were stopped at a gas station just after he announced that we was going to run for President and he noticed the gas station attendant was her old boy friend. He said he told Michelle who the guy was and she got out of the car to speak to him. It was then that he noticed that not only was the old boy friend working in a gas station, he was also looking kind of worn and dusty. So he stuck out his chest and started feeling good about himself.

After the man pumped the gas and walked away he told Michelle: "See, if you had married him, you wouldn't be married to the man running for President now." He said she lovingly straightened his tie and said, "If I were married to him, **he** would be running for President now." You see, a good woman can help her man achieve great things. Also, any great man will tell you that you cannot achieve greatness without having experienced humility. A virtuous woman has a lovely way of keeping a great man humble.

Note: I have a habit of telling on myself whenever I tell a lie. I needed to provide an example so I just made that story up... but it could have happened!

Single Mothers and Sons

The Truth about Submission

Many good men have ruined and missed the opportunity to access the power of virtuous women because they tried to follow the false religious doctrine of submission. The manufacturer of the universe gave us a book with the operating instructions for our lives. Misinterpretation of these operating instructions as a result of the devil's desire to oppress women has caused a deep rift in male/female relationships.

There is a Bible paragraph that reads "Wives submit yourselves unto your own husbands as unto the Lord (Ephesians 5:22)." This instruction was taken out of context and used to try to subordinate women to men. However, just before that paragraph a balancing instruction was given that is wholly ignored: "Submitting yourselves **one to another** in the fear of GOD (Ephesians 5:21)." Reading these instructions together shows us GOD's original intent: both the man and woman are to submit to each other, not just her to him. This is critical for men to understand because he actually needs a virtuous wife in order to be successful in life more than she needs him.

GOD put the man and woman together to add strength and power to one another. The wife was given as provision (pro = for; vision) to help her husband complete or fulfill the vision or mission that GOD established for his life and their family. The Bible describes the wife as a help **meet** (a suitable, proper or fit helper) or someone who was created to help another complete their mission. A man must have a wife with gifts, talent, and abilities that complement his to help him in complete his mission. A wife, in effect, carries the equipment that a man needs to achieve success. A man can become rich with a mate but he will be

Single Mothers and Sons

wealthy when his wife is meet. The family is the primary organization designed by GOD for wealth generation. A couple who is **meet** for each other are more likely to achieve victory and become wealthy!

It is very important, then, for a man who seeks wealth to understand that the Bible instructs men to submit to their wives. Every man who wants to be King needs a powerful Queen. He must make sure that she is free to move and use her power on his behalf however she sees fit. He has to learn to just let her do her thing because he won't understand what she is doing or why until after he sees the results. Then he will still be scratching his head trying to figure out how she did what she got done. It didn't make sense that Moses' mother would float him down a river filled with alligators but ended up in the King's palace and became a Prince (Exodus 2:3-5). So, a man must submit to his wife if he wants her to submit to him and have the value in her virtue work for him. Being submitted to one another is critical for a marital union to work as well as create wealth. He submits to her, she submits to him; she has his back, he has her back; he supports her, she supports him. They work together to strengthen and empower each other.

When a couple is in complete submission, the two of them are submitted to each other in a way that neither of them is superior to the other. President and Mrs. Obama is the perfect example of a couple in that is submitted to one another. He is in submission to her and she is in submission to him; he supports her and she supports him and that's why he's president. If you find a virtuous woman, my brother, you might not become President of the United States but she can at least help you to be president of something.

Chapter 12
The Question of a Man's Covering

"A wonderful [or astonishing] and horrible thing is committed in the land; the prophets prophesy falsely, and the priests bear rule by their means; and my people love to have it so: and what will you do in the end thereof (Jeremiah 5:30-31)."

GOD is saying that the people are twisted so far away from the truth of HIS word that it would be funny if it wasn't so horrible. The people want to believe so much that they are following an anointed man or woman of GOD that they can't see the truth. The preachers are constantly breathing out false prophesy, ruling GOD's people by their own means, and the word of GOD doesn't enter their consideration. The thing that breaks GOD's heart is the people love to have it that way. So GOD sends someone to straighten things out by calling the people and their leaders to repentance. But, they become even more rebellious seeking to kill GOD's message by destroying or discrediting the messenger.

So, GOD is saying to you now: What are you going to do after I am through protecting you? HE is saying, I see you like worshipping a preacher and having him lead you instead of ME. I see you like having a man "cover" you instead of ME. Well, if it's a preacher that you want, a preacher is what you'll get. But, he is going to be a man, not my true messenger, who is just as corrupt as you are!

Give us a King!
Many preachers or teachers have quoted the clause of scripture from **Joshua 24:15** which says "...as for me

and my house, we will serve the Lord". However, very few teach the reason why Joshua made that statement and why he was trying to lead the people into making a commitment to serve GOD. The reason Joshua did this is because GOD was **not** going to appoint another leader **over** the people anymore. GOD did **not** have Joshua pass the mantle of leadership to another man, as Moses did with him. The reason GOD did this is because HE was ending the centralized governance of the nation of Israel.

The nation was about to be split up across the entire region of the Promised Land so there would be no need for centralized governance. GOD had now set it up for each individual man to take control of a separate portion of the land for his inheritance which would be under his own governance. Each man would have the power or grace of GOD to fight his own battles, govern his own territory, and lead his own family. Each man would in effect become a king so that Jesus could come back to earth as the King of kings. GOD was preparing every husband and father leading and caring for a family among the children of Israel to be able to speak directly with HIM. They were being prepared to become the priest of their own homes. Being able to hear the voice of GOD themselves, they could go before GOD to seek guidance and direction on behalf of their families on their own. GOD was to beginning the process of fulfilling the gospel and leading HIS people back to the garden relationship that HE had with Adam before the fall. However, because the men of Israel were still weak and dependent they didn't want the responsibility of being empowered by GOD to operate on their own. They wanted another man to help or lead them.

Single Mothers and Sons

"Now after the death of Joshua it came to pass, that the children of Israel asked the Lord, saying, who shall go up for us against the Canaanites, first, to fight against them? And the Lord said, Judah shall go up: behold I have delivered the land into his hand. And Judah said unto Simeon his brother, come up with me into my lot, that **we** may fight against the Canaanites: and I likewise will go with you into your lot. So Simeon went with him (Judges 1:1-3)."

Here we see proof of the children of Israel going directly to GOD after the death of Joshua to receive guidance and direction on their own. Notice, GOD is speaking to them directly and giving them prophetic knowledge as HE did with Moses and Joshua. But we also need to take note the children of Israel did not do exactly as GOD said. HE said Judah should go up and fight <u>first</u> because HE had already delivered the land into **his** hand. However, Judah sought Simeon, another man, to go up with him. Practically every time the Bible refers to the nation of Israel as "the children" it is because they are either in rebellion or acting as immature children would. GOD told Judah the land was his, all he had to do is go in faith and take it. Instead, he operated in fear by asking someone else to go with him to <u>cover</u> him. The power of GOD's covering is all Judah needed but he thought he needed the covering of another man instead.

Knowing Judah was immature, GOD let that one pass. However, GOD's patience with the children of Israel's immaturity and failure to follow instructions finally runs out. After neither Benjamin, Manasseh, Ephraim, Zebulun, Asher, Naptali nor Dan did as they were supposed to do, GOD was tired of talking to them so HE sent an angel to speak against them.

Single Mothers and Sons

"And an angel of the Lord came up from Gilgal to Bochim, and said, I made you to go up out of Egypt, and have brought you unto the land which I swore unto your fathers; and I said, I will never break my covenant with you. And you shall make no league with the inhabitants of this land; you shall throw down their altars: but you have **not** obeyed my voice: why have you done this (Judges 2:1-2)?"

The people cried and lamented but by this time a whole generation of the children of Israel had stopped following The True and Living GOD, once again, to worship idol gods. So, GOD allowed their enemies to oppress them until they became greatly distressed. Being the merciful Father HE is, GOD could not stand to hear their constant suffering so HE sent judges to deliver them from their oppressors. These judges of GOD protected the people, heard from GOD on their behalf and fought their battles. Yet, the children of Israel would always return to the protection or covering of their idol gods whenever one of the judges died. Instead of being strong men and warriors for GOD, the adult males of Israel always looked for another man to cover them.

"Then all the elders of Israel gathered themselves together, and came to Samuel unto Ramah, and said unto him, behold, you are old, and your sons walk not in your ways: now make us a king to judge us like all the nations. But the thing displeased Samuel, when they said give us a king to judge us. And Samuel prayed unto the LORD. And the LORD said unto Samuel, hearken unto the voice of the people in all that they say unto you: for they have **not** rejected you, **but they have rejected ME**, that I should not reign over them (1 Samuel 8:4-7)."

Single Mothers and Sons

Here we find the men of Israel confronting the prophet of GOD to appoint a Judge to be their king. GOD appointed a Prophet over the children of Israel and here they were rejecting GOD's appointment. So GOD directs Samuel to tell the people the type of leader they were going to get. You see, when we reject the leadership GOD wanted us to have, we get exactly what we deserve, in that we get a leader who is just like we are. When you think about it every U.S. President ever elected either revealed what is in the heart of American men or he exposed it.

GOD told Samuel to tell the people: If you really want a king, since you are corrupt, you are going to get a corrupt king. He is going to take your sons, daughters, the first fruits of your fields, vineyards, and olive yards. He will take a tenth of your money and take your men, maidservants, and asses to do his work or support his vision, and so on. Samuel delivered the warning from GOD but they said: Naw! Give us a king that we may be like all other nations, so our king may judge us, go out before us, and fight our battles. In Joshua 24:21 they were pledging **"Nay; but we will serve the Lord"** while GOD was trying to wean them off of man's leadership. But again we see, the man sized boys of Israel backslide into irresponsibility and fear by choosing to have a man in authority over them instead of GOD HIMSELF.

The all seeing, all knowing, all powerful, ever present GOD wanted to lead and guide HIS people, but they chose to have a man who cannot protect them unless GOD allows him to. GOD wanted each man to be the king and priest of his home and have the right to come before GOD himself. If the men of GOD today did not continue to carry on the customs of the children of

Single Mothers and Sons

Israel and allowed GOD to be their covering, perhaps we would actually have the peace and prosperity that the charismatic movement leads us to seek. If we allow GOD and Jesus to be our covering, they will lead us to where they want us to be and we will receive exactly what they promised we would have. We won't need to engage in all the spiritual hocus-pocus of the charismatic movement if Jesus, instead of a preacher, was **truly** the head of our lives. We were all sent into the earth to achieve a purpose or to execute a specific mission. We can never know what that purpose is or get the job done unless we each go before GOD, ask HIM to reveal it to us, and allow **HIM** to guide us through it. The veil of the temple has been removed therefore a preacher cannot do this for you.

Charisma vs. the Anointing

"Wherefore the law was our schoolmaster to bring us unto Christ, that we might be justified by faith. But after that faith is come, we are no longer under a schoolmaster; for you are **all** the children of GOD by faith in Christ Jesus (Galatians 3:24-26)."

As children of GOD every person has the authority to go before GOD on behalf of their selves and their family any time they are ready. However, men would rather have another man go to GOD for them. The reason men of GOD today continue to be as weak and powerless as the men of Israel was is their preachers constantly lead them to be as the men of Israel were. GOD wants men to come to HIM on their own to receive power, protection, and provision but preachers teach that having direct access to GOD is not good enough. They need a preacher, a "mand" of god, to

Single Mothers and Sons

cover them just like they were spiritually weak little boys.

The way preachers convince men that their teaching is legitimate is by continually teaching from the Old Testament. That testament is called "old" for a reason. GOD gave it to us so that we can see all the mistakes the men of Israel constantly made so that we won't make the same mistakes. The Old Testament was intended to be used as a schoolmaster to lead us to come to Christ. Then, after He came and ushered in the New Testament will of GOD we were supposed to put the Old Testament aside. It is supposed to be used as a historical reference so that men of future generations will learn by wisdom rather than through experience. But preachers keep leading the men of GOD to believe that experience is the best teacher. Therefore, we condemn ourselves to experience the same problems and issues of the men of Israel because we keep doing what they did and we keep getting the same results.

The idea that a man needs the covering of another man is false Old Testament based teaching that came out of the charismatic movement. A lie always travels faster than truth so most preachers are now teaching that a man is in rebellion if he is not covered by a preacher. However, we are going to see from the word of GOD that the men and women who did the **greatest** work for GOD did **not** have a "covering" and was **not** subject to the authority of anyone but GOD. The problem with man is he has a tendency to follow that which is popular especially when it is not ordained by GOD or consistent with the word or will of GOD. When those in authority begin to follow a certain course, even when it is off course, the majority of people will convince themselves that GOD is doing a new thing

Single Mothers and Sons

and blindly follow. This is precisely the reason Jesus calls them sheep. It is also why He said let the blind lead the blind so that they can both fall in a ditch. But I have to at least try to make you see. I always hold out the hope that if my people knew better they would do better. However, since the average person doesn't really read or study the word they don't know better. Therefore, they blindly follow their preachers to certain destruction for a lack of knowledge.

The problem with following men the way we do today is our actions are setting our children up to follow the anti-Christ tomorrow. The way we bow down and give deference to men with mega ministries today will lead our children to bow down to the anti-Christ who will have a global ministry in the future. He will come as a man and a super mega preacher. He will perform what appear to be great miracles and will proclaim that he is god. Men from around the world will flock to his conferences and will want to be seen with and known of him. Giving great deference to man, making them idols gods in the way we do today, will lead our children to bow down to the image of the beast and the adversary of Jesus tomorrow. They will believe that the anti-Christ is the second coming of Jesus because preachers will proclaim that he is the Christ.

In the book of Daniel we find a prophet of GOD who refused to bow down before the king or the image of an idol god the king set up. Daniel was subsequently thrown into the lion's den to be eaten up. **But GOD**, shut up the mouths of the lions and they refused to eat him. They didn't have a problem eating the preachers that were thrown in after him though. There were three Hebrew boys who lived in the king's palace with Daniel. As a result of observing Daniel's principled

Single Mothers and Sons

obedience to the will of GOD, the boys developed the staunch determination to follow the will of GOD also, even when Daniel was no where around. So, they had to confront the dilemma of bowing before the king and his idol god as well or be thrown into a fiery furnace. Instead of bowing down, the boys stood up before the king and proclaimed that they would not bow down. Consequently, they were tossed into the flames. **But GOD**, removed the power of the fire and because the boys didn't bow, they didn't burn! Men of GOD have to be an example for our children as Daniel was for the Hebrew boys. If we allow men to lead us off course today, our children will be led astray tomorrow.

"And then if any man shall say to you, lo, here is Christ or lo He is there; believe him not: for false Christs and false prophets shall rise and shall show signs and wonders to seduce, if it were possible, even the elect (Mark 13:21-22)."

Whenever preachers are leading the people off course, GOD will invariably raise up a strong voice to call the leaders back into righteousness. This individual is an ambassador from GOD who is sent into a hostile environment to speak truth to power, call leadership to repentance, and call the people back into the order of HIS will. I was able to gather 74 examples from the Bible of men and women whom GOD sent to do this. None, not one, of these Judges of Israel, Prophets of GOD, or Ministers of GOD submitted themselves to the authority or covering of **any** man. They received instruction from GOD and they executed those instructions. Men were out of order so it would have been counterproductive for them to submit themselves to other men. They were submitted to the power and authority of GOD only. They had a righteous assignment and they breathed righteous indignation from the mouth and the mind of GOD through their mouths. The people would repent, although only for short periods of time, due to the courage of these men and women to speak truth to power and power conceded.

"Now HE which established us with you in Christ, and has anointed us, is GOD (2 Corinthians 1:21)."

One of the reasons Jesus died on the cross is so that we could have access to the power of GOD, by the Holy Spirit. GOD intended for each of us to have access to the anointing, not just preachers. But since the corrupt leaders have gained more power than righteous leaders after Jesus was resurrected, GOD's people have not had access to HIS anointing. With the advent of the charismatic movement, the truth that we are supposed to have access to the anointing has been revived. However, because most preachers who subscribe to the **false** teachings of that movement are out of order, GOD's men still do not have access to GOD's power.

Wherever there is a proclamation of truth you will always find a demonstration of power. We know then that most preachers are not proclaiming truth because we see no demonstration of power. In an effort to demonstrate (demon-strate) they have power many charismatic preachers are faking it. They "lay hands" on people's heads and **push** them to the ground to give the **false** impression that the power of GOD came through them and caused the person to be "slain" in the spirit. Slain in the spirit is a phrase that you won't find in the Bible. But since many of these preachers don't study the Bible they don't even know that people who come in contact with the power of GOD who are

HIS friends fall forward in HIS presence. Those who are GOD's enemies fall backward.

"But they hearkened not, nor inclined their ear, but walked in the counsels and in the imagination of their evil heart and went backward and not forward (Jeremiah 7:24)."

"Yet heard I the voice of HIS words: and when I heard the voice of HIS words, then was I in a deep sleep on my face, and my face toward the ground (Daniel 10:9)."

"They answered Him, Jesus of Nazareth. Jesus said unto them, I am He... As soon then as He had said unto them, I am He, they went backward, and fell to the ground (John 18:5-6)."

The people see the preacher's ability to draw crowds, stir their emotions, and manipulate the word so they believe that what they see is the power of GOD in operation or the anointing. What they are actually seeing is charisma. The anointing is the power given by GOD to equip him to do a job on behalf of the believer, not to make preacher appear special. When preachers employ their fake **demon** stration of power it only inures to their benefit. The people get emotional hype but they walk away empty of word, empty of spirit, and empty of pocket.

The Greek word for the English word anointing is "charisma". In a Greek man's mind, charisma is the power of GOD. However, in America we understand charisma to be the personal magic of a leader to arouse special loyalty or enthusiasm for himself. Charisma is the special magnetic charm or personal appeal that one has. The church really doesn't know the difference between charisma and anointing so they are confused. The devil is the author of confusion. You see, the devil

Single Mothers and Sons

will tell you exactly what he is doing to you and then dare you to do something about it. He calls his movement charismatic but lead you to believe that it is anointed. So, what GOD's people see operating in the charismatic preacher is charisma, not the anointing. The charismatic preacher uses his ability to arouse special loyalty to himself to seduce people into submitting to his will. This is why they crafted the guile of a spiritual "covering"; to seduce GOD's men into giving up their authority and steal their inheritance. It is a trick of the devil to control true men of GOD and to seduce their preachers to be as he is and to do his work for him. This is why we see preachers of smaller churches following charismatic preachers in droves and are leading their people to follow them as well.

"Let no man beguile you of your reward in a voluntary humility... (Colossians 2:18)"

The charismatic preacher appeals to the vanity of the smaller preacher to have a "big" world-wide ministry or to be as well known he is. These smaller preachers become blinded by the glamour and glitter of the charismatic preacher's ministry. They are seduced into becoming star gazers or a type of spiritual groupie. So they follow these men from place to place and city to city like they are rock stars. The charismatic preachers even act like rock stars, they have security guards, and you need a backstage pass to see them. Smaller preachers get caught up in the amusement park atmosphere of charismatic conferences, where they get conned into deferring to the mega minister, and end up losing their ability to think and see clearly.

Many of the charismatic ministries are actually a demonstration of the power of satan! You see, the devil owns churches in every denomination and he has preachers like GOD has because he wants to be GOD. However, the churches he creates and the preachers he ordains are corrupt. They look good on the outside, but they are rotten on the inside. The people and smaller church preachers look at the "big" ministries of satan and believe they are seeing a great move of GOD. We get sucked into following the doctrines of these ministries even though we know subconsciously that something is wrong. But we ignore what our spirit is telling us because our emotions convince us that GOD is getting the glory. The question is which god? The devil is a god to his followers. The difference between the Most High GOD's followers and satan's is that his people rarely uses the name of Jesus. They like to say "Christ". The name "Jesus" is poison on their tongue and a thorn to their flesh so they rarely use it.

Too many of the mega ministries are not the result of a great move of GOD as we are led to believe. They are the result of men having the knowledge or skill to build a big business. That is, they didn't build a ministry under the power of GOD. They built a business under their own power in the same manner as men built fortune 500 corporate conglomerates under their own power. The reason I know this well is because I made the same mistake. I promoted a concert that was hugely successful. As I was standing at the side of the stage I prayed and thanked GOD for the success. HE answered and said: "I didn't do that you did!" People don't know that fortune 500 corporations are actually built and are sustained on the principles of GOD. They tithe and give offerings, gifts, and alms, for example, through their charitable foundations. The principles of GOD will work if you work them whether you are good,

Single Mothers and Sons

bad, or indifferent. This is why they can appear to be good on the surface, yet are corrupt below the surface.

I didn't know then that the devil builds and sustains his churches on the principles of GOD as well. Hence the reason they appear to be of GOD. The devil does this because he wants to trick us into serving him instead of GOD. We must ever be mindful that the devil has transformed himself and his ministers into angels of light. When his son, the anti-Christ, manifests himself, he will claim to be the son of GOD. So, if satan pretends to be GOD and his son will pretend to be Jesus, don't be amazed that he has preachers who pretend to be ministers of GOD.

Satan is in Control

"Behold, I [Jesus] stand at the door, and knock: if any man hear my voice, and open the door, I will come in to him, and will sup with him, and he with me (Revelation 3:20)."

Listen, we have deluded ourselves into believing that GOD has been in charge of the church over the last 2000 years, when the devil has actually been in charge of it. It is not that GOD didn't want to be in charge, we didn't allow HIM to. The devil's disciples, leaders of the church, killed all of the apostles, prophets, and ministers of GOD and scattered the people. Instead of the people fighting against the devil's disciples and defending GOD's right to rule the church, they ran and hid themselves from the face of death. So the devil's disciples were able to take control over the church. Jesus came to give us control, but we didn't take it then and we still have not taken it even unto this very day.

Evidence that satan was in control of the church before Jesus came is revealed in the story where he tried to tempt Jesus to bow down and worship him in Matthew 4. The devil took Jesus on top of the highest pinnacle of the church and told him He could have all the kingdoms of the world, if He would bow to him. It is obvious that satan was in charge of the world at the time or Jesus would have rebuked him for offering something he didn't own. Most people can see the fact that satan was in control of the kingdoms of the earth, but they reject the fact that he had to have been in charge of the church too. Yet, we see him stand on top (in authority) of the church of GOD to seduce Jesus into worshipping him. This joker takes the Son of GOD into the city of GOD, stands Him on top of the church of GOD, and tries to get Him to defy the Most High GOD. The fact that he stood on top of the church without fear in the face of the Son of GOD is scriptural evidence that satan is in control of the church.

The leaders of the church were his disciples. This is one of the reasons why Jesus had to come in the first place. They controlled the church and he controlled them. Therefore, satan controlled the church which is why there was strong opposition to Jesus by church leaders. The fact that they were sons of satan is the reason they lied, schemed, and plotted to kill Jesus. Jesus gave GOD's people a chance to take control of the church but they never took it so satan is still in control today. Now, through the charismatic movement satan is controlling not just his disciples but also all the people who truly have a heart for GOD. He has snared everybody including preachers who started independent churches to give GOD control. They are now being taken captive through the seduction of their desire to be mega ministry stars.

Single Mothers and Sons

Satan is developing new disciples via the charismatic movement. Too many people, today, are claiming to have a call to preach because they see the big charismatic preacher as a star and they want to be a star too. There is one church here that has as many as 60 ministers in training at any given time. You have got to know that there is something wrong when you have 60 people in one church that claim to have a call to preach. This is the result of people star gazing. Most of these star gazers are puny little people with puny little lives who are nobody at home and nobody at work who want to be somebody. They see the church as an opportunity to be somebody only they don't want to pay the cost to be the boss so they claim to have a calling.

The service in a charismatic church is conducted in a carnival like atmosphere. There is a lot of jumping, shouting, and merrymaking. The object is to **amuse** people in the pew to the point where they lose their ability to think clearly in an effort to draw out of them the largest offering. This is why preachers get upset if you don't show up until after the worship portion of the service and when you sit looking sober while he is trying to get you to jump and shout. If the object was to teach the word of GOD, preachers would follow the example of a secular school teacher. She does not let anyone jump and shout when she is trying to teach because she knows that no one will learn anything in that atmosphere. They may be entertained but they won't learn anything.

The star gazer gets hooked in the carnival atmosphere because he doesn't realize that he is being amused and not taught. So he watches the charismatic preacher like he or she is a rock star. Then, he becomes amused into believing he can be a star too. Next, he begins to scheme, plan, and maneuver to get to preach. Now GOD's people will become subjects to another corrupt preacher. Why does he do this when he knows it is ungodly? He has been amused therefore he has lost his mind. His mind has been blinded from the light of the truth. Now he can only see the light of the preacher and not the glory of GOD.

"And no marvel; for Satan himself is transformed into an angel of light (2 Corinthians 11:14)."

Everybody knows the games on the midway of an amusement park are rigged, but we play them anyway. Have you ever thought about why we do that? It is as a result of being amused. The etymology of the word "amusement" reveals its true meaning: "a" means to take away, "muse" means the mind, and "ment" means the act or process. Therefore, amusement actually means "the act or process of making one lose their mind." We become amused, lose our minds, so consequently we spend lots more money than we intended to spend. People feel "led" to give more money than they intended in church because they became amused. The small church preachers have had their ability to think clearly taken away. So it becomes easy to trick them into believing their star will shine in GOD's time, if they just wait on the "lawd". The truth is, if they would just truly serve GOD they would receive the anointing they need and would not have to be subject to delayed gratification. When their hearts are right and their motives are pure GOD will exalt them in "do" time; when it is time for them to "do" what HE called them to do.

Single Mothers and Sons
Man Covering Man is an Affront to GOD

"Jesus, when he had cried again with a loud voice, yielded up the ghost. And behold, the veil of the temple was rent in twain from the **top** to the bottom: and the earth did quake, and the rocks rent (Matthew 27:50-51)."

As Jesus died on the cross the veil of the temple was rent in two. It was torn from **top** to bottom and <u>not</u> from bottom to top while it was still hanging so the world would know it was **GOD** who did this and not man. Man would have torn it from bottom to top. Prior to this only the High Priest could go behind the veil of the temple. Tearing the veil was a signal to us from GOD that Jesus is now our High Priest. We no longer needed a man to go behind the veil or before the throne of GOD for us. This meant that each and every man is now free to approach the throne of GOD, in the name of Jesus, on our own behalf. We don't need another man to go before us to talk to GOD for us and our families. We only need Jesus to know us so that He can introduce us to GOD and usher us into HIS throne room.

The problem with the "covering" teaching of the charismatic movement is man is saying that what Jesus did wasn't good enough. He just died for our sins so that we can be forgiven if we give another offering after we sin. These preachers are trying to convince us that GOD didn't know what HE was doing when HE tore the veil in two. They are teaching, by saying man still needs a covering of another man between him and GOD, that GOD was wrong. They are, in effect, trying to sew the veil back up! Charismatic influenced preachers are trying to keep the average man out of the Holy Of Holies by making us believe that **they** are the only ones entitled to enter in. The power of GOD rests in their hands alone because they are the only anointed men of GOD. We are still sinners and lowly dirty worms. We are filthy rags so we can't go before GOD. They alone are the righteousness of GOD. We have made these preachers our high priests instead of Jesus. They are now standing between us and GOD and GOD is not amused!

You might object to what I am saying but you know it is true. Why else would Jesus teach us to pray to GOD for ourselves, yet the charismatic preacher encourage us to send our prayer request to him? Don't pray for yourself, call me on my prayer line and we'll pray for you! Just have your credit card handy when you do. Don't pray for yourself and your family on your own. Just send your prayer request to me! Tuck your best "love" gift in the envelope and send it to us. We will lay hands on the letter and pray to GOD for you!

We have to realize that, when we are out of the will of GOD, the leadership that we get is going to be a reflection of the condition of our hearts. We have been conditioned to be lustful and greedy for money and things because we have preachers who are greedy and lustful for money and things. Preachers are taking our sons, daughters, and wives and leading them to help manifest their vision for their ministry rather than helping us manifest our vision for our family. Men have a hard time fulfilling the vision that GOD has given them for their family because their wives want to help the preacher with his vision more than their own husband's. The husband says we need to do this and the wife will say: "Pastor didn't say that!" and families are breaking up as a result. The preachers are taking a tenth of the income we need to lead our families to financial freedom and the provision that we need to bring our vision into fruition.

The charismatic movement or charis/manic (showing wild or deranged excitement) movement is making class B dependants out of the people of GOD. Its preachers are keeping adults, who need to grow up in GOD, spiritual children. Hence, the people who "sit under" these preachers love the milk of the word and cannot tolerate strong meat. Sitting "under" a man is the position of a boy **not** a man. Adult males are locked in spiritual childhood so they won't have a desire to be a man, take authority, ergo they are continually fed milk and not strong meat. Babies might chew on meat a little, but they will eventually spit it out. The charismatic preacher does not have any strong meat to give them anyway so he leads the people to desire only the milk of the word. He keeps them hyped up on what I call gossip, feel good, and you know how "they" do messages. Those messages are usually accompanied by one verse of scripture which may or may not have anything to do with what is being taught. The object is to give the illusion that the message has some scriptural authority. This would be funny if it wasn't an evil affront to GOD.

The blood that Jesus shed on the cross is the only covering that men need in addition to the power and authority of GOD covering our lives. Jesus was a type of Passover lamb. He was sacrificed for us so that any hurt, harm, or danger would pass over us as long as we remain under His blood. My question to those who believe that each man needs to have a "covering" of another man is: Why isn't the blood of Jesus enough to provide the protection we seek? Why isn't having direct access to GOD to receive guidance and direction for

Single Mothers and Sons

our lives from HIM enough? Why must we go through another man to get to GOD when the word is clear that HE set it up for **men** to come **boldly** before HIM ourselves? Why must we have other men teach us when it is clear that GOD wants to teach us HIMSELF? Man covering man is an affront to GOD because it makes the <u>blood</u> of Jesus of <u>none</u> effect.

"Seeing then that we have a great high priest, that is passed into the heavens, Jesus the Son of GOD, let us hold fast our profession ... Let us therefore come **boldly** unto the throne of grace that we may obtain mercy, and find grace to help in the time of need (Hebrews 4:16)."

"But the anointing which you have received of Him that abides in you, and you need **not** that **ANY** man teach you: but as the same anointing teaches you of all things, and is truth, and is no lie, and even as **it** has taught you, you shall abide in Him (1 John 2:27)."

WHAT IS A COVERING:

Frankly, I can't answer that question, in terms of the way the word is being used in the church. Charismatic preachers describe a covering as "one who is in authority over or has had someone submit themselves to their authority for the purpose of giving or receiving spiritual, professional, and personal guidance and direction." My problem is, I can't find the word "covering" being used with that meaning in the Bible. Charismatic influenced preachers say it is unscriptural to not have a covering. That is, some other man in authority over you. However, you cannot find in the Bible where GOD makes that assertion. There are some references where people are being reminded to operate within the bounds of civil or governmental authority,

Single Mothers and Sons

basically to follow the law. But I find no scripture where any man is commanded or remanded to have or keep another man as a "covering" over them. In Genesis where GOD lists everything man has dominion over other men are **not** on the list. To be respectful I say that I can't find a scripture. However, the truth is it is not in the Bible. The direct opposite of what they teach **is** in the Bible.

"...the chief priests and the scribes sought how they might take Him [Jesus] by craft [Greek: dolos = guile or deceit], and put Him to death (Mark 14:1)."

The same way preachers plotted to take out the Son of GOD they successfully crafted a scheme to control the men of GOD. The goal of the scheme is to capture the minds of men and essentially turn them into women and children. The objective is to get men to relinquish what GOD gave them authority over to them, like satan did with Adam, including their wives, children, and their finances. This is just as offensive to GOD as Adam yielding to satan or as Esau giving up his birthright. The word says GOD hated Esau for doing that. Satan tried to get Jesus to let him be His covering. He promised to give Jesus the kingdoms of the world if He allowed him to be in authority over Him instead of GOD. Do you think GOD would have been happy if Jesus had made Satan His covering? No! Likewise, GOD is **not** happy with **YOU** when you allow satan or a man who is a de-facto representative of satan be your covering. Let's see what the Apostle Paul says about a man being a covering for other men in **1 Corinthians 11:3-16**.

"But I would have you know that the head of **every** man is Christ; and the head of the woman is the man; and the head of Christ is GOD."

Single Mothers and Sons

Paul is clearly saying that the **head** or the one who is supposed to have headship, cover or be in authority over every man is Christ. He is bluntly saying in a matter of fact way "I, as a spiritual leader, am **not** your head or covering". He is also saying the head of the woman (meaning the married woman) is her husband not her preacher. A married woman should never allow a preacher or some man other than her husband to ever be in authority over her. An unmarried woman's head or covering is her father. Her father remains in authority over his daughter until he passes authority over her to her husband when he gives her away at her wedding. Next, Paul says the head, covering, or the one in authority over Christ is GOD.

"Every man praying or prophesying having his head covered dishonors his head [Jesus]..."

But every [married] **woman** that prays or prophecy with her head uncovered dishonors her head [husband]: for that is even all one as if she were shaven [or didn't even have a husband]."

Praying is talking to GOD and prophesying is speaking on behalf of GOD. Paul just told us that the head of man is Christ and the head of the **woman** is man. GOD set every individual man to not only be in authority but also to be held accountable for whatever occurs in his household. When his wife prays it should be in conjunction with what her husband prayed or consistent with his vision for the family. When his wife prophesies it should be conformation of a conversation that her husband already had with GOD. If she prays something contrary to his vision or has a prophesy that does not coincide with what GOD is saying to her husband it reveals that she has stepped out from under his authority and dishonors him.

Single Mothers and Sons

So, the Apostle Paul is also saying here that when a man talks to GOD or speaks on behalf of GOD with another man covering or in authority over him, that man dishonors Jesus. When a preacher demands that you as a man submit and be obedient to him, to let him be a covering for you, he is trying to lead you to voluntarily take the position of a woman? Some men are falling for this so deeply that they even develop the desire to lay with their preacher like a woman.

"For a **man** indeed ought **not** to cover his head, forasmuch as he is the image and glory of GOD..."

Paul said that a man ought not or should never have another man cover his head or be in authority over him because he is the image and glory of GOD. It does not seem to click in the minds of charismatic preachers that when GOD said HE made man in **HIS** image and after **HIS** likeness, HE was telling us that HE made **every** man to look like and to **act** like HIM!

So, men don't need another man to cover or be in authority over us when we walk in the image and likeness of GOD as HE intended. Glory means to hold up in high honor. The only way the world can see GOD and come to know that HE is a good and faithful Father is through us. The world cannot see us and therefore cannot see GOD when we allow the sons of satan to be a cover over us.

"But if any man seems to be contentious, we [the followers of Christ] have no such custom, neither the churches of GOD."

The summation of Paul's teaching is that Jesus is the covering or spiritual authority of every man. The word contentious means to be in dispute or in strife. The word custom here comes from the Greek word "sunetheia" meaning mutual habitation or usage.

Single Mothers and Sons

Therefore, the Apostle Paul concludes instructing GOD's people on whether a man covering another man is of GOD by saying: "If any man seems to be in dispute or in strife over what I just taught, then we followers of Christ have no use for him and neither does the churches of GOD."

Chapter 13
Fight Back!

"Be sober, be vigilant; because your adversary the devil, as a roaring lion, walks about seeking whom he MAY devour (1 Peter 5:8)." "Neither give place to the devil (Ephesians 4:27)."

The adversary seeks to attack anyone who will ALLOW or give him permission to devour them. The law of Natural Selection dictates that a man only has a right to that which he can defend. If a man cannot defend a wife he has no right to one. If he cannot defend a family he has no right to one. The adversary knows that the foundation of every nation, community, or organization is strong families. Family is the source of men's support, wealth and strength. Since the 60's the adversary has challenged our right as men to have a wife and children by forcing us to defend them. With 53% of all marriages failing and nearly 41% of all American babies being born to single mothers it appears that as men we have lost our spiritual power and allowed him to devour our families. Therefore, it is time to fight back!

The easiest way to disarm a strong man is to hold a gun to his family's head. The devil has been using this tactic to defeat men going all the way back to the Garden. Every time he wants to break the will of a man to fight he goes after that which the man loves most which is his wife and children. He wanted to take Adam's dominion and authority in the earth so he held Eve hostage. In an effort to demoralize David and his band of fierce fighting men the adversary burned their homes and kidnapped their wives and children.

Single Mothers and Sons

"...it came to pass, when David and his men were come to Ziklag... that the Amalekites had... burned it with fire; and had taken the women captive that were therein: they slew not any, either great or small but carried them away... and their wives, and their sons, and their daughters were taken captive (1 Samuel 30:1-3)."

When a lion attacks a herd for lunch he doesn't go after a bull he will hunt down one of the ladies or babies. The bull usually runs leaving the women and children to be devoured or he sometimes just stands by and watches it happen. GOD's plan for man's strength and prosperity is designed to come through the family structure. Man's seat of authority was programmed by GOD to be at the head of the family table. Family is GOD's primary organization for wealth generation. The key to that result lies in how well a man organizes his family for wealth creation.

In an effort to defeat the plan of GOD and take possession of man's wealth and authority, the adversary set out to destroy the family. Families without a man at the head are more likely to be poor and children are more likely to be maladaptive behaviorally which causes low performance academically. Like a lion looking for lunch, the devil has not been going after men to take possession of their prosperity and authority he has been going after women because it's easier for him to devour them and strip a man of his wealth and authority in the process.

Adam was not spending enough time with his wife so Eve was lonely and had a desire to be wise **like** her husband. The adversary used that desire to lead her to away from her husband which allowed him to take her into sin captivity. Adam had to put down his armor and go down into sin to rescue his wife from captivity. The devil has been able to destroy the family because of women's desire to be like men. Men allowed the devil to devour women and children because we left them alone too long and and treated them wrong too long. Our wives never should have had to struggle for equality. In effect, we gave satan place, room to enter and attack our families. So, it is time for men to fight back, bring our women out of captivity, and free our children to life in abundance and leave a powerful legacy.

Brothers, we opened the door and gave the devil an opportunity by going overboard on the issue of submission and it caused women to rebel and break free from domestic captivity. GOD could see that we were not utilizing the help meet HE had given us to her full capacity. So, GOD established the Women's Movement to free HIS daughters from oppression and give them equality in order to prevent another Eve. Whenever GOD creates something good you can count on satan to twist it into something evil. The devil twisted the Women's Movement into the Women's Liberation Movement. Whenever satan devises a plan to hurt you he always gives it a name that makes it seem like it is going to help you. GOD made the Women's Movement to give HIS girls equality within the family. The devil designed the Liberation Movement to give women the power and freedom to break up the family.

It may sound like I am blaming women for liberation but it's not their fault it is our fault. Men created the environment in the home for satan to enter in. We allowed the liberation movement to flourish because it gave us the benefit of having sex without responsibility.

Single Mothers and Sons

Women began giving up sex freely and we started taking all we could get willingly. The 3 power tools that satan always use to cause men to fall are: power, money, and sex. He always uses them because they always work. The allure of men being able to have sex freely and the desire of women to have men who were more sexually appealing opened the door for the Jezebel spirit to enter the family. Wherever the spirit of Jezebel is you will always find a desire for power and illicit sex.

A statement that was prominent in the liberation movement ideology among many women was that being treated like a woman was demeaning. Many women, in their quest for equality, were demanding to be treated "like" men. The attack on the family had powerful material effects but it was in reality a spiritual attack. The evil spirit that satan dispatched to attack the family is called Jezebel. The reason the spirit of Jezebel hates being treated like a woman is because that spirit is **not** a female spirit. Yes, Jezebel is **not** a woman! The spirit of Jezebel is a **male** demon who does most of his work operating in women but through men and children as well. When he operates in women they take on a strong male persona. When he operates in men they become weak, laid back, and let their woman lead. When he operates in children they defy all authority.

Jezebel is a defiant spirit. You can identify his presence if you know what to look for. A kid can be disobedient and not be influenced by the Jezebel spirit. However, if the kid is defiant and maladaptive to civil, social, or parental authority he/she is being influenced by the Jezebel spirit. When youth are trying to bring righteous order by engaging in civil disobedience they

Single Mothers and Sons

are not being influenced by the Jezebel spirit. However, when youth who have no respect for any authority are engaging in acts of civil <u>defiance</u> they are being seduced into disorder by the spirit of Jezebel. When young men walk around with their pants below their butt cheeks; literally showing their ass, they are engaging in civil defiance and are under the influence of the Jezebel spirit. Getting tattoos all over their face and body is an indicator of maladaptive behavior, an expression of civil defiance, and another sign of Jezebel's influence.

"An evil man seeks only rebellion therefore a cruel messenger shall be sent out against him (Proverbs 17:11)."

You can see the Jezebel spirit, if you don't make yourself willfully blind, influencing the Black Lives Matter Movement. Their aim is not to engage in civil disobedience but rather to defy governmental authority by challenging and confronting police. Police are a civil society's tool to **force** people who defy civil order to come back into order. Young people who are under the Jezebel influence hate to be told what to do. They defy everyone in authority: parents, priests, politicians, and principals. Police are the only authority that they cannot defy and get away with it. This entire movement is an effort to prevent police from telling them what to do and to strip cops of the authority to force them do it if they refuse. These young people for the most part didn't have a father so they have never been forced to submit to male authority in the home ergo they fight to remain free of any and all authority. The issue has nothing to do with people being killed by police. Only 32 police deaths occurred between 2009 and 2014. The goal is to prevent police from using deadly force against a defiant Jezebel spirit.

"Foolishness is bound in the heart of a child but the rod of correction shall drive it out of him (Proverbs 22:15)."

Wherever you find the spirit of Jezebel, you will find people who are rebellious toward male authority and operating out of GOD's order. The spirit of Babylon is a demon that creates and thrives in chaos and disorder. This demon was present in the earth before GOD reorganized it in Genesis, which is why the earth was **"without form and void"**. Babylon is a principality type demon that rules over governments and systems. Jezebel is a powers type demon that rules over people. Jezebel works for Babylon and his job is to take authority over male leadership. The purpose is to gain authority over that which the man has authority over in an effort to create chaos and disorder.

Men, it is important that we understand this clearly. The woman was GOD's greatest creation which is why HE saved her for last. Everything that she would need to live and operate in this world had already been created before she arrived. She was GOD's plan for man's success in so GOD supplied her with all she would need to get the job done. GOD made woman to be her man's source of strength to help him retain his authority as he worked to fulfill his GOD ordained purpose and vision. The devil wants man's authority and the woman has the power to block him from taking it. Therefore, the DEVIL HATES WOMEN! Since the day GOD told him that the seed of the woman would bruise his head he has been afraid of women. Consequently, he has done everything he can to strip women of their power to defeat him by trying to destroy them.

GOD placed a power in the woman called virtue that is designed to equip her to protect the head of her husband. Virtue is a woman's spiritual power but it is connected to her sexuality in the same way that a faithful man's power is connected to his sexuality. A woman's power can operate at its peak when she can keep herself in righteousness sexually. The devil recognized that if he could move women into depravity sexually he could break the power of their virtue to do harm to him spiritually. So he dispatches **men** in whom he has influence to attack women sexually, especially when they are most vulnerable as young girls and babies, in an effort to strip her of her virtue. By the 60's satan had learned how to influence women to lead each other to strip their selves of their own power through the sexual revolution.

I believe in the root theory to problem solving. You cannot end a problem until you understand how it began and you cannot kill it permanently unless you pull it up by the root. We must end the feminist ideology in the minds of our women, protect her from physical attack, and restore her power to protect us from spiritual attack. To understand how to make it end we have to go back a ways in history to find out how it all began. Just remember though brothers if we had treated women properly they would not have felt the need to break out of domestic captivity. So the root of women's rebellion began with us.

The History of Feminism

The women's movement began around 1962 and started to grow in popularity globally in May 1968

Single Mothers and Sons

when French Poet and defender of women's rights, Simone de Beauvoir, began writing articles that explained why it was difficult for talented women to become successful. She wrote that the obstacles women face include an inability to make as much money as men in the same job, society's lack of support for talented women, and the fear that success will lead to a threatened husband or prevent them from even finding a husband at all.

De Beauvoir argued that women lack ambition because of how they are raised. She said girls are raised to follow their mothers but boys are challenged to exceed the accomplishments of their fathers. As a result of her writings the Women's Movement which began as a fight for equality erupted into the Liberation Movement. The Liberation Movement was led by a group of women who were determined to turn De Beauvoir's ideas and ideals into actions designed to free women from domestic captivity. Through liberation women were able to achieve few of the same rights as men such as the right to education, the right to work, and the right to vote.

The Liberation Movement gained momentum in 1969 when Gloria Marie Steinem, a columnist for *New York* magazine, published an article, "After Black Power, Women's Liberation," which brought her national recognition as a feminist leader. In 1972 she created a platform from which to position herself as the thought leader of the movement by founding *Ms.* Magazine. Nearly 50 years later women are still fighting for the same issues: equality of pay for the same job, the lack of support for talented women, men's fear of women's success, and the difficulty of finding and keeping a husband. Women are still fighting to find ways to empower themselves and they are still searching for new avenues to encourage their daughters to be more powerful.

Feminism's Impact on Men

There is a dissonance in the collective feminist mindset. While women are raising their daughters to be strong and independent they over protect their sons and inadvertently cause them to be weak and dependent. The primary issues women complain about obtaining and maintaining relationships with men are: irresponsibility, lack of ambition, low education, as well as professional and financial incompatibility. Women either cannot or refuse to see that these issues are a direct result of the way they raise their sons. They try to raise their girls to be strong enough to take over the world but girls cannot find a suitable partner in this endeavor because of the way they raise their boys. The girls are strong, independent, and powerful but the boys are not fit to marry anybody's daughter.

Boys are failing to launch into manhood by being allowed to live at home too long. They are failing to thrive professionally and financially because they have been conditioned to having a woman take care of them. Thus, they find it hard to commit to marriage for fear that the woman they love will discover the inadequacies they feel as a man; they are adult males but in many ways they still feel like a boy. So, when they produce children they have difficulty living up to that responsibility because know they do not have response ability. They cannot be responsible because they were not made response able. Boys learn how to be men from men because women do not have the knowledge on how to be a man. This is a reality that the feminist ideology simply refuses to accept. Yet, the two main complains that women have about men in relationships is their lack of willingness to commit and their tendency towards irresponsibility.

Feminist ideology led women to try to create men in their own image and after their own likeness. The 70's feminist proclaimed a disdain for "macho men" and began to influence men to become more like women. They didn't want a man's man who was tough and rugged instead they wanted men to be softer, more caring, and in touch with their feelings. Women attempted to build a better man as if men were model airplanes but then they complained because that joker they built didn't fly right.

Feminist ideology held the man who looks like a woman is most sexy. So men began getting their hair curled and permed, wearing tight pants, donning flowered and pastel colored shirts, wearing high heels, and some even started carrying little purses. The feminist woman didn't really want a man she wanted a wife. She began to work and allowed the man to stay home all day and do nothing. The problems begin when women grew tired of having to work all day, take care of the kids, and do all of the house work while he would just rest, and dress, and hang out with "the boys" half the night. They would get aggravated by his failure to take any responsibility and exclaim: "Be a man!" when in reality neither he nor she knows what a man really is. She fought so hard to undo the imagery and ideology of what men thought a man was supposed to be that now neither one of them has a clue as to what a man is supposed to be and do.

Single Mothers and Sons

The Power of Words to Transform

"So shall my word be that goes forth out of my mouth: it shall not return unto me void, but it shall accomplish that which I please, and it shall prosper in the thing whereto I sent it (Isaiah 55:11)."

America is a nation of laws, laws are built on words and words have power. Yet, as a nation of people we have not figured out that words have power that is separate from what we give them in the context of law. They have a spiritual power attached to them that was meant to do what GOD intended them to do as they were being used regardless of what WE meant for them to do or mean as we use them. Since we were made in the image and likeness of GOD and HE created the world by speaking, we have the power to create **our** world by speaking as well.

However, GOD retained power over what our words would **do** as we speak because people will try to make words have meanings other than what GOD intended. So GOD established a universal meaning to all words so that the universe would respond in a uniform way to each word and produce what GOD intended that word to produce as it is spoken. GOD said that words that HE, and by extension, we utter shall **not** return unto HIM void or without producing something. Our words will produce what GOD intended each word to produce regardless of what we intended or meant.

So now, if you look at the TRUE meanings of the words feminism and feminist irrespective of what **we** meant when we say them we can see the root cause of what the movement based on those words have produced. The word "feminine" means having the qualities or appearance traditionally associated with women. The suffix "ism" has two meanings in this context: 1) an abnormal state or condition resulting from excess or 2) adherence to a system of principles, doctrine, or theory. The suffix "ist" refers to a person who practices certain doctrines. Regardless of what we want these words to mean the word "feminism" actually means a system of doctrine or theory which holds the **belief** that men should have the qualities or appearance traditionally associated with women.

A feminist is one who <u>practices</u> the doctrines of the feminism to the point of excess where they reach an abnormal state or condition. Feminism has indeed reached a state of excess to where men are now having operations to turn themselves into women. The 70's feminist ideology asserted that being treated like a woman was demeaning so women are taking excessive measures as well and are having sex changes to turn themselves into men.

Now we should be able to see how the Lesbian, Gay, Bi-sexual, and Transgender (LGBT) Movement has gained so much power, influence, and notoriety in our society. The LGBT Movement is a natural conclusion to the Liberation Movement. It has taken on the doctrine or belief system of feminism that everyone should have the qualities or appearance of a woman to its natural end. The thing about any word that ends with the suffix "ism" is that after a while the doctrines and beliefs associated with it become a type of religion that is no different than Hinduism, Buddhism, Catholicism, Judaism, and so on.

The problem with religion or people who adhere to any religious doctrine is they become obsessed with trying to get other people to follow their doctrine or beliefs. This is why adherents to the LGBT ideology are not happy with just having equality they want everyone to accept their doctrine or beliefs. They don't understand that 50 years from now they will still be fighting over the same issues of equality that they are today just like the feminists have been since the 70's because people have a habit of holding on to their own doctrines and beliefs.

Feminism or Faminism

Brazil is about to make the transition from a 3rd world nation to become the world's 5th largest economy because men and woman are working together in traditional roles to move that nation forward as a society and it is paying dividends economically. America is becoming a 3rd world nation economically because men and women are in constant competition. The universe is designed by GOD to reward cooperation and to penalize competition. This is the reason that one rival corporations merge, the simple news of the merger cause the stock prices of both companies to shoot up.

The business world at the Fortune 500 level operates on spiritual principles. People talk about the Illuminati but never stop to ask the question: what are they illuminated about? They have been enlightened on the spiritual principles that GOD built into the universe that is designed to automatically produce wealth when they are diligently adhered to. This is why they have most of the world's money while we are still fighting with each other to achieve equality. Women who have grown weary of struggling financially need to recognize that their struggle economically is connected to their adherence to feminist ideology.

Feminism should be called what it actually is which is famine-ism because a famine in whole families, a

Single Mothers and Sons

famine in real men, a famine in real fathers, a famine in real relationships, and a famine economically is what feminism has led to. Ladies, you've come a long way baby! You can bring home the bacon and fry it in the pan but you have to do that now because you don't have a man. How much better do you think you and your baby's lives would be if you had a REAL MAN and a WHOLE family? Adhering to the doctrine of feminism has deprived you of that opportunity. Those who manage to get with a REAL MAN can't hold on to him because feminist ideology leads you to fight for supremacy in the family. Even real men leave their wives once they grow weary of having to fight for male authority in their family.

GOD intended for there to be only one head on each body and only one head of each family. Some women have the belief that they can be "co-head" of the family not realizing that anything with two heads is a monster. Monsters either die prematurely due to their abnormalities or they must be killed because they become dangerous to society. There is a spiritual power associated with the single head principle that when executed properly (a husband loving and honoring his wife as Jesus loves the church) is designed to lead a family to prosperity.

This may be a hard pill to swallow but it is a simple fact the feminist movement has not worked for women. It has in fact worked against them. Yes, GOD's girls have gained a few rights and society's permission to do what men do like staying out all night, drinking, drugging, and sexing, without being looked down upon. There is no more double standard. Ladies can now go to hell in a hand basket just like the men are. But the problem is the babies are going too.

Single Mothers and Sons

Prior to the feminist movement we did not have an epidemic of children being hooked on drugs, with ADD, ADHD, and other mental problems, committing mass murder, committing suicide, killing other kids, and so on. We didn't have a nation of women who believed that children don't need a father. We didn't have more than 16 million children living in families with incomes below the federal poverty level. 53% of the nation's households were not headed by a single female. We didn't have an epidemic of men leaving their families or walking away from women who were pregnant with their children. We did have high rates of men dying from heart disease, alcoholism, and suicide. However, we did not have women dying at alarming rates from heart attacks and strokes like men used to as a result of the stress and pressure from trying to provide for a family as the sole breadwinner.

Men must lead women to see that there is no positive future in continuing to follow this destructive course. With love we must lead them to abandon the feminist ideology and find a way to restore their families. There is no problem with continuing the fight for equality: equal pay for equal work, and so on. That was GOD's original intent for creating the women's movement. Men must join women in the fight for equality on behalf of their daughters. Men and women have to return to the system of cooperation and cast away the competition so that our children can grow up happy, healthy, and wealthy rather than in low self esteem and poverty.

Fight Back!

It is time to fight back, arrest the spirit of Jezebel, and kick him out of the lives of our wives and children.

Single Mothers and Sons

We must remember however that our fight is not against flesh and blood, our women and children, but against a power. We cannot therefore attack the ones we love in our fight with this demon. We have to reach out to them in love. Remember, any battle with satan is always for control over the mind. We must turn our wives and children's minds toward us so that we have their undivided attention and begin a conversation. The purpose of conversation is to produce conversion. The goal is to convert them back to a righteous way of thinking and lead them out of satanic detention.

Men must lead women to start a conversation among themselves and answer the question: Has feminism and the feminist movement really worked for working women? It is a quiet secret that while wealthy women believe in equality they do not adhere to the ideology of the feminist movement because they know that it will ultimately lead their children into poverty. Women who adhere to the feminist ideology get upset with wealthy women who stand by their man after he was caught in adultery. They don't realize that wealthy women do stand by the man for him they do it for their children. She is protecting her children from poverty and trying to preserve the size of their inheritance. You can see the impact of the feminist ideology as it relates to poverty more clearly by observing the lives of its staunchest adherents: Black women and poor White women.

Nearly 73% of Black children are born out of wedlock, only 35% of Black children live with both parents, and 43% of Black women have never been married. The feminist ideology leads them to believe that there is veracity in being strong and independent. The truth is there is no room for independence in a relationship as

Single Mothers and Sons

couples must move from independence as single individuals to interdependence as a couple in order to have a long lasting mutually satisfying relationship.

55% of the people in American poverty, on welfare, and food stamps are White women and their children. Among all groups of women who adhere to the feminist ideology, those over 40 are more likely to be struck by lightning than to get married. Hispanic women are rising economically because their ideology is "la famillia" or the family first. They believe in protecting the head of their family therefore they are prospering. With that knowledge then we must begin to ask the question: has the feminist movement really worked to women's advantage?

The movement promised things like equal pay for equal work. Has it delivered on its promises or do women now have to do even more work for less pay? When you read the results that the feminist movement has produced in studies such as "Changing Patterns of Non-marital Childbearing in the United States," released by the National Center for Health Statistics, from the Centers for Disease Control and Prevention, you can clearly see that it has not worked to the advantage of women or their children. If something is not working, is it not considered insanity to keep doing it and expecting a different result? It is time for men to get back in position and start the fight with the devil to end the feminist scourge against our women and children. Let's GO!

Essays

Can You be a Man Like Joseph?

"Now the birth of Jesus Christ was on this wise. When as His mother Mary was espoused to Joseph, before they came together, she was found with child of the Holy Ghost. Then Joseph her husband, being a **just** man, and not willing to make her a public example, was minded to put her away privately.

But while he thought on these things, behold, the angel of the Lord appeared unto him in a dream, saying, Joseph, you son of David, fear not to take unto you Mary your wife: for that which is conceived in her is of the Holy Ghost. And she shall bring forth a son, and you shall call His name JESUS: for He shall save his people from their sins... Then Joseph being raised from sleep did as the angel of the Lord had bidden him, and took unto him his wife (Matthew 1:18-25)."

Brothers, if a woman you were engaged to be married to came and told you that she was pregnant, what would you do? In the days of Mary and Joseph, by Jewish custom, Joseph had the right to have Mary stoned to death. Would you have been so hurt and upset that you would have had her stoned in public immediately? Or would you have been like Joseph and try to think about how to put this matter to rest privately?

The fact that Joseph didn't have her stoned to death immediately reveals something about his heart and character as a man. It also provides some insight into why GOD selected Joseph to raise Jesus. What kind of man would you have to be for GOD to choose **you** to raise HIS only begotten Son? We know that a boy will

Single Mothers and Sons

take on some of the qualities, characteristics, values, and beliefs of the man that raises him. It is only natural for a boy to look up to his daddy and allow the man to guide him into his destiny.

If GOD decided to have Jesus' return come through a woman again, do you think that HE could trust **you** to raise Jesus? Could GOD depend on you to see that HIS Son was guided into the completion and fulfillment of his destiny to be the Savior of all humanity?

As far as we know, Joseph had never had an angel speak to him before this incident. Yet, we see that he was obviously faithful in addition to being a just man because he did exactly what the angel instructed him to do. There was no hesitation or mental reservation; he simply got up and took responsibility for the baby and his mommy. It appears to me that responsibility or response ability was another quality in Joseph's character that led GOD to choose him. He had response ability or the ability to respond properly in each situation. Instead of reacting wildly, he thought to put Mary away privately. Rather than abandoning Mary and her baby, and be done, he decided to take care of her and her son.

"And when they were departed, behold, the angel of the Lord appeared to **Joseph** in a dream, saying, arise, and take the young child and His mother, and flee into Egypt, and be you there until I bring you word: for Herod will seek the young child to destroy Him (Matthew 2:13)."

"But when Herod was dead, behold, an angel of the Lord appeared in a dream to **Joseph** in Egypt, saying, arise, and take the young child and His mother, and go into the land of Israel: for they are dead which sought the young child's life (Matthew 2:19-20)."

Single Mothers and Sons

These two scenes are strange in light of how we would conduct ourselves in this situation. Mothers today who are married to a man that is not their child's father would want to make decisions about what should be done to protect her son. They don't trust the man to make those decisions because, after all, he isn't the boy's real daddy so (in her mind) he couldn't possibly love "her" son as much as she does.

However, this should be a lesson to all liberated women. The child may be your baby but if you are married GOD intends for your baby to be your husband's responsibility. While he may not be they boy's natural father as your husband he is that boy's daddy. Therefore, GOD is not going to instruct you on what to do with the child. HE is going to tell your husband. This is crucial because it is a man's responsibility to guide a child into their destiny. A woman can nurture and guide a child to grow up righteously but the child needs a daddy to guide him or her into their GOD ordained destiny.

Now, there is something else strange in these verses related to Joseph. We can surmise from the context as to the type of man he was but the Bible doesn't really tell us much about him. Since I couldn't find much in the Bible I began searching historical records and zip, nada, nothing much there either. Then I finally realized why the Bible didn't tell us much about Joseph. It's because it tells you everything about Jesus. You see, a good man hides his life in his children's lives so that to know the child is to know the father **(John 8:19)**. This is the same reason the Bible doesn't tell us much specifically about GOD. The Bible teaches us more about the faith, character, and integrity of Jesus than it does about GOD. Since we know all of the

Single Mothers and Sons

characteristics and qualities of Jesus, we can know the attributes of His Father because GOD breathed or inspired HIS life into HIS Son.

"Now after the death of Moses the servant of the LORD it came to pass that the LORD spoke unto Joshua the son of Nun... (Joshua 1:1)"

Joshua is the first book of prophecy that teaches us about the coming of Jesus. Joshua and Nun are merely an allegory for GOD and Jesus. The book of Joshua constantly refers to him as the son of Nun. Yet, it never tells you anything about Nun. But that is because it told you all about Joshua. Nun was a faithful father. A faithful father hides his life in his son's life so that the son represents or re/presents the father to the world wherever he goes. We know all about Nun because we heard all about Joshua. We know all about GOD because we heard all about Jesus. Similarly, the world should be able to learn everything they need to know about you once they have heard all about your children.

Whenever Jesus' name is called, most of us begin to think about the impact that GOD has had in our lives. We love Jesus but we immediately begin to give GOD credit. When your name is called what impact will people see in their lives as a result of the children you gave birth to? GOD intended for every father to be like Jesus Christ and for every child to be like his or her dad. Then every man, woman, boy or girl would know who Jesus is, have a life worthy of emulating and grow into the image and likeness of Jesus. If men handle our responsibility faithfully and guide our children into their GOD ordained destiny, the impact of their lives will resonate throughout the earth into eternity.

Single Mothers and Sons

The way GOD measures a man is in whether or not he led his wife and children to reach their GOD ordained destiny. A husband and/or dad is responsible for what the people he is given charge over do or don't do **(Hosea 4:4-12)**. It does not take a special type of man to lead his family to into their destiny. It simply takes a man who has obtained victory over himself and who will yield himself to the knowledge and wisdom of GOD in order to complete this responsibility successfully.

Joseph was the type of man who yielded himself to the wisdom and knowledge of GOD. This is another reason GOD selected him to be the dad, caretaker, and administrator of the Savior. Joseph proved that he would be led of GOD and demonstrated that he was a man of wisdom as he did what GOD instructed him to do in order to keep Herod from killing his son. If Joseph had not done what GOD instructed him to do, Jesus would not have lived to reach his GOD ordained destiny. Jesus needed Joseph to fulfill his created purpose and to take on the responsibilities of being his daddy which is to guide, guard, and govern; direct, correct, and protect Him as a baby so that He could reach His GOD ordained destiny. Every time we thank GOD for Jesus we should also give thanks for Joseph.

Prisoner to Prime Minister

"If you let me draw the best man you can be out of you, the best athlete that you can be will come out too."
~ Dr Will

Every man wants to be a successful husband and father and every coach wants to win a championship. Any man can be a successful husband and father and **ANY** coach who was last in his league can go from worst to first if they use the power that GOD gave us all effectively. The average man struggles to be successful because nobody told him that he has spiritual power available to help him succeed.

"...have you not heard that the everlasting GOD... faints not neither is weary? He gives power to the faint; and to them that have no might he increases strength. Even the youths shall faint and be weary, and the young men shall utterly fall: But they that wait upon [serve] the LORD shall renew their strength; they shall mount up with wings as eagles; they shall run, and not be weary; and they shall walk, and not faint (Isaiah 40:28-31)."

Every entity on earth from the biggest down to the smallest atom has 3 main components. Humans are comprised of a spirit, soul, and body. Every physical entity has a spiritual property. We work hard to strengthen the physical entity but we neglect the spiritual property. Men who don't strengthen the spiritual property, over time weaken the physical entity and even with the ability to succeed they will fail. Men that learn to use spiritual power effectively can be like Joseph, the son of Israel, who used spiritual power to go from prisoner to Prime Minister.

Single Mothers and Sons

"And it came to pass after these things, that his master's wife... caught him by his garment, saying, lie with me: and he... fled... she called unto the men of her house... saying... he came in unto me to lie with me and I cried with a loud voice... when he heard that I lifted up my voice and cried... he fled ... And Joseph's master took him and put him into the prison (Genesis 39:7-20)."

"Pharaoh said unto Joseph, I have dreamed a dream... and I have heard say... that you can understand a dream to interpret it. And Joseph answered... saying, it is not in me: GOD shall give Pharaoh an answer of peace (Genesis 41:15-16)."

"And the thing [interpretation] was good in the eyes of Pharaoh, and in the eyes of all his servants. And Pharaoh said unto his servants, can we find such a one as this is, a man in whom the Spirit [power] of GOD is (Genesis 41:37-38)?

"And Pharaoh said unto Joseph... you shall be over my house, and according unto your word shall all my people be ruled: only in the throne will I be greater than you... he made him ruler over all the land of Egypt (Genesis 41:39-43)."

Now, I made a long story short so that you can get the gist. If you want the full story, please read Genesis chapters 39 to 41.

The lesson here is Joseph had the physical ability: knowledge, strength of character, and experience to handle the duties of Prime Minister. But it was knowing how to use spiritual power effectively gave him the opportunity to go from prisoner to Prime Minister. Knowledge, strength of character, integrity, and the ability to occupy the position effectively is the stuff that successful coaches and fathers are made of

Single Mothers and Sons

but spiritual power is the stuff men add to their other assets to become champions.

Joseph ended up in prison because he refused to have sex with the Pharaoh's wife. Rich men usually have gorgeous wives. How many men have the integrity or strength of character to refuse the sexual advances of a gorgeous woman? If the boss's wife tried to seduce you, could you refuse? Men who lack character and integrity would give in because nobody told them that their personal deficiencies will impact the success of their family or team members.

The truth is a woman cannot cause a man to fall to temptation if he could not have been tempted. Men who never smoked for example cannot be tempted to smoke a cigarette but men who are "trying" to quit smoking can. A man caught in error where it exposed his lack of integrity must take the full weight and responsibility in order to improve his character. Otherwise, he will never grow into maturity, will be a consummate loser, and will cause his whole family or team to fail. Here is a prime example of how one man can impact a whole team's success.

"But the children of Israel committed a trespass... for **Achan**... took of the accursed thing: and the anger of the LORD was kindled against the children of Israel (Joshua 7:1)."

Again, I am chopping up the verse to make a very long story short but please read Joshua Chapter 7 in its entirety in order to feel the weight and gravity of the whole story.

GOD instructed Joshua that none of the children of Israel were to take any of the spoils of war after they defeated Jericho because their goods were cursed. Taking cursed things into your house makes you, your

Single Mothers and Sons

whole house, or your entire camp cursed. When GOD confronted Joshua about this the verse says Achan had taken the accursed thing (he stole some money, gold, and clothes) yet it says the children of Israel committed a trespass. The anger of the Lord was not kindled against Achan alone but rather against the entire family of the children of Israel.

When the men of Israel went out to fight again, against a smaller and weaker opponent, they got their hats handed to them. The spiritual power to win left the team because of what one man did. The children of Israel still had the physical ability and the mental capacity to win but lacking spiritual power produced an imbalance in their attack which caused them to lose. Ultimately, Achan, his family, and everything he owned (even the family pet) was destroyed.

"Joshua, and all Israel with him, took Achan... the silver, the garment, the wedge of gold, his sons, his daughters, his oxen, his asses, his sheep, his tent, and all that he had... to the valley of Achor... And all Israel stoned him with stones and burned them with fire... (Joshua 7:24-25)."

The 3 things that make a successful sports team also make a successful family: teamwork, conditioning, and determination. The conditioning required is mental, physical, and spiritual. If one of these types of conditioning is neglected or missing there will be an imbalance. Permitting an imbalance to exist in one area creates weaknesses or over use in another area. Imbalance never goes away on its own. It must be corrected or it can become a permanent part of a family's or team's culture. This is the reason most NFL teams never reach the Super Bowl. Teams who live with imbalance will have consecutive mediocre seasons

Single Mothers and Sons

and families will produce consecutive generations of mediocre children. Any achievement beyond mediocrity will become a cause for celebration and glory.

Tall buildings don't topple over because they are built in a very deep hole and upon a solid foundation. Before you build up you have to dig down. Men only become tall in character and stature once they have dug deep inside of themselves and laid the proper spiritual foundation necessary to handle both the glory and attack that comes with being a winner.

Teams that win championships rarely win two or three years in a row because there is a spiritual weight that comes with the glory of winning. Every individual on a team must have the proper spiritual foundation to support the weight of glory. Losers love to challenge a winner. Something in the adverse nature of humans makes us want to see men who have reached great heights take a great fall. They love to stand over a winner who is down and exclaim "Oh, how the mighty have fallen!" Therefore, each person must be built up spiritually in order for a team to have the spiritual power to overcome the spiritual pressure to fall at the feet of the opposition.

Most championship teams fail to repeat the following season because they try to combat the spiritual attack that comes with being a champion with mental and physical opposition. However, spiritual opposition cannot be overcome by physical means. Championship coaches that want to repeat next season must understand how to condition their team to overcome mental, physical, and spiritual attack. Failing to strengthen a team spiritually creates an imbalance which leads to physical injuries, mental fatigue, and loss. Winning consecutive championships requires adding spiritual power to a team's physical and mental abilities.

"...the kingdom of heaven suffers violence and the violent take it by force." ~ Matthew 11:12b

Championship teams suffer violence so they must take the next championship by spiritual power or force. Religious men are taught to glory when under spiritual attack as if they can learn a great lesson through affliction. However, real men know that they must fight through affliction with spiritual force because that attack is designed to strip them of the spiritual will to win.

True glory in life comes from being up not down. Although celebrated in the valley, true glory resides on top of the mountain not in the valley. Men who are determined to reach the top of their metaphoric mountain, whether they are leading a team or a family, must have great physical abilities and mental tenacity. But unbeatable champions add spiritual power to their physical and mental mix. They win again and again because they have the mental tenacity to overcome all opposition, the physical capability to go from the pit to the palace, and the spiritual audacity to grow from worst to first.

We Need More Uncle Toms

"It's a matter of taking the side of the weak against the strong, something the best people have always done."
~ **Uncle Tom**

The African American community uses the term "Uncle Tom" to describe a Black man who demonstrated that he would betray other Black people. It was my understanding that the term become widely used during a time before the book "Uncle Tom's Cabin" (Harriet Beecher Stowe, 1852) was published. I learned about this book when I was in grade school. However, I refused to read a book written by a White woman who I thought was denigrating Black men. Some 30 years later while doing research on a project for Black History, I decided to read the book. Once I started reading it was so fascinating that I could hardly put it down.

The theme of Uncle Tom's Cabin is centered primarily on the Black family; how they were separated during slavery and their heroic faith, hope, and struggle to remain together. I absolutely fell in love with a character named Eliza. She was the type of intelligent, courageous, and faithful woman that any man would want in a wife. The character I found most impressive of course was Uncle Tom. He had the qualities of a family man, dedicated husband, dedicated father and faithful Christian. He was physically strong, courageous and had the characteristics of a king, warrior, mentor and a friend; character qualities that every man should have.

Uncle Tom risked his life to save a little White girl who was drowning although he couldn't swim.

Single Mothers and Sons

Everyone who spent any time around him was influenced by this strength, convictions and godly manner. Uncle Tom was also a martyr who sacrificed his life so that two women could go free that were being raped and abused by the wicked Slave Master Simon Legree. When they escaped Legree figured Uncle Tom knew where the women were heading or hiding so he had his Black plantation overseers, Sambo and Quimbo, beat Uncle Tom to make him confess. Uncle Tom did know where they were but even while being beaten mercilessly he never revealed where they were hiding. Ultimately, he died from the beating.

When Sambo and Quimbo finally realized that this was no ordinary man they had beaten, and seeing that he was just about to die, they kneeled down and asked him for forgiveness. While he lay there dying, Uncle Tom led them to commit their lives to GOD.

I understand that the term Uncle Tom has traditionally been used as a pejorative. However, from what I have observed in the Black community it appears that we need more Uncle Toms. When I see young women looking lost without the love and guidance of strong male leadership, using their bodies to advertise brand names because their daddy didn't give them a name, we need more Uncle Toms. When I see young men looking like desperate strays, no better than throwaways, struggling to find a sense of manhood, walking down the street with their pants hanging down because their daddies aren't around, we need more Uncle Toms.

Uncle Tom was a strong heroic figure who would be a man that we would try to elevate as a role model today. He would be someone revered, like Mandela, not reviled. Uncle Tom was the type of Black man who was

Single Mothers and Sons

hated, feared, and despised by wicked men like Simon Legree. This is how Uncle Tom's name became a dirty word. Evil men like Legree saw a man like Uncle Tom's strength of character as a threat to order and discipline. He would whip other slaves if he thought they were trying to be courageous like Uncle Tom. Legree saw Uncle Tom's strength as something that had to be tamed so that other slaves would not become strong too.

I came to realize that most Black folks did not understand the history of why men who were troublesome to slave owners are called Uncle Tom. Uncle Tom, to slave owners, made it tough to keep the slaves docile and under control. The common remedy for handling a strong Black male slave was not to totally break him because they needed him to breed strong babies. So they used to punish other slaves in order to make him conform. Since men like Uncle Tom were sometimes seen by other slaves as trouble makers Black folks assigned that term to all Black men who caused them trouble. Then, of course, the term morphed into a label that described the type of man who would betray his people but that was not Uncle Tom.

I understand, now, that the negative connotation assigned to the name of Uncle Tom was misapplied. Therefore, we must stop applying that moniker to Black men who are enemies to the community. The image of a Black man like Uncle Tom, whether fictional or real, needs to be preserved with dignity.

Cowardly opportunists who would sell out their constituents to gain an advantage with modern day "Massas" should not be called an Uncle Tom. Guys at work who side with management to obtain favor by

Single Mothers and Sons

betraying labor, should not be called an Uncle Tom. Young men who deal drugs, shoot wildly in the streets, kill their brothers, burglarize homes and commit robberies should not be named in the same breath as Uncle Tom.

If a name is required with which to label men like them, then perhaps Sambo or Quimbo would be apropos.

Afterword

"But I have prayed for you that your faith fail not: and when you are converted, strengthen your brothers (Luke 22:32)."

Each time I write a book that is intended for men only women run to get it immediately. Women can't wait to get their hands on it because they love to know what men are thinking. I have one book entitled "Healing the Wounded Woman" which I make sure that women can't get their hands on. However, it struck me suddenly that single mothers need to know what men are thinking so that they can teach their sons. I wrote another book that was designed to encourage men to get actively involved in raising their sons. Yet, I know a lot of men are not going to what is right for their sons so I came to the conclusion that mothers need this information so that they can teach, train, and guide their son's into manhood.

Single moms, I want you to know that I did not write this book **to** you but I did write it **for** you. One of the primary issues women have is difficulty in not only finding a man but also one who is godly. The underlying cause of this issue is men are not born godly so they must learn how to BE godly. They are not learning to be godly, even while going to church regularly, because the average preacher has **no** clue about how to teach a man to be godly. If the truth were told, most preachers are struggling with being godly themselves. Therefore, this book is intended to not only provide the essential knowledge every young boy needs to become a successful man, husband, and father but also a godly man. Good Christ centered women

Single Mothers and Sons

need to have a large pool of godly men to chose from. Men who are godly that marry a good woman have a better chance at becoming wealthy.

Church has been successful at leading men to be saved but failing at teaching them how to be godly and obtain the same characteristics and qualities as Jesus. Church going people have been conditioned to defend preachers when they come under criticism. The problem women have with finding the godly man that they both want and need is never resolved because they refuse to recognize that the man who is charged by GOD to teach men to be godly: to be better men, husbands, and fathers has not been doing his job. When you refuse to recognize the problem you cannot realize the solution. Women must begin to put pressure on their preacher to produce godly men that know who they are in Christ, have a vision for their family, and understand how to lead their family into its divine destiny.

50-75% of the average church membership is either single or divorced. When surveyed nationally as to whether they would rather be single or married the vast majority responded married. All of these single people are going to church together and sitting in the pews together so why can't they get together? Why is it so hard for women to find a godly man in church?

The issue is simple: men are being led to **GO** to church but they are not being taught how to **BE** church. The truth is the average preacher knows that he struggles to be a godly man himself so it affects his pride and self-esteem when he is in the presence of strong or confident men. Therefore, rather than building all the men in his church up he tries to keep strong men <u>under</u> or <u>obedient</u> to him. As a result, there

Single Mothers and Sons

is no room in church for a man to be a man because the position of being **under** a man is for a woman and being obedient to a man is the duty of a BOY not a man. A preacher can't teach men to be a man when he needs him to be a boy; his "spiritual son". No man can teach another man to be what he doesn't know how to be himself.

A strong man that is godly, has the knowledge of who he is, why he was created, and the power of GOD to execute his purpose is a threat to the average preacher. He finds strength in being the strong man's shepherd because in his mind there is only one shepherd over a flock and there can only be ONE Alpha male in a church. Thus, many strong men find it hard to remain in church. And the majority of the men that remain in the flock are not taught to be godly therefore they are not strong enough to embody the character and qualities of Jesus.

Sadly, the reason men are sometimes not taught to be godly, powerful men of GOD, simply comes down to money. In a flock there are male and female sheep; rams and ewes. The value of a shepherd's flock is not measured by the number of rams he has but by the number of ewes. When there are multiple rams in a flock fighting and competition arises over which one will be the alpha. Once the alpha emerges the shepherd castrates or kills the others. He leaves the alpha intact to inseminate the ewes and produce strong healthy lambs. The ones he castrates are used to help defend the flock from outside predators or intact rams from other flocks. I can always tell a church going man who is a castrated ram. He is quick to defend preachers also. The type of preacher must maintain control over the ewes to keep them from running of with a strong

Single Mothers and Sons

man or an intact ram. This is why the preacher, as both shepherd and alpha male of the flock, periodically gives this message to the ewes: "You better watch out for these men, all of them didn't come to church for the right reason!" Now a man who wanted to invite one of the women in church out for lunch can't do that for fear of being viewed as a pew predator.

One of the main issues men are having (which is making them angry in their core being but hidden under a happy exterior) is they are being effeminized by society and emasculated in the church. They are made to be a boy in church and treated like one of the children at home. The solution is to train men to **BE** men but also godly men so they can come into both the knowledge and power of who they really are and who GOD created them to BE. This is what women really need. However, there are not many men, preachers included, who know how to train men to be godly men. This is why I wrote this book. I have tried to provide men with the knowledge they need to BE godly men and become better husbands to their wives and better fathers to their children. Now I need to provide the same knowledge to single mothers so that they can share it with their sons and help them take the journey and make the transition into manhood.

Young men, this book is written for you to use as a reference tool and obtain all the knowledge you need to become a successful man, husband and father. It is critical for young men to learn early in life that it is not weak to admit that you need help. It does not make you a lesser man to seek the knowledge you need to be the man that you want to become. I wrote this book for you to read so that you can lead. A man who won't read can't lead.

Single Mothers and Sons

I know that some young men love to act like they don't need anybody. Due to pride they cannot bring themselves to go to another man and admit that they do not know some things. So I have tried to include in this book everything a man would need to know about how to live his life, love his wife, and raise his children. I have also included everything a man needs to know to put his self on a path to discover and achieve his GOD ordained purpose which is the key to finding three things that every man needs: a good woman, great wealth and true glory. So please use this like a reference book to study alone and get what they need on your own.

Finally, my brothers, having the knowledge you need to function successfully as a husband and father physically will do you no good if you do not transform yourself spiritually. GOD left us one of the 8 Wonders of the World to remind us that we have this duty. The Sphinx is the head of a man on an animal's body. Every man is born with a lower or animal nature. The thing that separates man from an animal is our intellectual capacity. Our duty before GOD and before we try to take on the responsibility of leading a family is to transform our lower animal nature up to its higher spiritual or godly nature. Jesus' call to repent (re/pent; as in pent/house) means: go back to the top! Go back up from a lower level of thinking so that you can have a higher level of existence. The top is where men discover who we are, where we can see a larger vision of ourselves, achieve success, and obtain wealth. Men who don't learn to repent will remain in one place, like the Sphinx, looking big and powerful but never able to be successful. I'm going to the top are you coming? Let's GO!

About the Author

For over 30 years Dr Will has helped men repair their personal and professional relationships. He holds a PhD in Religious Studies and authored many books: including Strengthening the Family, Relationships 911, How to Avoid Bad Relationships, Healing the Wounded Woman, Money DOES Grow on trees, Secrets of the Fortune 500, and more. Dr Will used the power of excellence in relationships to lead thousands of men to become successful by helping them see a bigger vision and create a better version of themselves. He used this skill to produce highly proficient employees, build championship sports teams, and influence drug dealers to turn their illegal operations into legitimate businesses. Dr Will also conducts award winning seminars for men in the areas of domestic violence prevention and awareness, personal power development, and family enrichment, along with wealth creation and management. See www.drwillspeaking.com for more information.

Single Mothers and Sons
Recommended Reading

Secrets of the Fortune 500 - www.drwillspeaking.com
Money Does Grow On Trees - www.drwillspeaking.com
Relationships 911 - www.drwillspeaking.com
The Small Stuff – www.drwillspeaking.com
Action has no Season – Michael V. Roberts
The 7 Habits of Highly Effective People – Stephen Covey
The 8th Habit - Stephen Covey
Awaken the Giant Within – Anthony Robbins
The 4 Hour Work Week – Timothy Ferris
Change Your Thoughts, Change Your Life - Wayne W. Dyer
Goals: Setting and Achieving Them on Schedule – Zig Ziglar
How to Win Friends and Influence People – Dale Carnegie
The Art of the Deal – Donald Trump
Live Your Dreams - Les Brown
Lessons on History – Will Durant
Lessons on Philosophy – Will Durant
The Fatherhood Principle – Myles Munroe
Teamwork 101 – John Maxwell
Leadership 101 – John Maxwell
The Master Key System - Charles F. Haanel
Psycho-Cybernetics - Maxwell Maltz
The Success Principles - Jack Canfield/Janet Switzer
Think and Grow Rich – Napoleon Hill

www.ingramcontent.com/pod-product-compliance
Lightning Source LLC
Chambersburg PA
CBHW070551100426
42744CB00006B/259